MIGRANT MUSES:

MENNONITE/S WRITING IN THE U.S.

John D. Roth
Ervin Beck

Editors

Mennonite Historical Society

Goshen, Indiana

1998

Published by the Mennonite Historical Society
1700 South Main Street, Goshen, IN 46526

Typesetting by Stuart W. Showalter and John D. Roth
Cover Design by Andy Wetherill and Dee Birkey

Manufactured in the United States of America
Printed by Herald Press, Scottdale, PA 15683

TABLE OF CONTENTS

FOREWORD

For most of their 300-year history in the United States, Mennonites have regarded literature with some ambivalence. On the one hand, narrative texts like the *Martyrs' Mirror* and *The Wandering Soul* have long held a quasi-canonical status in many Amish and Mennonite households and were reprinted frequently throughout the eighteenth and nineteenth centuries. Supplemented by the ballad hymns of the *Ausbund*, a rich body of genealogical lore and a host of didactic stories serialized in periodicals of the twentieth century, a Mennonite literary tradition developed that has often been overlooked by students of the period.

On the other hand, the more culturally mainstream forms of literary production–fiction, poetry, literary criticism, etc.–frequently met with hostility in Mennonite communities. For many Mennonite leaders, literary activities suggested a culture of learnedness and leisure in tension with a tradition that valued simplicity and manual labor. Literature seemed to promote flights of imaginative fancy over concrete deeds of human kindness and the transparency of letting your "yea be yea." Perhaps most troubling of all, the individualism of the authorial voice in fiction and poetry seemed to challenge the Anabaptist ideal of yieldedness to the larger community.

Today this ambivalence seems to have virtually disappeared. During the past twenty years a flourishing body of literary and cultural creativity has emerged among Mennonites in the United States that suggests a fundamental shift in Mennonite attitudes toward the literary arts. As Mennonites have become more culturally assimilated–and as the number of Mennonite university students enrolled in creative writing programs has increased–we now have a significant number of writers who find publishers and audiences outside denominational circles. Moreover, teachers and critics at Mennonite colleges increasingly find Mennonite writing deserving of the same serious attention they normally have given to longer-established classics.

On October 23-26, 1997 the English department of Goshen College sponsored a conference on Mennonite/s Writing in the U.S., which brought some 300 poets, novelists, playwrights, teachers, literary critics and readers together for a celebration and critical assessment of Mennonite literature in the United States. The number and quality of presentations at the conference suggest that the event represented a kind of coming-of-age for Mennonite creative writing and literary criticism. This collection of essays offers a sampling of the rich variety of ideas, criticism and theoretical reflection that found expression at the conference.

The methodological approaches and thematic considerations presented at the conference and reproduced here ranged widely. **John Fisher**, for example, places Julia Kasdorf's *Sleeping Preacher* in the rich philological context of the pastoral elegy, especially as practiced by John Milton and Seamus Heaney. **Ervin Beck** and **Carroll D. Yoder** seek out archetypal patterns–the former in the broad sweep of Mennonite experience and literature and the latter in a close study of the journey motif in a recent novel by Omar Eby. **Dan Lehman** raises a host of ethical issues in his study of recent depictions of the Amish in fiction and on television; **Phoebe Wiley** addresses a different set of ethical questions concerning Mennonites attitudes toward domestic abuse that are implied in Christmas Carol Kauffman's popular novel *Light From Heaven*. In a more historical vein, **Jane Hostetler Robinett** traces antecedents for Mennonite narrative fiction in the travel writings of Sanford Calvin Yoder, while **Laura Schmidt Roberts** reflects upon the theological themes of creation and redemption woven into a cycle of new poems by Jean Janzen.

Reflecting recent critical modes of analysis, **Jessica W. Lapp** brings insights from French feminist theory into conversation with Janet Kauffman's first novel; **Beth Martin Birky** analyzes the language of the body in the poetry of several Mennonite women; and **Paul Tiessen** highlights the deconstructive, postmodern characteristics of the published works of Dallas Wiebe.

Rounding out the sampler are a variety of topical and theoretical studies. Thus, **Todd Davis** highlights the theme of work in the poetry of Janet Kauffman; **Edna Froese** compares perspectives on the community of faith in novels by Rudy Wiebe and Jeff Gundy; **David Wright** articulates the poetics of community found in Gundy's poetry and *A Community of Memory*; **Ann Hostetler** considers the tension between faith and ethnicity in Mennonite poetry; **Hildi Froese Tiessen** challenges Mennonite writers to lay aside the false dichotomies of individual versus community, while **Jeff Gundy** celebrates the ambivalent status of the writer within the broader religious and ethnic community.

The volume concludes with tributes to three pioneers in the production and study of Mennonite literature and then offers readers seven book reviews, all focusing on recent Mennonite fiction or poetry.

Despite this broad range of interest and approaches, the conference neglected certain kinds of literature produced by Mennonites in the United States. With the exception of the studies of Christmas Carol

Kauffman and Sanford C. Yoder, Mennonite literature prior to the 1960s is inadequately represented--understandably so in light of critics' interest in the recent literature that more nearly conforms to the taste of educated readers. Yet if we are interested in the way literature relates to an ethno-religious community, then our critical studies will need to become more anthropological and focus more on the "popular" literature of earlier Mennonite culture as it was read and appreciated by the mass of Mennonite readers.

And we will need to go even further than that, into the literature of oral tradition. Just as we now realize that the "true" early literature of marginalized groups such as women and African-Americans is to be found in the folk literature created by those groups, so we need to recognize that the same situation also prevailed for Mennonites prior to their accepting of higher education, and is still largely the case for Amish and other conservative groups today. A proper understanding of Mennonite literary culture warrants attention to both popular and folk literary forms, even if it means developing skills and approaches different from those called for in the analysis of "elite" literature. Such new directions are fully supported by recent postmodern literary theory and practice–especially as found in the interdisciplinary approach of cultural studies–which tends to ignore the traditional borders between folk, popular and educated literary expressions.

The conference may also represent a turning point in regard to a discussion that has dominated Mennonite literary criticism since 1970: namely, the relationship of the Mennonite writer to the core values, or "center," of his or her community. That discussion was shaped in a formative way by Al Reimer and John Ruth, representing the Canadian/Russian Mennonite and the U.S./Swiss Mennonite traditions, respectively. In this issue, Hildi Froese Tiessen moves the conversation to a new level by denying the binary oppositional positions–such as "center" versus "margin"–and calling on us to recognize the multiplicity of views within the Mennonite church and the corresponding positions from which Mennonite authors might express themselves while still remaining in community. **Denise Levertov** universalizes Hildi's point by acknowledging that the literary muse flourishes in many different homes, including nation, region, ethnicity and even the language itself.

Although Froese Tiessen is clearly inspired by current literary critical theory and practice, the evident evolution of Mennonite churches during the past twenty years toward more diversity and less conformity also supports her thesis. What that means for the Mennonite church is not entirely clear. Yet the weakening of the frustrating tensions between center and margin, preacher and poet, conformity and individuality may bode well for creative writers in the Mennonite community.

The geographic border that has traditionally divided the evolution of Mennonite literature along the 49th parallel is also weakening. The title of the conference in Goshen deliberately imitated the groundbreaking Mennonite's Writing in Canada conference held in 1990 in Waterloo, Ontario. Four of the presenters at the Goshen conference–Rudy Wiebe, Edna Froese, Paul Tiessen, Hildi Froese Tiessen–were Canadian Mennonites. Three of the seven reviews in this collection are of books by Canadian Mennonite writers–Di Brandt, David Bergen, Rosemary Nixon. With such gestures we recognize the truly international nature–and cross-fertilizing influence–of Mennonite writing on both sides of the border.

Hence it gives us great pleasure to announce that an international conference on Mennonite writing is tentatively being planned for the fall of 2002 at Conrad Grebel College, Waterloo, Ontario by Hildi Froese Tiessen and others. Perhaps this book of essays will serve as the inspiration and sounding board for the many essays to be prepared for that conference when Canadian and U.S. creative writers and literary critics will, at last, meet as equals.

—John D. Roth and Ervin Beck, co-editors

THE MIGRANT MUSE: ROOTS AND AIRPLANTS

DENISE LEVERTOV*

It is generally agreed that an artist who has deep roots in a landscape or in a culture, particularly a regional culture with well-defined values and traditions, has an advantage. Cézanne could paint a masterpiece at the Lake of Annecy, but his relationship with the environs of Aix, and with Mont Ste. Victoire in particular, was nurtured from birth through his entire life and surely gave a special authority to his work. Hardy's intimate knowledge of the group of English southwestern counties he called, collectively, Wessex — a knowledge of architectural detail, agricultural customs (which in his day still differed subtly from one county to another), dialect variations, the appearance of lanes and hedgerows, woods, heaths and vales peculiar to that part of the country — was not merely a backdrop for the tales he told but gave his work its palette, its tone or (to switch to musical analogies) the keys in which he wrote and the orchestration that gave his work its unmistakable Hardy-ness. When folk elements are incorporated in a composer's work we feel, I think, a difference between those who appropriate exotic elements and those for whom the same motifs are not exotic but are part of their inheritance.

William Carlos Williams dug into his native and lifelong New Jersey, demonstrating his own dictum about finding the universal in the local; yet he could never be dismissed as a regional writer in the restricted

---

*Denise Levertov, distinguished American poet, presented this essay as the keynote address for the conference Mennonite/s Writing in the U.S. She died of lymphoma on Dec. 20, 1997.

sense. A major artist like him finds in the local a firm ground on which to stand and from which to leap and fly. Wendell Berry's deep roots in rural Kentucky inform his poetry, his fiction and his essays and have an inseparable relationship to the values he articulates. A probably minor, but charming and still young fiction writer like Allegra Goodman in *The Family Mankowitz* gets the Jewish-American "tone" just right; her exactitude is in itself a pleasure. But she has psychological wisdom and perceptiveness which makes me feel she could, if she wished, write convincingly about quite different people and places. Her rootedness is a potential springboard.

The down side of belonging so definitely to a place and a culture—I should say a place *or* a culture, because of course many cultures persist in diaspora, independently of geography—is that it can be restrictive. Perhaps the most obvious problem (in the past more than recently) is the writer's decision to use dialect; and this is not because of the grammar and usage of dialect but because the attempts to convey its sounds by spellings which are supposed to approximate them often only present an insurmountable barrier to the reader. Now and again a writer will with real skill overcome whatever difficulty dialect itself may present. Robert Morgan in *The Truest Pleasure*, for instance, has a narrator who is a North Carolina hill farm woman and a "holy roller" at the turn of the century; he uses no transliteration of sounds, but she does say "we was," not "we were," and she and her family think of molasses as a plural. Although at times she rises to heights of eloquence, her voice is perfectly credible throughout. I recommend this small masterpiece to anyone who has not come across it. John Edgar Wideman often uses Black English but without any "funny spelling," and he can move with complete smoothness from dialect to standard English. The reader thus is enabled to make swift, almost unconscious adjustments. But often the use of dialect is problematical—restrictive to the writer and uninviting to the reader.

There is also the matter of provinciality—of a narrow outlook, or rather, of an outlook not only lacking in a broad experience of other ways and places but unaware that it is narrow; an outlook lacking not only curiosity about what lies beyond its experience but in respect for it when encountered. Such provinciality is not a primitive innocence but the philistine enemy of art, and indeed of personal growth. Hideous sentimental greeting cards and calendars and other "religious" goods purveyed both by the organs of the fundamentalist right wing churches and those of a certain conservative segment of the Catholic church demonstrate the link between this kind of provinciality and aesthetic atrophy. However, a more recent problem of restriction affects the culturally and ethnically, but not necessarily geographically, rooted

2

writer, namely an oppressive sense of obligation in regard to content, whether that sense sprang from within or was imposed by a peer group. Thus some of the young African American poets two decades ago could hardly write a poem about a tree or a lake or Greta Garbo or Gutenberg's press or spinach and hope to publish it unless it made a point about slavery, racism and poverty—and preferably were written in ghetto English even if the writer habitually spoke perfect standard English. The historical reasons for this imposed restriction are clear and understandable, but it was a situation not conducive to the artistry of a generation or two of young writers. Happily, a greater freedom ensued and there are now many fine young Black poets who, without any denial of their history, clearly feel the right to write about anything and everything, just like anyone else. I have not observed just how and if parallel phases have occurred among other minorities. A number of Japanese-American writers have written about the World War II camps, of course—notably Lawson Fusao Inada. Among Chicanos there is a thriving, often bilingual literature imbued with a sense of a painful, oppressive past and present but not restricted by a domineering sense of "ought" in regard to subject matter.

These, then, are some of the advantages and disadvantages of belonging firmly somewhere, geographically and culturally; and the positive aspects outweigh the liabilities, I believe, since the advantages are available and sustaining to all who inherit them, while the truly gifted can usually manage sooner or later to get past the disadvantages.

But what of those who, like myself, don't really belong anywhere? My own case is already familiar to those who read my work; I summed it up in an autobiographical essay included in *New and Selected Essays*:

> The reading I did myself, and the reading aloud which was a staple of our family life, combined to give me a passion for England—for the nuances of country things, hedges and old churches and the names of wildflowers—even though part of me knew I was an outsider. Among Jews a Goy, among Gentiles (secular or Christian) a Jew or at least a half-Jew (which was good or bad according to their degree of anti-Semitism); among Anglo-Saxons a Celt; in Wales a Londoner who not only did not speak Welsh but was not imbued with Welsh attitudes; among schoolchildren a strange exception whom they did not know whether to envy or mistrust: all of these anomalies predicated my later experience. I so often feel English, or perhaps European, in the United States, while in England I sometimes feel American—and certainly as a poet have been thought of for decades as an American, for it was in the United States that I developed, though my first book had been published in England before I crossed the Atlantic. But though I was quick to

3

scornfully protest anti-Semitic remarks, or references to the Welsh language as a "dialect," these feelings of not-belonging were positive for me, not negative. I was given such a sense of confidence by my family, *in* my family, that though I was often shy (and have remained so in certain respects) I nevertheless experienced the sense of difference as an honor, as a part of knowing (secretly) from an early age—perhaps seven, certainly before I was ten—that I was an artist-person and had a destiny.

I sometimes feel like an exception because the cultural strands united in me were manifest in a household I find very difficult to describe. It seemed to have a culture of its own, but I suppose I would have to be a writer of short stories or novels to convey its atmosphere or tone; but then again, it may be that everyone feels that way, and even siblings may not have formed identical impressions of their family. Then, too, just as the individual character and atmosphere of such an atypical family remains a source for the adult's later development, so the succeeding influences—the persons, places, affiliations and salient events of a life—form a rich, unique compost for persons for whom place-roots and a sense of ethnic or other defined social identity is lacking. I will merely mention class identity, so strong a determinant in England and some other countries, and though vaguer and more transmutable in the U.S., nevertheless a factor in forming the sense of self. It is, however, not so strong an influence anywhere for people with an active artistic vocation, who have almost always come to form a class of their own, able to pass through the usual barriers and float up and down the social scale—if not fully acceptable yet recognized as undefinable.

Who, then, are some of the others—writers in general, poets in particular—who seem to have had to *make do* without the profound and prolonged shared relationship to a place and its human ways which is sometimes urged as a sine qua non, in disregard of the fact that "if you ain't got it, you ain't got it"?

I think first of the very great: of Rilke. Rilke certainly had *European* roots; but they were, so to speak, diffused. He was a German-speaking Czech, one could say, but as his birthplace Prague was part of the Austro-Hungarian Empire and he was not part of the Czech nationalist movement, he is more accurately categorized as Austrian. He lived and worked in Austria, Germany, France (Paris in particular) and the French-speaking area of Switzerland, and traveled for prolonged stays to Italy, Egypt, Sweden, Russia. His visits to Russia had a deep and lasting influence on him, although they were not of long duration. The castle of Duino, where he wrote most of the famous Elegies, is in the often disputed area around Trieste, which has been at different times Austrian, Italian and in more recent times Yugoslavian. Paris was to him a place much beloved, his enforced absence from which during World War I symbolized all his pain at that senseless slaughter, just as his return there after the war symbolized spring and a precarious, precious renewal. Throughout his life he did not settle anywhere permanently; most often he was a guest in other people's houses. He has been criticized for this, but since his hosts were always people with lots of space who could easily afford to be hospitable, I have always found this critique uncalled for. All artists have to try to find the circumstances in which they can best serve the muse. This has often led to their exploitation of other people; but there is every reason to suppose that Rilke's hosts were delighted to have him occupy some part of their often enormous castles. Such reciprocity is not exploitative.

Since he had no physical home, and since virtually all his travels yielded him poems, where were his roots? I've said they were, in a diffuse way, European, and that is true; but where beyond that? The answer seems to be, unquestionably, in the German language. Rilke was very much at home in French, to the point of writing quite a number of poems in that language. But German was his essential locus, and such an intimate one that he felt free to treat it in unique ways, drawing forth from it untapped resources—somewhat as Hopkins did with English.

Another great artist to place beside Rilke is Joseph Conrad, who for political reasons, and because English seamen and adventurers were so stimulating to his narrative impulse (and also I suppose because he sought a wider audience) chose to abandon his native language and not to make Poland the scene or subject of his major work. This act of choice contrasts strongly to Rilke's peregrinations. Rilke's French poems were in no way an abandonment of German but a graceful tribute to French civilization—and in some degree to the fact that at the time most or all of what he heard around him daily was French speech. Peregrinations is an apt word to use of Rilke, for his travels constituted a lifelong pilgrimage rather than expatriation. Conrad, in switching to English and settling in England, was deliberately undertaking a kind of metamorphosis. In his seagoing years he had come to know a great many English men whose lives inspired a majority of his fictions. This I think was the reason he chose English and not French, although as an upper-class Pole he must have been fluent in French. That a native language is an essential root for any writer (not only those who don't have place and ethnicity to support them) is demonstrated by the fact that Conrad, although he wrote marvelous English prose, often betrays, in turns of phrase and sentence structure, the fact that it was not his first language—that his experimental metamorphosis was incomplete. This failure, although he himself might have deplored it, not only did not detract from the majesty of his style but subtly added to it, in my opinion.

5

A third major writer whom it may be relevant to consider is Henry James. Socially, and I suppose one may say genetically, James certainly had every right to claim roots in place and culture: in New York and in the New England of Transcendentalist intellectual tradition. And he did not deny them by his voluntary expatriation, for physical distance often provides an important vantage point from which to perceive and engage with the society of which one is a part. But the intensity and refinement of his aesthetic understandings not only demanded such a distancing, which visits home only reinforced, but also resulted in his developing an equally strong relationship to England, and in certain ways to France and Italy too. His sensibility was perhaps more French than English; yet to me while growing up in England he was completely acceptable as an English writer (as he was generally regarded in England when I was young) and it was quite a shock to discover him claimed as one of their own when I first met American intellectuals just after World War II. He developed a style which, unique and increasingly refined, cannot be called typically English and was certainly not typically American either, though one might see in Hawthorne's elaborations some prefigurings of it. Indeed, since the nearest cousin to his style seems to be that of Proust, who was influenced by Ruskin; and since in sheer analytic complexity James's sentences and paragraphs have something in common with German writers such as Thomas Mann and Herman Broch, one might say that James formed a *European* style in the process of pursuing the utmost precision possible in the rich and flexible English language.

Our century's convulsive history has cast many writers into exile from their lands, their cultures and their languages. These have not necessarily lost their roots, for cultural roots are portable and even place can be carried in memory. But in regard to language these writers have had to face a peculiarly painful choice: to continue creating their poems and fictions in their mother tongue, but without access to readers in their homelands, while relying on translation to link them to readers in their place of exile; or to attempt the so rarely successful transfer of their creative allegiance to a new language. The best solution for writers in this dilemma — especially for poets, since prose is always more susceptible to satisfactory translation than poetry — is the one Czeslaw Milosz has fortunately found: a devoted translator who himself is of high poetic caliber and intelligence, like Robert Hass, with whom the author (presuming him to have, as Milosz has, a good knowledge of English) can collaborate, while continuing to write in his own native tongue. Milosz is also fortunate in that he has never entirely lost touch with readers in Poland. Many others have not had good translators and have been more completely cut off from their former readers.

But neither voluntary expatriation nor involuntary exile constitutes the category I most wanted to consider—of someone like myself who has neither a clear ethnic identity nor an intimate relationship to a particular place. I have already spoken of Rilke, the one great poet I can think of who was a floater or airplant except in his relationship to language. But there must be others on a less exalted level. Of myself I've written that:

Without a terrain in which, to which, I belong
language is itself my home, my Jerusalem.

The most obvious danger for such floaters is that one may find oneself writing "tourist poems." I have thought about poems by various people that have struck me as having fallen into that trap, and about what distinguishes them from other poems derived from the visits and travels away from the writer's own usual surroundings. The tourist poem, I have concluded, is one resulting from a kind of journalistic alertness to "good copy." Perhaps the poet has set out to find "good subjects." Such poems may be written with that deadly "competence" taught in the MFA programs, but it will reveal to an acute reader its origin in base intention. No authentic revelation takes place. However, other poems about places and events to which the poet has no previous connection, no birthright claim, but stumbles upon without prior intention of "using" them, can constitute authentic revelations because they were unpremeditated responses—both subject and poem taking the poet by surprise. It is a subjective judgment, of course, for the reader. But for the writer it is a matter of conscience. You *know* that the trap exists and you must be wary of falling into it—more wary than writers who have place-roots, for to the poet who is at home nowhere and everywhere, every place has a potential for exotic effect or for a seeming neutrality that might tempt one to cast over it the veil of one's own agenda. The writer lacking the advantage of roots in anything but language has to cope with their absence, with the danger of sounding touristy, with the risk of appropriating other people's turf.

But does the floater or airplant—not, mark well, a parasite!—have any special advantages? Just possibly their necessary reliance on language itself as their "one home" causes that relationship to be more of a romance than it is for people secure in their marriage to a locale and its customs. I don't assert this as a fact—it just occurs to me as possible. Then again, if one is never a full and recognizable member of any community but brushes the edges of many, one experiences a sense of freedom rather than of isolation. One is not deprived of friendships; but one does not become a unit of a collective. I'm straying here across the border between what belongs to art and what to daily living; it is, of course a "wandering border," hard to discern. Living, for the forever migrant poet, is perhaps more of an adventure? But if so, one must not think too literally of migration, for the most famous of stay-at-homes, Emily Dickinson, traveled as far as anyone has gone. Deaf Beethoven plumbed new depths of music. Blind Homer . . . blind Borges . . . the tribe of seers, of shamans, deaf and blind in trance, who travel on eagles' wings or in the minds of wolves—the inner world is where the most profound adventures, journeys of discovery, magical transformations take place, whether or not the pilgrim undertakes migrations in the outer world.

But as many of you are members of a faith community with its own strong traditions, I feel I should not conclude these reflections without turning to the question of what role religious allegiances may play in the life of migrants, floaters, airplant artists—poets in particular. When faith is the overwhelming dominant impetus and subject of a poet's work, as it is in the case of, say, George Herbert or Gerard Manley Hopkins, each of whom wrote (or anyway preserved) hardly any poems other than devotional ones, then their faith *is* their cultural, emotional, intellectual root. The context of Herbert's poems is the English countryside, but he is not a poet of place. Hopkins was passionately in love with nature and with the visual world, and again it is the English and Welsh countryside that in his case is more than context, forming the whole surface, sometimes, of poems that at the core are prayers. His poems, so sensuous to the ear and the mouth, are full as well of the most precise and astonishing visual observation. But for all his concrete imagery, no one could categorize him as a "nature poet."

One must count such poets as having deep roots in religious faith, in addition to whatever cultural or ethnic or geographic origins they may have. Does this mean that a floater or migrant poet who happens to be a believer—in whatever faith—can claim that faith as a root? Yes and no: for that poet may or may not be part of a community of fellow believers. Every religion and every subdivision of it has its social dimension, its customs and mores. Individuals may not have grown up within that dimension, and if they are adult converts they will rarely if ever share in that dimension except superficially. They will have a cordial sense of entering into a community of belief when they worship together, but sharing a theology does not bring them within the social fold, regarding which they will remain at the edge, looking in, as they remain in relation to other such folds or enclaves. Perhaps to some people, hungry to "belong," this is painful. To the artist, however, it is not a matter of regret—and I speak from my own experience. To be aware of sharing Eucharistic communion with fellow believers, and to have individual friends who share the same faith, is of course a great joy to any Christian; yet poets who are not rooted in the cultural dimensions of their religious affiliation will not look to it for social life, and will never feel completely at home in that aspect of it.

There is a tension in any artist's life between the claims of the collective and the claims of art. It is probably a useful and necessary tension. For those who do belong within an ethnic cultural collective, the tensions concern restrictions, problems of self-censorship. For those who do not belong within a group, but whose beliefs (both religious and political) nevertheless impose moral demands on them, self-censorship is unlikely to be the focus—except when deciding whether or not to publish something that might be hurtful to some individual. Rather, it will concern the division of time and energy—how much to allot to activities that constitute the "works" that must validate faith, how much to the service of art. This must be a problem for those within a group as well as for solitaries, of course. And ultimately it comes down to how strong a sense of artistic vocation one has, and how one *can* find a way to balance it with other demands and imperatives.

The advantages and disadvantages of those with nourishing social and geographic roots and those rooted only in their art itself—in language if they are poets, in the sense of story if they are fiction writers, in music if they are composers, and so on—seem on reflection to be about equal. The solitary has less nourishment already in place to draw upon and must seek equivalents in the accidents of pilgrimage—but by the same token is freer, and has available (if capable of drawing upon it) a wider range. The *depth* that either kind of life will reach in artistic works will in either case depend on the individual's unique gifts and the strength and persistence with which he or she pursues them.

BEYOND THE BINARY: RE-INSCRIBING CULTURAL IDENTITY IN THE LITERATURE OF MENNONITES

HILDI FROESE TIESSEN*

Abstract: Mennonites tend to perceive their cultural existence in binary terms: center/margin or insider/outsider. Although Mennonite creative writers have tended, also, to adopt these binary categories in their critical writing, some of them, in their creative work, have escaped the fixed, binary categories that seem to prevent Mennonites from articulating the complex nature of their cultural identity. Writers like Jeff Gundy and Julia Kasdorf, for example, have undertaken compelling explorations of what cultural theorists call an "in-between" world that binary understandings prevent us from naming or claiming. By exploring and re-mapping the diverse worlds that contemporary Mennonites occupy, creative writers like these have begun to inscribe the multiple and unfixed "locations of culture" that most contemporary North American Mennonites occupy, and so have begun to re-inscribe Mennonite cultural identity.

In a compelling article published in 1997,[1] poet Julia Kasdorf quotes the closing lines of a prose poem by her Canadian Mennonite literary colleague Di Brandt: "I hate having to choose between my inherited identity & my life: traditional Mennonite *versus* contemporary Canadian woman writer, yet how can i be both & not fly apart?"[2] Commenting, some years earlier, in 1992, on the imminent publication of her own first book of poetry, *Sleeping Preacher*, Kasdorf observed that many of the poems in that collection had been "written from the perspective of an outsider—either a Mennonite outside American culture, or a critical sheep in the Mennonite fold. I've had it both ways," she said, "to be in the community and in the world—which, of course, means to have it neither way. Alienating as it sometimes feels, this non-home is my home."[3] Writers like Kasdorf and Brandt, and others who in recent decades have chosen to write both creatively and critically about Mennonite experience from a Mennonite perspective, have given a good

---

*Hildi Froese Tiessen, Academic Dean at Conrad Grebel College in Waterloo, Ontario, has edited several volumes of work by and about Mennonite writers.

1. Julia Kasdorf, "Bakhtin, Boundaries and Bodies," *MQR* 71 (April 1997), 169-88. Note Kasdorf's unselfconscious use of the term "outsider" in this piece.

2. Di Brandt, quoted in Kasdorf, ibid., 185.

3. Julia Kasdorf, "Bringing Home the Work: Thoughts on Publishing a First Book," *Festival Quarterly* 19 (Spring 1992), 10.

deal of attention to the question of what it means to be "inside" or "outside" a community that once represented for them a fairly unqualified "home."[4] In the process, they have tended to foreground general questions of Mennonite cultural identity and to probe, more specifically, questions about how their writing might be regarded as a means of "locating" themselves (and, presumably, other contemporary North American Mennonites) relative to the two monoliths Brandt once referred to as "the Mennonite world" and "the worldly world out there."[5]

Of course, neither Mennonite writers nor Mennonites in general have a sole claim to the tensions involved in an individual's trying "to be true to two worlds" (to quote the University of Pittsburgh Press's release announcing Kasdorf's *Sleeping Preacher*) or to more general experiences of displacement or deterritorialization in the closing years of this century. "The migrant's sense of being rootless, of living between worlds, between a lost past and a non-integrated present," cultural studies critic Iain Chambers has observed, is, after all, "perhaps the most fitting metaphor of [our] (post)modern condition."[6] It is not surprising, then, that a good many contemporary theorists should attempt to come to terms with, and to theorize, what novelist Michael Ondaatje and others have referred to as "the migrant's double perspective."[7] As writers and critics have struggled to make sense of what it means to live between cultures, they often have revealed the human tendency to try to understand the complexly intertwined several contexts they occupy in

---

4. This paper is concerned with Mennonite "cultural identity," a category not restricted to, and not to be confused with, Mennonite "ethnic" identity, which we have come to understand as generally either "Russian" or "Swiss." I happen to have in mind here the critical observations and creative work of "Swiss" writers like Julia Kasdorf and Jeff Gundy. Their exploration of issues of cultural identity tend to be particular to their personal circumstances; the questions to which they give voice are not, however, unique to them. Mennonite writers who move among two or more cultural subject positions, no matter what their ethnicity, would presumably share with Kasdorf, Gundy and other writers questions about how they might locate themselves relative to the several cultural sites on their lives' itinerary.

5. Di Brandt, "how i got saved," in *Why I Am a Mennonite: Essays on Mennonite Identity*, ed. Harry Loewen (Scottdale, PA: Herald Press, 1988), 27.

6. Iain Chambers, *Migrancy, Culture, Identity* (London: Routledge, 1994), 27. Contemporary literary critics, cultural theorists, anthropologists and other commentators on the worlds we live in observe that displacement—migration between cultures through physical dislocation "as refugees, immigrants, migrants, exiles or expatriates," or by colonization—is, indeed, as literary critic Angelika Bammer has observed, "one of the most formative experiences of our century."—Angelika Bammer, *Displacements: Cultural Identities in Question* (Bloomington: Indiana U. Press, 1994), xi.

7. Michael Ondaatje, in conversation with Linda Hutcheon, *Other Solitudes: Canadian Multicultural Fictions* eds. Linda Hutcheon and Marion Richmond (Toronto: Oxford U. Press, 1990), 197.

simple, binary terms: center/margin, home/exile, community/individual, insiders/outsiders, and so on.

Such a tendency to perceive one's contexts — or, one might say, the locations of one's personal or cultural existence — in binary terms has contributed to the emergence of a monolith Mennonites conventionally refer to as "the Mennonite community." In fact, such a monolith has been projected in numerous commentaries on Mennonite writing, at least since John Ruth's landmark lectures on "Mennonite Identity and Literary Art" in 1976. Moreover, "the Mennonite community" (or "the Mennonite world") has, in recent decades at least, become a powerful trope that has dominated both critics' and writers' thinking about the role of the writer among Mennonites.[8] This trope of the essentialist, monolithic center has had a significant function in the provisional resolution of issues related to Mennonite cultural identity. In Mennonite literary circles at least, the trope of "the Mennonite community" has in fact come to represent an unproblematized cultural identity which, to borrow the words of theorist Stuart Hall, is suggestive of "a sort of collective 'one true self'. . . which people with a shared history and ancestry hold in common." As a trope, "the community" reflects

---

8. The trope of "the Mennonite community" has been developed and sustained in literary circles by what Jeff Gundy has referred to as the Mennonites' "seemingly endless preoccupation with individual/community relations."—See Jeff Gundy, "U.S. Mennonite Poetry and Poets: Beyond Dr. Johnson's Dog," *MQR* 71 (January 1997), 5-41; Warren Kliewer's essay on art and artists, "Controversy and the Religious Arts," *Mennonite Life* 20 (January 1965), 8-11; John Ruth's Menno Simons Lectures on "Mennonite Identity and Literary Art" in 1976, published with the same title in *Mennonite Life* 32 (March 1977), 4-25 and in *Mennonite Identity and Literary Art* (Scottdale, PA: Herald Press, 1978); my own "The Role of Art and Literature in Mennonite Self-Understanding," in *Mennonite Identity. Historical and Contemporary Perspectives*, ed. Calvin Redekop and Samuel J. Steiner (New York: U. Press of America, 1988), 235-52; Jeff Gundy's "Humility in Mennonite Literature," *MQR* 63 (January 1989), 5-21; my introductions to *Liars and Rascals: Mennonite Short Stories*, (Waterloo: U. of Waterloo Press, 1989), xi-xiii and to *The New Quarterly* [special issue on Mennonite/s Writing in Canada] 10 (Spring/Summer 1990), 9-12 and to *Prairie Fire* [a special issue on Canadian Mennonite Writing.] 11 (Summer 1990), 8-11; Al Reimer's *Mennonite Literary Voices: Past and Present* (North Newton, KS: Bethel College, 1993); Elmer Suderman's "Mennonites, the Mennonite Community, and Mennonite Writers," *Mennonite Life* 47 (September 1992), 21-26; Julia Kasdorf's musings anticipating the publication of her first collection of poetry, "Bringing Home the Work: Thoughts on Publishing a First Book," *Festival Quarterly* 19 (Spring 1992), 7-10; Jeff Gundy's "Some Words on Poetry, Band Camps, Guitars, Gifts, Transgression, Community, Mennonite Art, Etc.," *Mennonite Life* 48 (December 1993), 15-16; and the epigraph chosen for the web page announcing the 1997 conference at Goshen College on Mennonite/s Writing in the U.S.—a quotation taken from the closing paragraph of Julia Kasdorf's essay on the Martyrs' Mirror titled "'Work and Hope': Tradition and Translation of an Anabaptist Adam," *MQR* 69 (April 1995), 178-204. All these critical reflections, each of them a signpost along the trail of Mennonite literary history, speak of "the tension between the artist and community" in Mennonite literature.

the common historical experiences and shared cultural codes which provide us, as 'one people', with stable, unchanging and continuous frames of reference and meaning, beneath the shifting divisions and vicissitudes of our actual history. This 'oneness' underlying all the other, more superficial differences, [has been perceived as] the truth, the essence,[9]

presumably, of Mennonitism.

This way of defining ourselves in terms of monolithic and binary categories is, of course, reflected in identity politics as we find it expressed around the world. It is central to the kind of "imaginative re-discovery"[10] advocated by commentators like John Ruth in his 1976 lectures on Mennonite identity and in his review of *Liars and Rascals* in the *Mennonite Reporter* in 1989—a review for which, Julia Kasdorf remarked in 1992, Ruth "had read [the collection of stories by Mennonite writers] searching for a single expression of the 'communal soul' that would somehow offer a standard interpretation of our collective experience."[11] The imposition of such an "imaginary coherence"[12] onto Mennonite identity results in the emergence of a master narrative (rooted in binary thinking) that has, in fact, become a principal resource of resistance for dissenting voices. That is, John Ruth's "unique center of covenant-conviction"[13] or what he has called the "very soul-drama" of the "covenant community"[14] of the Mennonites becomes the ground *against* which the "outsider-prophet" or "iconoclast of the imagination"[15] —Al Reimer's terms for the Mennonite artist—speaks. In such a typically hierarchical binary opposition, one party is seen to be ascendant: for Ruth, the "covenant-community"; for Reimer, "the new Mennonite literary prophet."

This kind of dualistic thinking, in which one dynamic is privileged, the other diminished by implication, is familiar enough to those individuals who grew up among North American Mennonites in the years on either side of World War II: those who were nurtured in a Mennonite world where the lines between "insiders" and "outsiders" were fairly clearly drawn and the categories of identity, as they

---

9. Stuart Hall, "Cultural Identity and Cinematic Representation," *Framework* 36 (1989), 69.

10. Ibid., 69.

11. Kasdorf, "Bringing Home the Work," 10. John L. Ruth's review, "Stories reveal individual psyches offended by stingy heritage,'" appeared in *Mennonite Reporter*, June 26, 1989, 11.

12. Hall, "Cultural Identity and Cinematic Representation," 70.

13. Ruth, "Mennonite Identity and Literary Art," 5.

14. Ibid., 25.

15. Reimer, *Mennonite Literary Voices*, 59.

experienced them, rigid and relatively stable.[16] But in late twentieth-century North America, urbanism, evangelicalism, and easy access to travel and information have precluded the sustaining of this kind of "oneness." Nevertheless, still compelled by the paradigm of binary opposites, Mennonites insist on referring to something they call "the Mennonite community" and persist also in accepting the notion that any voices that do not emerge from what they have conventionally regarded as "the center" must be perceived as "marginal" at best.

In the 1960s Rudy Wiebe, Warren Kliewer, Dallas Wiebe and a few others were representing in fiction analogues for the Mennonite communities they had come to observe. These communities were, in the imaginations of these writers at least, dominated (and defined) by a relatively stable religious and cultural orthodoxy. Rudy Wiebe's *Peace Shall Destroy Many* suggests something of the inherent destructiveness of such monoliths. In 1962 Wiebe found no recourse for Joseph Dueck (the compelling dissenter in Wiebe's first novel) but for this insightful man to abandon the community that had been the object merely of his good will. The most significant difference between Joseph Dueck and today's "Mennos on the margins" or Mennonots—so christened in this decade by poet and editor Sheri Hostetler—is that Dueck had no recourse but to leave his communal home once he had given voice to his dissent. The Menno*nots* (or Mennonites who want to lay claim to their heritage, even though they may be ambivalent about much that it represents), as Hostetler declared at the "Quiet in the Land?" conference in Millersville in 1995, "have no intention of going away." In her editorial comments in the first issue of the magazine *Mennonot: For Mennos on the Margins* (Fall 1993), Hostetler wrote: "perhaps *Mennonot* can . . . help articulate what it means to be a biworldly Mennonite, for those of us still claiming that name for ourselves."[17] In effect echoing Brandt and Kasdorf, she declares: "I found myself in that crevice between worlds I've fallen into many a time since leaving home 10 years ago. I sometimes felt that I'd taken the Mennonite dictum to 'be in the world but be not of it' one better: I was living in two worlds and wasn't a part of either of them."[18]

---

16. The categories were stable, although with occasional, jarring exceptions here and there where stratification along lines of class—a category conveniently obscured by other predominant paradigms—provided "insider" status to some who would otherwise be cast out. Much work needs to be done on the operation of class in the Mennonite communities in North America.

17. Sheri Hostetler, "The Story of *Mennonot*," *Mennonot: For Mennos on the Margins* (Fall 1993), 2.

18. Ibid., 1.

Hostetler's comments speak to particular, contemporary identity issues. But they also reveal the degree to which she and other self-defined Mennonots have come to perceive their community of origin in terms of a binary logic that identifies insiders and outsiders, home and exile, center and margin—Mennonites and Menno*nots*—and sustains these categories in a posture of opposition. It is true that in *Mennonot* Hostetler, like other writers who have situated themselves "in the margins," has cleared a space for herself and others to speak. But there is an inherent weakness in her "marginal" position as she defines it, a weakness rooted in the very binary assumption underlying her work and the title of her magazine.

As long as Mennonite literary critics and writers continue to accept the limiting, inherently hierarchical binary paradigms of center and margin, insider and outsider we are examining here, they give credence to the persistent and prevailing notion that the territory the writers nurtured among the Mennonites occupy is, well, marginal. Margins consist, of course, of peripheral space, of that which is allowed beyond what is necessary. Texts of the margin, although they might offer illuminations and/or annotations, tend to be determined and limited by the primary texts—the master-narratives, if you will—to which they refer.[19]

The point I am making here is this: the critics of Mennonite writing—and several of the writers who themselves comment critically on various aspects of the creative process and/or the creative condition—have tended to place the Mennonite writer in the context of a binary paradigm, with its inherent hierarchical structure. That is, they have accepted that those writers who have offered alternative readings of Mennonite cultural identity are appropriately perceived as marginal (and they have, in large measure, presented themselves that way). To be sure, Julia Kasdorf has argued recently for a corrective dialogic paradigm for the interaction of all Mennonite voices (and, specifically, for the integration of the voice of the creative artist)—a paradigm based on the work of Bakhtin, that ideologically eschews the hierarchies binary paradigms imply and allows both sides of a dualistic model to be given equal weight. But her model actually (in true Bakhtinian fashion) merely inverts previously held hierarchical assumptions about the community and the artist. In Kasdorf's dialogic universe, that is, the world remains divided along binary lines, and the writer simply takes the place of the community in subsuming and embodying all contradictions.[20] Kasdorf's

---

19. See Gloria Anzaldua, *Borderlines/La Frontera: The New Mestiza* (San Francisco: aunt lute books, 1987), esp. 78.

20. In Kasdorf's model the individual would, in effect, embody the community: "The point is not how we remain part of the Body of Christ—or of the Mennonite community—"

thoughtful essay is extraordinarily valuable in that it suggest a way for all who identify themselves as Mennonite to interact in "form-giving conversation."[21] But it leaves intact the persistent, problematic binary categories that have governed Mennonite identity politics (inclusive of center and margin, insiders and outsiders). Her views, like the views of other writers and critics who have spoken about the role of the writer relative to the Mennonites, have been shaped, first of all, by binary hierarchies that have tended to oversimplify the nature of the "precarious discursive construction"[22] so often referred to as "the Mennonite community."

The overwhelming power of the center, as Mennonites have acknowledged it, has been usefully interrogated or challenged by some Mennonite writers who have argued from the margins, as it were. However, it is in Mennonite writers' creative work—not in their own and others' critical observations—that they have in fact escaped not only the binary categories that support the assumption that the center is fixed and unified but also the politics of the margins. It is in their poems and stories that writers like Julia Kasdorf and Jeff Gundy, for example, have been able to move us into the productive territory of what might be described as "the politics of difference,"[23] for it is in their creative writing that they confront their readers with what cultural theorist Iain Chambers refers to as "a continuous disbanding and dispersal of the terms that claim to represent us, them, and reality."[24] In their creative work, these writers have been prepared to trust to fragments, as Canadian postmodernist literary critic Robert Kroetsch would say, "letting them speak their incompleteness."[25] Here the fixed construction we have come to designate as the center defers to that which is unstable and diverse, and issues of identity that were once invariably controlled by limiting binary categories are allowed some flexibility.

Kasdorf observes, "but how the Body remains part of us and acts through us in the world" ("Bakhtin, Boundaries and Bodies," 185). She concludes: "Outsiders or those who inhabit the margins of the community would be valued for their ability to offer consummating images of the Body in relation to its context, views impossible to grasp from an interior perspective" (188). The binary paradigm of outsider/insider (with its implied limiting essentialism) persists in Kasdorf's otherwise valuable model.

21. Kasdorf, "Bakhtin, Boundaries and Bodies," 188.

22. Paul Gilroy quoted in Chambers, *Migrancy, Culture, Identity*, 86.

23. Chambers, ibid., 86.

24. Ibid., 86.

25. Robert Kroetsch, "Disunity as Unity: A Canadian Strategy," in *The Lovely Treachery of Words: Essays Selected and New* (Toronto: Oxford U. Press, 1989), 24.

"Identity," British author Jeffrey Weeks has observed, "is about belonging, about what you have in common with some people. . . . At its most basic it gives you a sense of personal location. . . ."[26] Identity, Stuart Hall has observed with acuity, is formed "at the unstable point where the 'unspeakable' stories of subjectivity meet the narratives of history, of a culture."[27] This "unstable" intersection where identity comes into being—or, more accurately, this series of intersections—is what Homi Bhabha calls "a contingent 'in-between' space," an "intervening space."[28] Postcolonial and postmodern theorists like Bhabha and Hall eschew the notion that center and margin or insider and outsider might be acceptable as absolute categories. On the contrary, identity—or a sense of cultural and/or personal location—tends to be found in what Gloria Anzaldua refers to as a "place of contradictions,"[29] a "wholly new and separate territory."[30] Moreover, the site of identity is "in a constant state of transition."[31] Anzaldua refers to it as a borderland and speaks of it as a place of empowering hybridity. This is a place, "that has to be engaged," Homi Bhabha argues, paraphrasing Salmon Rushdie, "in creating the conditions through which 'newness comes into the world.'"[32]

During a time when cultural boundaries are generally acknowledged as fluid rather than fixed, identity—this place of "perpetual transition," as Stuart Hall has observed—undergoes "constant transformation." "Far from being eternally fixed in some essentialized past," Hall argues, identity is "subject to the continuous 'play' of history, culture and power":

---

26. Jeffrey Weeks, "The Value of Difference," *Identity: Community, Culture, Difference*, ed. Jonathan Rutherford (London: Lawrence & Wishart, 1990), 88.

27. Stuart Hall, quoted by Bill Schwarz in "Memories of Empire," in *Displacements: Cultural Identities in Question*, ed. Angelica Bammer (Bloomington: Indiana U. Press, 1994), 157.

28. Homi K. Bhabha, *The Location of Culture* (London: Routledge, 1994), 7. Bhabha states that "the borderline work of culture demands an encounter with 'newness' that is not part of the continuum of past and present. It creates a sense of the new as an insurgent act of cultural translation. Such art does not merely recall the past as social cause or aesthetic precedent; it renews the past, refiguring it as a contingent 'in-between' space, that innovates and interrupts the performance of the present. The 'past-present' becomes part of the necessity, not the nostalgia, of living."

29. Anzaldua, *Borderlines/La Frontera*, [n.p.].

30. Ibid., 79.

31. Ibid., 3. Anzaldua, who writes about the U.S.-Mexico border "where the Third World grates against the first and bleeds," speaks of a border culture as a site where "the lifeblood of two worlds [merge] to form a third country—a border culture." She continues: "Borders are set up to define the places that are safe and unsafe, to distinguish us from them" (3). This paper borrows from a number of critical paradigms, including Anzaldua's; the "border cultures" posited here that Mennonites might encounter tend to be cultural and/or chronological.

32. Bhabha, *The Location of Culture*, 227.

> Far from being grounded in a mere "recovery" of the past, which is waiting to be found, and which, when found, will secure our sense of ourselves into eternity, identities are the names we give to the different ways we are positioned by, and position ourselves within, the narratives of the past. [33]

Surely this speaks to the heart of what Mennonite writers like Jeff Gundy and Julia Kasdorf and others are doing in their creative work. Gundy has remarked that many writers find their art "in the difficult space where faith, doubt and real, lived experience cohabit or collide."[34] This is not unlike the "'in-between'" space of which Bhabha speaks, the contingent, provisional space from which the occupant can apprehend the continual, ultimately arbitrary re-positioning or re-siting of the border itself. This is the place of cultural hybridity that "resists unitary paradigms and dualistic thinking,"[35] a place where transient, versatile, multiple and unstable boundaries of difference are "re-mapped" and "re-named."[36] The act of writing in this interstitial space consists, as Julia Kasdorf has observed,[37] of an attempt to locate herself relative to the dislocations of contemporary life. And as writers negotiate this indeterminate middle-space and construct ways to make sense of the complex worlds we occupy, they offer those constructions to others "as one possible form of existence."[38] It is liberating to recognize that movement within that space, as Paul Carter has observed, might be regarded not as "an awkward interval between fixed points of departure and arrival, but as a mode of being in the world."[39]

---

33. Hall, "Cultural Identity and Cinematic Representation," 70.

34. Gundy, "U.S. Mennonite Poetry and Poets: Beyond Dr. Johnson's Dog," 8.

35. Carol Boyce Davies citing Anzaldua, in *Black Women, Writing and Identity: Migrations of the Subject* (London: Routledge, 1994), 16.

36. I take these terms from Juan Flores and George Yudice, cited in Davies, ibid., 10: "The view from the border enables us to apprehend the ultimate arbitrariness of the border itself, of forced separations and inferiorizations. . . ." Flores and Yudice speak of an inclusive society that "has to do with nothing less than the imaginative ethos of re-mapping and re-naming in the service [of]. . . all claimants."

37. In "Bringing Home the Work: Thoughts on Publishing a First Book," Kasdorf observed that "Paradoxically, a precarious sense of location is exactly what has fueled much of my writing so far" (10).

38. I draw here on Linda Martin Alcoff's "The Problem of Speaking for Others," in *Who Can Speak? Authority and Critical Identity*, ed. Judith Roof and Robyn Wiegman, (Urbana: U. of Illinois Press, 1995), 97 - 119. See especially 109.

39. Paul Carter, quoted in Iain Chambers, *Migrancy, Culture, Identity*, 42. The paragraph containing this statement, from Paul Carter's *Living in a New Country: History, Travelling and Language* (London: Faber & Faber, 1992), quoted in Chambers, 42, is instructive here: "An authentically migrant perspective would, perhaps, be based on an intuition that the opposition between here and there is itself a cultural construction, a consequence of

The fixed categories of identity that Mennonites once believed they could slip into unproblematically are no longer useful. The binary oppositions inscribed in their literary-critical writing and thinking over the past half century serve them ill. Those who talk about Mennonite cultural identity must now learn to read the expanded text (or "assemblage of texts") that creative writers have begun to inscribe.[40] The place that Mennonite writers are writing from, like the place most of us occupy, is not eternally fixed but is "somewhere in motion"[41] — between the early twentieth-century world of George and Clara in Jeff Gundy's *A Community of Memory* and the world of Gundy's self-conscious, sometimes postmodern narrator, for example; or between the modest sensibility of conservative Mennonite market vendor Emma Peachey and the ambivalently urban/e consciousness of the speaker in Julia Kasdorf's "Green Market, New York," the opening poem in *Sleeping Preacher*. Poems, Jeff Gundy has observed, "probe areas that the credos leave untouched, they insist that all experience and all feeling deserve attention, they work toward the messy inclusiveness of life itself."[42] Creative works like Gundy's and Kasdorf's are compelling explorations of that "in-between" world the Mennonites' binary understandings have not allowed them to name or claim: a place of re-territorialization, re-connection, re-inscription, re-membering.

In their critical work writers like Gundy, Kasdorf and others have not entirely escaped the fixed, oppositional essentialisms that have, for decades, confined the Mennonites and their writers; but literature, by its very nature, eschews the fixity and essentialism that binary propositions imply. In their poetry and stories, Mennonite writers have demonstrated that the conventionally bounded and hierarchical binary categories of insider and outsider, home and exile reveal little about the complex personal and cultural situations in which contemporary Mennonites live. By exploring and re-mapping the "postmodern world of indeterminacy and undecidability" in their creative work[43] Mennonite writers have begun to inscribe the diverse, multiple and unfixed "locations of

thinking in terms of fixed entities and defining them oppositionally. It might begin by regarding movement, not as an awkward interval between fixed points of departure and arrival, but as a mode of being in the world. The question would be, then, not how to arrive, but how to move, how to identify convergent and divergent movements; and the challenge would be how to notate such events, how to give them a historical and social value."

40. In *The Predicament of Culture: Twentieth-Century Ethnography, Literature, and Art* (Cambridge: Harvard U. Press, 1988) anthropologist James Clifford refers to culture as an "assemblage of texts, loosely and sometimes contradictorly united" (41).

41. See Jonathan Rutherford, ed., *Identity: Community, Culture, Difference* (London: Lawrence & Wishart, 1990), 9-27, esp.13.

42. Gundy, "U.S. Mennonite Poetry and Poets: Beyond Dr. Johnson's Dog," 8.

43. Ibid., 30.

culture"[44] where contemporary Mennonites inevitably find themselves, and hence to re-inscribe the Mennonites' cultural identity. "I believe that we will benefit from listening to our poets," Jeff Gundy remarked recently. "I doubt that they will save us," he continued modestly, "but I believe they can make us a little less lost."[45]

---

44. I borrow the phrase from Homi K. Bhabha's collection of essays by the same name, *The Location of Culture.*

45. Gundy, "U.S. Mennonite Poetry and Poets: Beyond Dr. Johnson's Dog," 39.

IN PRAISE OF THE LURKERS (WHO COME OUT TO SPEAK)

JEFF GUNDY*

Abstract: Mennonite writers may be compared to Internet "lurkers," who are in their worldly and religious communities but not entirely of them. Philosophers from Plato to Kierkegaard, and writers such as Wallace Stevens and William Stafford, have worried over the relation of writers to their community. Mennonite writers such as Keith Ratzlaff, Dallas Wiebe, Julia Kasdorf and Jean Janzen indeed serve the Mennonite community by bringing back the discoveries of their inner and outer travels, by complicating and expanding the communal sense of what is true and real, and by providing the leaven of laughter as a counterbalance to whatever views are accepted too readily.

From Joseph Joder to Julia Kasdorf, to be a writer among Mennonites has been a strange calling. We have little practice at how to treat them, and Mennonite writers have struggled to know what to do with Mennonites as well. I suppose little of this should surprise us. After all, many — perhaps most — writers and artists have always had some kind of borderline position in their communities. Borrowing a term from the new Internet lexicon, we might call them "lurkers." Like Walt Whitman and Emily Dickinson, those prototypical lurkers, Mennonite writers are in their world — and often their religious community — but not quite of it. Controversial or beloved, tolerated or ignored, they are bound to be at least partly "other." We might, then, take that marginality as a given and explore some of what it means, for writers and for the community.

I want to look briefly at the social functions of lurkers, at their role as inner and outer travelers and the news they bring, at their relation to what I will call, loosely, "truth" and "imagination," and finally at the strangely linked topics of angels and laughter. I will briefly discuss some Mennonite writers and texts, but I will also examine some ways that writers from a much wider sphere have explored these issues. They are our concerns, but not only ours.

SOCIAL FUNCTIONS

Reading Plato's *The Republic* this summer, I had the eerie feeling that I was overhearing two good, upstanding, traditional Mennonite men of a slightly earlier era — a preacher and a college president, say — discussing

---

* Jeff Gundy is Professor of English at Bluffton College, Bluffton, Ohio.

how to keep their institutions in order. Consider this part of the discussion between Glaucon and Socrates, who speaks first:

> "But if you receive the honeyed Muse [of poetry] in lyric or epic, be sure that pleasure and pain will be kings in your city, instead of law and whatever reasoned argument the community shall approve in each case to be best."

> "Very true," he said.

> "So much then," said I, "for our defence . . . we were justified before in banishing [poetry] from our city. For it was reason which led us on. And lest she condemn us as rather harsh and rough, let us tell her that there is an ancient feud between philosophy and poetry."[1]

Plato refuses the poets entry because he knows they can't be trusted to be reasonable, rational and helpful. He accuses them, quite rightly, of saying things that are neither orthodox, nor strictly true, nor calculated to maintain the social order. The traditional Mennonite view of imaginative literature repeats Plato's caution: the most powerful poets must be kept out of the city, lest they lead the people astray with their wild, seductive images and stories. Only "the more austere and less pleasing poet and storyteller," who will limit his work to pious, edifying tales of the sort useful for the instruction of children, can be safely admitted.[2]

A long time later, Kierkegaard took up similar questions and came to similar conclusions about the utility and danger of poetry. In *The Concept of Irony* he argues—following Socrates—that poetry provides only an illusory sort of truth:

> Poetry opens up a higher actuality, expands and transfigures the imperfect into the perfect, and thereby softens and mitigates that deep pain which would darken and obscure all things. To this extent poetry is a kind of reconciliation, though not the true reconciliation. . . . Only the religious . . . is capable of effecting the true reconciliation, for it renders actuality infinite for me.[3]

As you might expect, I'm not content to let either Plato or Kierkegaard have the last word here. Poets have always sensed, and sometimes argued, that what they do has a social function, although one not easily defined or understood in purely rational or utilitarian terms. Here is

---

1. Plato, *Great Dialogues of Plato*, trans. W. H. D. Rouse (New York: Mentor, 1956), 407 (Book X).

2. Ibid., 196.

3. Søren Kierkegaard, *The Concept of Irony: With Constant Reference to Socrates*, trans. Lee M. Capel (Bloomington, IN: Indiana U. Press, 1965), 312.

what that prototypical lurker, poet and insurance executive Wallace Stevens, had to say:

> What is [the poet's] function? Certainly it is not to lead people out of the confusion in which they find themselves. Nor is it, I think, to comfort them. . . . I think that his function is to make his imagination theirs and that he fulfills himself only as he sees his imagination become the light in the minds of others. His role, in short, is to help people live.[4]

With these rather contradictory claims in our heads, it is time to look at some real Mennonite lurkers. Of course, the purest lurkers never say anything; they are in deep cover, for reasons that range from shyness to schizophrenia to pure self-preservation. We should not need reminding these days about the human and Mennonite capacity to ostracize and persecute anyone we perceive as too different from ourselves. Despite the risks, of course, some lurkers do sneak out and speak; others, even in their silence, strike a chord in those around them.

One example of the latter is a man named John Nachtigall, whom Keith Ratzlaff remembers living in the middle of his hometown of Henderson, Nebraska. In his essay "The Poet as John Nachtigall" Ratzlaff describes Nachtigall's lonely life in the old train depot, known to everyone but talking to nobody, spied on through the windows. Ratzlaff argues that Nachtigall, even in his silence, performed an important communal function:

> I've come to see John Nachtigall's role in my home town as a kind of allegory of the role of the poet in the larger world, as an answer to the question of whether art and artists matter. That Nachtigall lived in the very heart of town, not on the edge of it or on a farm by the river, forced us to think differently about ourselves. We had to include him because he lived with us and we had to account for what it meant to include him. We didn't have to like him or talk to him, but he made us think inclusively — as a community not a tribe.[5]

A lurker who did choose to speak, and was estranged although not quite shunned as a result, was the poet, farmer and part-time schoolteacher Joseph Joder (not to be confused with another classic lurker, the J. W. Yoder who wrote *Rosanna of the Amish*). Joseph Joder's universalist beliefs and poems like "Die Frohe Botschaft" helped to trigger the Stuckey Amish schism in the 1870s in central Illinois. Well into his eighties, long after he had been excluded from communion for

---

4 Wallace Stevens, "The Noble Rider and the Sound of Words," *in The Necessary Angel: Essays on Reality and the Imagination* (New York: Vintage, 1951), 29.
5 Keith Ratzlaff, "The Poet as John Nachtigall," *Mennonite Life* 46 (Dec. 1991), 23.

the dangerous idea that God loves all his children too much to torment any of them throughout eternity, Joder was still driving his buggy into the village of Carlock for the mail, stopping the children to quiz them on their German and exhort them to learn the old tongue, studying his Hebrew and Greek, hoping someday to get to the heart of the Scriptures. He was with his people, deeply engaged in their lives and their efforts to be faithful to their tradition, their God and their destiny. Yet he was also set apart by his particular, unconventional, perhaps heretical vision.[6]

TRAVELS, INNER AND OUTER

Joseph Joder became a lurker largely because he traveled—not physically, but intellectually—into places that his fellows were content to leave alone. This seems to me one of the most universal qualities of lurkers: they leave the valley, cross the mountains, go on reckless physical or mental journeys and come back changed. Lurkers are always crossing cultural boundaries of one sort or another; what they return with, whether or not it has anything to do with poverty or oppression or salvation, may be powerful and even life-changing.

Lurkers find themselves outside the sanctioned channels, in the company of junkies and rock musicians and adulterers and homosexuals and assorted other Bad People. They encounter Rumi or Mirabai, Leonard Cohen or Sappho, Adrienne Rich or Allen Ginsberg or the Grateful Dead—I could name fifty other names, and we all could make our own lists—and realize that they will never again be able to live without ideas and images and words that originate in traditions and cultures wildly different from—and opposed to, in major ways—their home communities. They discover human beings who are not Mennonite or Christian or heterosexual or white or American but still seem smarter and clearer and deeper than just about anybody in Bluffton or Goshen or even Lancaster County.

It does not take much of this, if you are of the true lurker character, to destroy forever the idea that everything you will ever need is right there inside any one tidy enclave. And so lurkers live out their lives in more than one world, even if they live in places like Bluffton, Ohio and Pella, Iowa and Camp Hill, Pennsylvania. In those other worlds they find what Kenneth Burke called "equipment for living"—images and ideas that enable, or condemn, them to live in ways just a little—or a lot—out of the ordinary. They live in worlds of the head and the heart that make phrases like "keeping salvation ethical" or "the discipling community"

---

6 See Olynthus Clark, "Joseph Joder, Schoolmaster-Farmer and Poet 1797-1887," *Transactions of the Illinois State Historical Society* 36 (1929), 135-65, for a biographical sketch of Joder. For an imaginative reconstruction of Joder, see my *A Community of Memory* (Urbana: U. of Illinois Press, 1996).

or "official denominational position" sound bizarre and unreal, the way words do if you say them ten or twelve times in a row.

Lurkers come back from those other worlds the way children come back from the creek, with treasures that their parents are not sure should be in the house. Sometimes they come home in fact, sometimes in story, sometimes soon and sometimes late. Dallas Wiebe spent a good part of his life trying to get as far from his Kansas Mennonite roots as he could. In one of his Kansas Poems he puts it this way: "When I visit Kansas / I take the slow train out / and fly back."[7] Yet after writing one of the archetypal Mennonite kiss-it-goodbye novels, *Skyblue the Badass*, and spending many years teaching and working in Cincinnati (which might in a strange way be as much like a Mennonite city as one with only a handful of Mennonites can be), he wrote a wonderful novel about his Russian Mennonite roots. *Our Asian Journey* is both postmodernist and deeply traditional, and I think it's safe to say we wouldn't have it if he hadn't spent that long period of lurking and traveling.[8]

The central dynamic of Julia Kasdorf's *Sleeping Preacher*[9] is the strain that develops out of her travels, physical and imaginative, between the two worlds of New York City and Big Valley, Pennsylvania. The book's first poem "Green Market, New York" describes a wonderful, strange, familiar moment when the speaker and an Amish woman who is also from Big Valley play the Mennonite game on a New York street. Her speaker knows that in some ways she can never go home again, but that in other ways, as the title of "I Carry Dead Vesta" suggests, she will always carry that ancestral home within her. And so, the poem suggests, lurkers may have their own interior lurkers, figures of memory and desire and imagination that haunt and tempt, obsess and infuriate and inspire them.

TRUTH AND IMAGINATION

I have lived for a long time under the institutional motto "The truth makes free." But I have also lived for a long time with the sense that "the truth" was much too complicated and messy to ever get my head around. William Stafford said part of it in a poem about teaching: "Well, Right has a long and intricate name / And the saying of it is a lonely

---

7. Dallas Wiebe, *The Kansas Poems* (Cincinnati: Cincinnati Poetry Review Press, 1987), 34.

8. Dallas Wiebe, *Our Asian Journey* (Waterloo, ON: MLR Editions Canada, 1997).

9. Julia Kasdorf, *Sleeping Preacher* (Pittsburgh: U. of Pittsburgh Press, 1992).

thing."[10] Wallace Stevens also muses on the relation between truth and imagination:

> We have been a little insane about the truth. We have had an obsession. In its ultimate extension, the truth about which we have been insane will lead us to look beyond the truth to something in which the imagination will be the dominant complement. It is not only that the imagination adheres to reality, but, also, that reality adheres to the imagination and that the interdependence is essential.[11]

Stevens insists here that imaginative constructions have a kind of value, a kind of use, that is different from the uses of truth but equally important. His long meditation on such issues led him into speculation about a "supreme fiction," something we could believe in even though we knew we had made it up ourselves. I am not sure I accept that idea, but as a fellow lurker I share his sense that "truth" — especially in the narrow sense of adherence to common-sense "realism" or some abstract, credal version of orthodoxy — is considerably overrated. And the lurkers' function, perhaps above all, is to make their strange and sometimes dangerous visions of that complicated, inexhaustible reality available to us.

As examples of Mennonite writing that follows along these lines, I might quote almost any of Jean Janzen's poems, which cumulatively represent a deep and rich world of memory, knowledge and desire. "Cover Me," for example, moves unobtrusively from the simplest memory to far deeper levels of meditation:

> When I offered to wash dishes after supper
> you sent me to practice the piano.
> I wonder now whether you wanted the music
> to take me to places you had never seen,
> playing Mozart and Rachmaninoff in the scents
> of my first cologne from my first boy,
> your hand waving me off into danger.
> You knew that my dresses moved like water
> when I walked, or was it fire, our true covering?
> The way you now let your good dresses hang
> unused, your skin so thin and translucent,
> it wants to flare and rise.[12]

---

10. William Stafford, "Lit Instructor," in *Stories That Could Be True* (New York: Harper/Colophon, 1977), 78.

11. Stevens, *The Necessary Angel*, 33.

12. Jean Janzen, *Snake in the Parsonage* (Intercourse, PA: Good Books, 1995), 54.

There is much here that is unsaid, or only intimated, and yet very firmly present. The poem says a great deal about the movement of a girl from innocence to experience, about music and feeling, about the knowledge that passes between mothers and daughters, with or without words. It is a poem about love, sex and death that never uses any of those words, a poem that moves toward an imaginative apprehension far deeper and more complex than the mere surface reality of a woman and a girl in a room. There we are, lurking with her in that strange, deep new room of the imagination, where the physical details are only a blurred shadow of the human reality the poem directs us toward.

ANGELS AND LAUGHTER

The great romantic lurker, visionary and heretic William Blake said, among many other reckless things, that "without contraries is no progression." Wallace Stevens likewise insists that reality and the imagination are necessary to each other, that "reality adheres to the imagination and that the interdependence is essential."[13] Stevens, Blake and the great Czech writer Milan Kundera all write of angels and devils. Kundera's *Book of Laughter and Forgetting* proposes a sort of Manichean vision that associates angels with order and devils with individualism, recklessness and artistic creativity. He insists that both are necessary:

> Angels are not partisans of Good, but of divine creation. The Devil, on the other hand, denies all rational meaning to God's world. . . . If there is too much uncontested meaning on earth (the reign of the angels), man collapses under the burden; if the world loses all its meaning (the reign of the demons), life is every bit as impossible.[14]

Kundera suggests that the laughter of angels rejoices in order and harmony; that of devils, in chaos and absurdity. They are not always easy to distinguish. Which sort of laughter comes from the lurkers? Both, I suspect. I also suspect that lurkers often feel compelled to take whichever side seems least popular. When the communal order becomes too powerful, they cry out for freedom and the individual; when order breaks down, they sing of the harmonious community. Finally, perhaps the lurkers are here to be a counterbalance, to remind us of what would otherwise be lost in consensus and conformity and majority rule, to allow and insist that we laugh as well as mourn, dance as well as sing, not forget whatever is counter and spare and strange and yet also within

---

13. Stevens, *The Necessary Angel*, 33.
14. Milan Kundera, *The Book of Laughter and Forgetting*, trans. Michael Henry Heim (New York: Penguin, 1980), 61.

our circle. Let me end in that spirit by quoting the great Sufi Mennonite poet, mystic and lurker, Rumi:

> There is a community of the spirit.
> Join it, and feel the delight
> of walking in the noisy street,
> and being the noise.
>
> Drink all your passion,
> and be a disgrace.
>
> Close both eyes
> to see with the other eye . . .
>
> Why do you stay in prison
> when the door is so wide open?
>
> Move outside the tangle of fear-thinking.
> Live in silence.
>
> Flow down and down in always
> widening rings of being.[15]

To be a lurker is to walk the streets knowing at once that you are in the community, inseparable from it, and at the same moment in a world far away, one where strange voices whisper brilliant, frightening sentences and demands—the most frightening demand of all being that you listen even when you know that doing so will mean that you must change your life. It is to feel yourself a disgrace to both worlds, knowing that you really are at home in neither, and that you can never do justice to either one. To feel responsible and alien, bound and free, sinful and prophetic, at the same moment. To sense that your work in the world may be, not to find some pure, true Word and sing it once for all, but to bend the hints and glimpses and obstinate questionings that come your way into some shape that might be of some use to a few others. That is not such an easy way to spend a life, but not such a bad way either.

---

15. Maulana Jalal al-Din Rumi, *The Essential Rumi*, trans. Coleman Barks (New York: HarperCollins, 1995), 3.

THE UNOFFICIAL VOICE:
THE POETICS OF CULTURAL IDENTITY AND
CONTEMPORARY U.S. MENNONITE POETRY

ANN HOSTETLER*

Abstract: Contemporary poetry by writers of Mennonite heritage has been receiving unprecedented attention from both the Mennonite and the literary communities. This essay discusses the role of the poet in relation to Mennonite culture and seeks to define Mennonite poetry as ethnic literature in a broader sense. Drawing on a model of culture articulated by Stuart Hall, I suggest that the "unofficial voice" of the poet can portray complex internal differences within Mennonite culture that are not articulated in official constructions of Mennonite identity. Furthermore, Mennonite poets can be viewed as cultural translators who thrive at cultural crossroads. Poems by Mennonite writers Sheri Hostetler, Jean Janzen and Julia Kasdorf illustrate the ways that ethnic poetry simultaneously addresses Mennonite readers and non-ethnic readers, challenging the former to re-examine their cultural heritage and the latter to see their own humanity in the representation of ethnicity.

During coffee hour one Sunday morning at church shortly after I began editing an anthology of Mennonite poets, I fell into a conversation about the poetry of Jean Janzen with a Mennonite businessman who has a Ph.D. in English. He asked me whether I knew that Janzen's father had been a Mennonite minister. "I find her poems more meaningful than her father's sermons, however," he confided. At that moment, coffee cup in hand, participating in one of the informal but vital rituals of Mennonite community, I saw with new clarity the seemingly ambiguous role of the poet in the Mennonite community. Poetry is the unofficial voice. It is what one might think during the sermon, but never say aloud. Only after the sermon is over, sometimes long afterwards, are such private thoughts recollected in tranquility and shaped in language by the poet for another audience: individual readers of poetry. Such readers of poetry are increasing among U.S. Mennonites, and poets from Mennonite origins are, for the first time, contributing to a sense of collective Mennonite identity both inside and outside of the Mennonite community.

---

*Ann Hostetler is Assistant Professor of English at Goshen College. She is currently editing an anthology of Mennonite poetry in North America.

Janzen has written a number of poems about her father. In "Order" she shows the difference between her and her father's relationship to language as well as the difference between their delivery of the "word" to an audience. This juxtaposition mirrors the relationship of poet and preacher in the Mennonite community:

> Saturday afternoon, father in his study
> hunts and pecks the Order of Service.
> I can still see it, the invocation,
> hymn of praise, the growing columns of words.
> Rock and fortress, he will say tomorrow,
> wings over us. And set on a table
> between the pillars is his sermon,
> a pitcherful shivering until morning.
> Keys clatter, the return bar swings down
> to the benediction, his arms over the people.
> They will stand like these inked letters,
> surrounded by silence, a whiteness
> that vibrates like the ceiling in his study,
> which sometimes rises and opens, books
> towering on all sides — *My Utmost for His Highest,*
> *The Cloud of Unknowing* — the pages
> like slippery steps, and forever turning.[1]

As the vehicle for representing her father's sermons, Janzen has chosen the private moment of composition (the silence in which the already written sermon awaits an audience like a "pitcherful shivering until morning") rather than the performative moment of delivery. Thus she recasts her preacher-father as poet (albeit of the predictable) and herself as predictor of the poem's effect on the audience. Although she writes about one whose vocation is to voice the official word of the church, she renders him in a private act, that of composition. Yet his public sermons are delivered to an audience who "will stand like these inked letters/ surrounded by silence." The official word, delivered from the pulpit, requires the audience to mute individual thought, marginalizing all that is not centered in the sermon. Poetry, on the other hand, provides a space for multiple voices and points of view. Those reluctant or unwelcome to stand behind the pulpit, or submit to its constraints, can deliver the Word through a poem. Thus it is not surprising that women are strongly represented among contemporary Mennonite poets.

A lyric poem is a personal statement. The poet invites readers to imagine their own lives as poetry, to engage in imaginative dialogue about the experiences of being alive that mostly fall outside of official

---

1. Jean Janzen, *The Snake in the Parsonage* (Intercourse, PA: Good Books, 1995), 22.

discourse. Yet the poet's audience can extend far beyond the bounds of the preacher's Sunday morning listeners to include those outside of the community. (Of course the poet will not reach all or even most of the Sunday morning listeners even though the poet's work is read by members of a broadly scattered literary community.) Thus, in cross-cultural perspective, the personal poem can serve as a bridge between cultures, whereas a sermon serves to ideologically re-center the practitioners of a particular culture. The poet invites the reader to become part of what anthropologist James Clifford terms "a cultural poetics that is an interplay of voices, of positioned utterances."[2] By focusing her poem on her father's Saturday sermon-making, Janzen positions his utterance within hers, bringing the marginal (the private voice) and the official into a new relationship or order not dependent on a hierarchy of margin/center.

The 1990s have seen an unprecedented flourishing in the United States of poets from Mennonite origins who have received recognition not so much from their communities of origin but from mainstream literary communities.[3] The recent recognition in the U.S. of writers from Mennonite contexts, preceded by an earlier recognition of Mennonite poets in Canada during the 1980s, seems startling because it heralds the emergence of significant poetry from an ethnic group that has scarcely had a tradition in the literary arts. In fact, Mennonite literature seems to be a category very much in the process of creation. It appears to have been developing behind the scenes for the past several generations, fueled by Mennonite higher education in the arts, which has trained both writers and their potential audiences. While Mennonite writers and scholars John Ruth and Al Reimer[4] have attempted to characterize the role of literature in Mennonite culture—the Swiss/American and

---

2. James Clifford, "Introduction: Partial Truths," in *Writing Culture: The Poetics and Politics of Ethnography*, ed. James Clifford and George E. Marcus (Berkeley: U. of California Press, 1986), 12.

3. In 1991 Julia Kasdorf received the Agnes Lynch Starrett poetry prize from the University of Pittsburgh Press for her first book, *Sleeping Preacher* (1992). Jeff Gundy's first full-length book of poetry, *Inquiries* (1992), was followed in 1994 by a second book of poetry, *Flatlands*, a finalist for the Cleveland State University Press poetry prize. Jean Janzen won a National Endowment for the Arts Grant in 1995 and published her first full-length book of poetry in the United States, *Snake in the Parsonage*, in the same year. In 1996 two poets from Mennonite background—Juanita Brunk and Keith Ratzlaff—won the Brittingham Prize (University of Wisconsin Press) and the Anhinga Prize (Anhinga Press, Tallahassee, FL) for their first books, *Brief Landing on the Earth's Surface* and *Man Under a Pear Tree* respectively. Betsy Sholl, the 1997 winner of the Felix Pollack Prize (University of Wisconsin Press) for *Don't Explain*, is also affiliated with Mennonites. A number of other Mennonite poets have been publishing regularly in literary journals during the same time.

4. See John Ruth, *Mennonite Identity and Literary Art* (Scottdale, PA: Herald Press, 1976) and Al Reimer, *Mennonite Literary Voices: Past and Present* (North Newton, KS: Bethel College, 1993).

Russian/Canadian strands respectively—little other serious critical attention has been paid to Mennonite poets in the United States until very recently.[5] On the other hand, outsiders' recognition of the poet's merit—a recognition that is just coming about—seems crucial to the Mennonite community's recognition of their poets. It appears that contemporary poets of Mennonite origin first have to establish their credentials outside of the Mennonite community before gaining a Mennonite audience. Thus poets of Mennonite origin seem to span the borders of the Mennonite and the literary communities.

MENNONITE POETRY AND THE CONSTRUCTION OF ETHNIC IDENTITY

What is a "Mennonite" poet? Does ethnic/religious context influence a writer's form or discourse? How and by whom is Mennonite ethnicity constructed? Is it possible for someone to be culturally Mennonite, although not a member of the church, when the church defines itself as a community of believers baptized as consenting adults? Jeff Gundy suggests that "poets of Mennonite extraction have radically varied experiences—almost one per writer."[6] In addition, the ways in which poets associated with Mennonites view the influence of their Mennonite background on their work varies widely as well. Janet Kauffman, whose father was raised a Mennonite and who grew up in an extended family of Mennonites, writes that "the Mennonite questioning of all cultural matters . . . in moral terms was crucial to me—the refusal to simply accept what the culture offers."[7] Patrick Friesen, on the other hand, whose upbringing in a strict and isolated Canadian Mennonite community might seem to provide a much stronger influence, writes "I have never thought of myself as a Mennonite poet. Just, a poet, who happens to come from Mennonite birth. . . . Yet, I have been utterly shaped by my Menno birth and upbringing."[8] Jean Janzen's poetry comes out of a life steeped in her vital participation in her Mennonite Brethren denomination. Shari Miller Wagner shares a similar commitment to her church community. Julia Kasdorf grew up in a Mennonite family, was baptized in the Mennonite church, and attended Goshen College for a few years before completing the remainder of her

---

5. Gundy, "U.S. Mennonite Poetry and Poets: Beyond Dr. Johnson's Dog," in *The Mennonite Quarterly Review* 71 (Jan. 1997), 5-442, and Ervin Beck, "A Reader's Guide to Mennonite Literature, " *Gospel Herald*, Oct. 14, 1997, 4-8. On October 23-26, 1997, a landmark conference, Mennonite(s) Writing in the U.S., was held at Goshen College in Goshen, Indiana. *The Mennonite* (Bethel College) and *Mennonot* have provided periodical forums for Mennonite poets.

6. Gundy, "U.S. Mennonite Poetry," 9.

7. Letter to the author, March, 1998.

8. Letter to the author, April 1998.

education at New York University. Currently she attends an Episcopal church and is a professor of writing at Messiah College. In their various relations to Mennonite community, I consider all of these poets as Mennonite poets, for each writes out of a profound and indelible experience of being Mennonite, whether or not he or she is currently an active member of a Mennonite congregation. Some things can be more clearly seen by ex-members or non-members, and I include their valuable perspectives in my broad definition of Mennonite poets.

Ethnic poets can be viewed as cultural translators who address a number of different audiences simultaneously. Their poetry, in its representation of ethnicity, can be viewed as a multi-faceted mirror. One facet reflects back to members of the ethnic group a portrait of their culture. Another facet at first appears to be a window providing a glimpse into Mennonite culture, but this window also serves as a mirror in which non-ethnic readers can recognize kindred aspects of their own experiences. According to anthropologist Michael M. J. Fischer, the definition of ethnicity arises in the borderland between the larger culture and the minority culture: "Ethnicity is a process of inter-reference between two or more cultural traditions, and . . . these dynamics of intercultural knowledge provide reservoirs for renewing human values."[9] Thus the very concept of ethnicity is predicated on an awareness of cultural boundary crossings.

This is clearly illustrated by the different ways in which Canadian and U. S. Mennonite poets have constructed their ethnicity in relation to a larger national identity.[10] Canadian Mennonite poets have received national recognition during the 1980s and 90s when Canadian government grants offered incentives for ethnic publishing. Although the funds are scarcer now, Hildi Froese Tiessen was nonetheless able to make the claim in 1989 "that among our 'minority literary communities' . . . few . . . are at present more productive — or more visible as a literary

---

9. Michael M. J. Fischer, "Ethnicity and the Post-Modern Arts of Memory," in *Writing Culture,* ed. James Clifford and George Marcus (Berkeley: U. of California Press, 1986), 194-233.

10. The broad outlines of Canadian and U. S. Mennonite ethnicity also differ. While Mennonites in Canada are not exclusively of Russian descent, the majority of Canadian Mennonites are and thus have a comparatively recent traumatic history of immigration, the effects of which are still alive in the memories of surviving members of the group who immigrated earlier in this century. This group of Mennonites also has a specific ethnic, cultural and communal heritage that is still viable both in language difference and cultural practice. Ethnic Mennonites (or "birthright Mennonites," to borrow a phrase used by Quakers to designate people whose ancestry is Quaker) in the U. S., while certainly not of exclusively Swiss descent, are predominantly of Swiss Mennonite heritage and tend to have immigrated much earlier — as long as 260 years ago. Though Mennonites have preached "separation from the world" for much of that time, nonetheless their communities have been bounded by a kind of semi-permeable membrane that permits, if not encourages, an ongoing exchange with non-Mennonites.

community—than the Mennonites."[11] Since the Vietnam War era in the United States, however, Mennonites in general—let alone Mennonite poets—have received little recognition from the surrounding culture beyond their immediate spheres of influence (such as in peace lobbying in Washington, MCC relief work, the business community in Lancaster County, etc.). The national construction of a multi-cultural literature during the past two decades in the *U.S. does not include Mennonite among its major categories: African American, Hispanic, Asian American, American Indian. In fact, within the broader context of U. S. culture, one must apparently make a case for the category of Mennonite poet as an ethnic, rather than a merely denominational one.[12]

How is it that Mennonites in the United States and Canada, who have been slow to recognize and value their own artists, have produced poets who speak to an audience beyond the boundaries of the Mennonite community? Because ethnic literature is a literature of intercultural translation, it depends on how much interest readers and writers on both sides of a cultural boundary have in crossing its border. The "translatability" of ethnicity in literature is predicated on the notion that the universal is in the particular, that the specific experiences of individuals in specific subcultures have corollaries in the experiences of other individuals in other subcultures. At the same time, there is a residue of particularity that is not translatable, that has a different sort of appeal to readers curious about other ways of life. Within the Mennonite spectrum there is such a high degree of diversity that even Mennonite readers from a particular part of the spectrum may encounter this residue of the untranslatable in literature by Mennonite writers from another part of the spectrum.

The interest in poets of Mennonite origin also comes at a time when the larger culture is interested in representations of specific ethnic experiences. Ethnic literature, as opposed to folk literature, arises at the point when members of a culture find it vital to translate their specific cultural experiences into language and discursive forms accessible to

---

11. Hildi Froese Tiessen, "Mennonite/s Writing in Canada: An Introduction," *The New Quarterly* [Special Issue: Mennonite/s Writing in Canada], 10 (Spring/Summer 1990), 9. Fine pioneering work in Mennonite literature has been done by Hildi Froese Tiessen, professor of English at Conrad Grebel College, University of Waterloo, Canada, and the vital arts community of Mennonite and formerly Mennonite writers in Canada, especially Winnipeg, Manitoba. Many U. S. Mennonite writers have been encouraged and inspired by the work of such poets as Di Brandt and Patrick Friesen and David Waltner-Toews, as well as Tiessen's critical articulation of a community of Mennonite ethnic writers. As an anthologist of a volume (currently in progress) of Mennonite poets, I am grateful for Froese Tiessen's example.

12. An exception is the inclusion of Julia Kasdorf's poem "Mennonites" in *The Many Worlds of Literature*, ed. Stuart Hirschberg (New York: Macmillan, 1994), as the sole entry in the category "Mennonite."

those outside of their ethnic group. Werner Sollors defines ethnic literature as "works written by, about, or for persons who perceived themselves, or were perceived by others, as members of ethnic groups, including even nationally and internationally popular writings by 'major' authors and formally intricate texts."[13] Ethnic writers, Sollors suggests, may be even more open to experimentation with language than mainstream writers because of their experiences with multiple languages, perspectives, and marginality."[14] Thus while ethnic literature may at first appear to hearken back to tradition and to develop apart from major literary movements and innovations, Werner Sollors convincingly argues that American "ethnic" writers are actually innovators.[15] Some poets from Mennonite background, however, have been cautious about the "ethnic" label. Some feel the term "Mennonite poet" to be reductionistic; others welcome the designation as an opportunity for Mennonite poets to emerge as one of the many ethnic strands in the complex symphony of North American voices. To complicate matters, the term "ethnicity" is construed differently in U.S. and Canadian contexts.[16]

I use the word "ethnic" to describe Mennonite identity, because the term implies a relationship between the Mennonite subculture and the culture that surrounds it. Through their practices of "nonconformity" and "nonresistance," Mennonites have formed communities that are necessarily apart intellectually and spiritually, if not always physically, from those of the larger culture. Thus, when writers grow up in the Mennonite community, their consciousness is shaped not only by a set of religious beliefs but by the intimate experience of cultural structures that have arisen from those beliefs. Furthermore, their world view is also shaped by the ways in which their community construes its relationship to the larger society.

Community among Mennonites, however, is not just an accidental result of commonly held beliefs, but is deliberately pursued as an expression of God's earthly presence in covenanted relationships. In its most holistic form—as embodied in its Old Order groups—Mennonite and Amish religious expression is inseparably intertwined with the particulars of practice in the formation and maintenance of community.

13. Werner Sollors, *Beyond Ethnicity: Consent and Descent in American Culture* (New York: Oxford U. Press, 1986), 243.

14. Ibid., 244-5.

15. "Introduction: Inventing Ethnicity," in *The Invention of Ethnicity* (New York: Oxford, 1989), xiii.

16. See Hildi Froese Tiessen, "Introduction: Mennonite Writing and the Post-Colonial Condition" in *Acts of Concealment: Mennonites Writing in Canada*, ed. Hildi Froese Tiessen and Peter Hinchcliffe (Waterloo, ON: U. of Waterloo Press, 1992). See also Linda Hutcheon on "crypto-ethnicity" in "Four Views on Ethnicity," *PMLA* 113 (January 1998), 28-33.

While such groups appear to be the "most ethnic" to outsiders, they are also the groups least preoccupied with the definition of their own ethnicity. This is because their boundaries are clearly delineated, and their encounters with outsiders clearly defined. In their communities the larger society is constructed as separate and "other."

The term "ethnicity" is not needed until the boundary between cultures becomes well-traveled, muddied, or even central to one's identity. The term—but not the phenomenon—originated with modernism.[17] The use of the term "ethnicity" by Mennonites themselves signifies a moment of self-consciousness in which the unity of faith and practice has already begun to unravel with the admission of multiple perspectives as a way of interrogating it.

FAITH AND ETHNICITY

From within Mennonite culture discussions of ethnicity in relation to faith often become perplexing. Certainly Mennonites have a unique history, stemming either from the Dutch/Russian/Prussian stream or the Swiss/Alsatian/Amish stream. But membership in the church has always been an adult choice—not one bestowed by legacy or birth. As a totality, Mennonites can be viewed more as a diaspora—a displaced and scattered global community—than as an ethnic group arising out of a particular national context. Yet, many Mennonites today are barely aware of the larger history and heritage of the group, even though history has been a primary disciplinary focus of Mennonite scholars for the past seventy or so years, as dated by the founding of *The Mennonite Quarterly Review*. While Mennonites originated in Europe during the Reformation, today they span the globe and their fastest-growing segment lives beyond the boundaries of North America.

In the broader context of global Mennonite identity, however, the discussion of ethnicity as a valid way of defining "Mennonite" might be offensive to some Mennonites, especially those who define their Mennonite identity on the basis of church. membership.[18] After all, ethnicity excludes. It is genetically and racially inflected. And it is a category that secularizes religious experience in the sense that it is a term, and thus a framing of experience, borrowed from the worldly discipline of anthropology. One might argue that when discussions of

---

17. Sollors, *Beyond Ethnicity*, 23. Sollors cites 1941 as the date of the first American use of this adjective.

18. Today's fastest growing Mennonite congregations are those in Africa and Latin America, where the surrounding cultures have influenced worship and community in ways that have nothing to do with the ethnic trappings of European-inflected Anabaptism.

ethnicity arise, they are often prompted by a desire to preserve the material manifestations of a no longer vital spirituality.

However, faith and ethnicity are not mutually exclusive terms in binary opposition, but categories created by different disciplinary perspectives, serving the needs of different audiences. Faith is a religious, spiritual, theological and psychological term that implies an ahistorical perspective; ethnicity is a cultural, historical, anthropological term used to describe the relationships of diverse subcultures within a larger national or cultural group. Those concerned more with faith within the Mennonite community tend not to concern themselves with the boundaries created by the perspective of ethnicity. By contrast, those invested in constructing Mennonite ethnic identity are highly sensitive to the *cultural* context of religious practice that makes translation not only a necessity, but an often exhilarating challenge as well.[19] In fact, to separate faith and ethnicity is to create a false dichotomy, for faith—or at least a faith tradition—is an indispensable part of Mennonite ethnicity.

Traditionally, poetry among Mennonites has arisen primarily from the internal needs of the faith community, either as a medium of religious expression or an aspect of oral folk culture: from poems by Dutch Renaissance urbanites to verses passed on through the generations in Plattdeutsch or Pennsylvania German, from hymns in the *Ausbund* to devotional poems for denominational publications. One can argue that the modern (or postmodern) literary poetry being written by poets of Mennonite origins today has arisen from the needs of Mennonites to make sense of their community and faith in dialogue with a complex postmodern society. Thus poetry that attempts to translate Mennonite ethnicity to literary readers outside of the Mennonite tradition is also serving the spiritual, artistic, and aesthetic needs of Mennonites educated and living in conversation with the larger society.

While the precedent among Mennonites for creating literary art for a wider audience has been scanty, a number of fine poets emerged from Mennonite communities in Holland during the Reformation. Some crafted ballads of dramatic intensity that were included in the *Ausbund* (1583). Others wrote devotional books in the style of Christian allegory that remained popular for several centuries. As Al Reimer notes, "most Anabaptist believers were arrested and sentenced for what they said and wrote rather than for overt actions."[20] Today again there are a significant number of literary artists among Mennonites who, like their Dutch

---

19. Ironically, the most conservative Mennonite groups along with the Amish, who appear most "ethnic" to outsiders, are probably least concerned with questions of ethnic identity. For them, faith and practice are integral and holistic.

20. See Reimer, *Mennonite Literary Voices*, 8.

Reformation counterparts, are actively participating in sophisticated cultural practices that are part of the larger society. These poets, through their work, have situated themselves at a cultural crossroads. Within the Mennonite community, their poetry privileges individual voices often suppressed by internal cultural values of the group. Such poetry offers the individual consciousness a way of interrogating the community values that have shaped it. Poetry enables the individual poet to use the community as a point of reference, without speaking *for* the community in an official capacity.

The tension between faith and ethnicity in the definition of the Mennonite writer is one of the first things Froese Tiessen addresses in her introduction to the special issue of *The New Quarterly*, "Mennonite/s Writing in Canada." Froese Tiessen's definition of "Mennonite" embraces both the center and the margins because "the artist's voice is one that is generally heard from the margins. In Mennonite terms, the artist has conventionally spoken from the very periphery of community experience."[21] Invoking theorist of post-modernism Linda Hutcheon, Froese Tiessen suggests that acknowledging our Mennonite writers means embracing our margins as "the frontier, the place of possibility." But she also suggests a possible hazard to the writers themselves from this situation: the threat of being reabsorbed into the center of the community and thereby losing their marginal perspective as Mennonite readers become more and more receptive to their representations of Mennonite identity. This is barely a threat to U.S. Mennonite writers at the moment, however, with the possible exception of Julia Kasdorf, who has been astounded by the receptivity of Mennonites to her work. Being a spokesperson for a group and being one of its marginal voices are two different vocations. To nurture their poets, Mennonites need to gently and loosely embrace the cultural margins where poets tend to lurk, without wishing to reabsorb and fuse them into a centripetal construction of Mennonite cultural identity. Such tension between margin and center is a vital pre-condition of writing, especially ethnic poetry; without it the poet cannot thrive.

The creative tension between faith and ethnicity can be reframed as embodied practice. Ethnicity has to do with the anthropological definition of bodies and boundaries as defined diachronically, or historically, through specific communal practices. Human faith cannot exist apart from the body, either the individual human body or the communal body. The dilemma created when one attempts to separate the body from the faith was clarified for me when a friend and colleague, an artist who is also a Yoruba priest, described his journey from the

---

21. Froese Tiessen, *Mennonite/s Writing in Canada*, 10.

Baptist church to the Nation of Islam to Yoruba, an African tribal religion now being revived in the United States and Haiti. "Religion is like a car: you use it to get you where your spiritual journey takes you. When it doesn't work anymore, you get out and get into a new car that works. Religion is simply a vehicle for your spirituality, its political and earthly body."[22] While I am not suggesting that Mennonite ethnicity is something to be discarded like an old Dodge that has thrown a rod, I am suggesting we view it as a form of spiritual and cultural embodiment. If we apply this metaphor for a moment to Mennonite faith and practice, we might see that many Mennonites polish, wax and care for their cars with intricate loving detail. One can become so invested in a particular make or model—a particular version of tradition—that one often fails to see the disparate sources and influences that have contributed to its evolution. How many Mennonites are aware that one of their most cherished "ethnic" practices, four-part a cappella singing, originated in the singing schools of the early 1800s and was only introduced into Mennonite church services at the turn of this century?

Ethnicity without spirituality can be compared either to an abandoned car or a restored antique, driven only on special occasions. The idea of spirituality without a formal body, a specific history and set of practices we might term ethnic, tends to instill anxiety in most Mennonites—perhaps because, as community-oriented people, Mennonites tend to distrust the concept of a disembodied voice. The idea of a spirit without a body conjures up images of ghostly presences, or more frighteningly, the cast-out demons of the biblical account who, in search of new bodies, possessed the wild pigs that hurled themselves over the precipice. Anthropologists, on the other hand, would view de-contextualized spirituality as a human impossibility. An apt metaphor for the Mennonite integrated in faith and practice might be the driver of the well tended, but not ornate, older car such as the well-tuned maroon Impala Julia Kasdorf inherited from her step-grandmother and poetic muse Bertha, who was not able, in spite of her faith, to take it to heaven with her. Religious forms, after all, are of this world. We have to leave them behind as others continue to shape the embodying traditions for future generations. Human faith must take on human form to exist, and culture is a necessary condition of human existence. The poet's work of image-making is one way of registering the ways in which embodied spirituality shapes the soul. It may also be contributing to a richer and more complicated portrait of Mennonite identity because of its unofficial character.

---

22. Conversation with Muneer Bahauudeen, Milwaukee, WI, May 1997.

POETRY AND THE ONGOING DIALOGUE
OF MENNONITE CULTURAL IDENTITY

Mennonites in the United States in the twentieth century have been preoccupied with the task of self-definition in relation to the larger culture, especially as they have shed the physical markers of religious difference such as plain coats, cape dresses and coverings. (In this they are not unlike their ethnic Swiss cousins, who today struggle to maintain their internal diversity even as they attempt to define a distinct identity from the European Community forming around them.) While not every Mennonite was raised in such a closed and restrictive community as the eastern Pennsylvania "called out" church district described by anthropologist Elmer Miller, most are familiar with its basic tenets in any one of a number of forms: nonconformity and nonresistance.[23] In defining Mennonite identity in terms of nonconformity to both insiders and outsiders, the tendency has been to emphasize common ground among Mennonites rather than their internal differences. Individual difference is suppressed in the service of maintaining a sense of homogeneous Mennonite identity. Identity theorist Stuart Hall suggests two different ways of viewing what he terms "cultural identity." The first way is that of "one, shared culture, a sort of collective 'one true self,' hiding inside the many other, more superficial or artificially imposed 'selves,' which a people with a shared history and ancestry hold in common."[24] This is reflected in the project of defining collective Mennonite identity, an ongoing process in Mennonite communities, especially those in urban areas or those who have frequent contact with people from other walks of life. Mennonite identity is also the ongoing work of Mennonite scholars, historians and theologians, as well as local congregations and communities. The desire to create "one true identity" is a form of nostalgia that has resulted in distortions for both Mennonites and non-Mennonites.

While Mennonites are organized at the congregational and conference level, and have distinctive local identities, viewed as a whole (including all the groups that answer to the name "Mennonite") they appear to be a complex and loosely affiliated aggregate of local communities. They are hard to define collectively because the many distinct and vital communities — simultaneously global and local — exist in complex dialogic relation to one another. Contemporary Mennonites are both rural and urban, often highly educated and articulate, with a wide

---

23. Elmer S. Miller, *Nurturing Doubt: From Mennonite Missionary to Anthropologist in the Argentine Chaco* (Urbana: U. of Illinois Press, 1995), 9.

24. Stuart Hall, "Identity and Diaspora," *Colonial Discourse and Post-Colonial Theory*, ed. Patrick Williams and Laura Chrisman (New York: Columbia U. Press, 1994), 393.

economic and social range; most are now indistinguishable by dress or habit from members of the larger culture. However, Mennonites who come into contact with the world have been obsessed with defining their own group identity partly because there is such diversity among Mennonites — from extremes of conservative to liberal — that the category threatens to erupt into meaninglessness. Nonetheless, the desire to create "one true identity" internally among Mennonites exacerbates many of the problems it is intended to solve. It causes splits, divisions, inclusions, exclusions from the corporate body of believers. It requires members of a community to support opinions and practices they do not necessarily believe in as individuals. It tempts its members to split themselves into the official Mennonite version and the unofficial one: a deadening solution for both the individual and the community because it preempts the dialogue so necessary to ongoing cultural vitality. Instead of viewing diversity, disagreement, or internal difference as sources of strength and mutually enriching dialogue, those who desire to construct a unified Mennonite identity force diversity through splitting — antagonistically instead of dialogically — proliferating the differences they intend to contain.[25] The mono-cultural model of "one true self" is clearly inadequate to describe the intricate network of dialogic relationships that exist between the many local Mennonite communities and conferences scattered across the globe among diverse cultures.

Those unfamiliar with Mennonites in the U. S. — even in the 1990s — often respond to the group by imposing a single simplistic symbol of otherness, attempting to define "one true culture" by drawing on the most extreme outward manifestations of a small minority of the denomination's most conservative members such as black cars, horses and buggies, coverings, plain coats and cape dresses — symbols shared by only a few strands of the manifold tapestry of Mennonite life. The tangible symbols of ethnic identity are so compelling that they overshadow any reasonable explanation of the culture in the imagination of outsiders. Distortions about Mennonite identity persist, even among the educated elite, as those who live at the cultural crossroads are well aware. At a luncheon for poet Galway Kinnell which I attended a number of years ago at the University of Pennsylvania, Julia Kasdorf was referred to as a Mennonite. One of the professors present asked whether she was "one of those people who don't vaccinate their children." Other times Mennonites are confused with the Amish, a group to which American Mennonites of Swiss origin are historically related. In a recent conversation at another educational institution a colleague asked me in a

25. This is the central theme of a recent issue of *MQR* devoted to the topic of conflict. — See especially "In This Issue," *MQR* 72 (April, 1998), 117-120.

multi-cultural discussion group how to relate appropriately to Mennonites: "Should I ask them to teach me how to weave, or should I offer to teach them how to use the computer?" When I responded by searching for "Mennonites" on the World Wide Web, he was amazed to see 6000 entries generated by my search, including many congregational web sites. When my family moved into our new house last year, my daughter—who had once worn Amish clothing to an ethnic day at school and has been teased about it ever since—came home from school one day upset because she had heard a rumor circulating at school that we had had all of the electric lines removed from our house. Those of us living in largely non-Mennonite contexts are certainly aware that Mennonites have an ethnic designation in the larger culture that exists apart from whether we are active or not in a congregation. Clearly the work of creating Mennonite cultural identity—both for outsiders and insiders—has not yet been completed.

Is it any wonder that Mennonites are hesitant to present internal differences to an already misinformed and prejudiced larger community? However, the work of communicating Mennonite identity to outsiders will not be complete or successful until the constructed definition of Mennonites reflects our diversity and complexity—and internal differences—rather than one unified image. Such a definition must consist of more than institutional history and tourist information brochures. It needs to include not only the outward symbols by which Mennonites have traditionally distinguished themselves from mainstream culture, but also the images of the poet and other imaginative artists who engage the complexities of the culture in their unofficial versions, exposing both the rugged beauties and the painful contradictions of Mennonite humanity.

THE ROLE OF THE POET IN THE CREATION OF CULTURAL IDENTITY

Poetic discourse in the contemporary literary and cultural climate invites the exploration of multiple voices and internal tensions through images, myths and stories that relate the particular Mennonite cultural experience to the experiences of those from other cultural backgrounds. It is a loom on which poets from Mennonite origins can weave a narrative of the encounter of two cultures, or two sensibilities: that of Mennonite and that of the larger world in which Mennonites find themselves situated. Poets' voices, as they explore Mennonite identity and sensibility, as they journey out from a Mennonite context, reflect what Hall defines as a second way of viewing cultural identity:

The second position recognizes that, as well as the many points of similarity, there are also critical points of deep and significant difference which constitute "what we really are"; or rather—since history has intervened—"what we have become". . . . Cultural identity, in this second sense, is a matter of "becoming" as well as "being." It belongs to the future as well as the past.[26]

Hall theorizes about the cultural identity of the Caribbean, but his distinctions aptly describe the situation of the Mennonite poet, whose project, whether consciously or not, is often to reinvent culture from the perspective of the second position:

In this perspective, cultural identity is not a fixed essence at all lying unchanged outside of history and culture. . . . The past continues to speak to us. But it no longer addresses us as a simple, factual "past," since our relation to it, like the child's relation to the mother, is always-already after the break. It is always constructed through memory, fantasy, narrative, and myth.[27]

Mennonite poets present the vitality of memory and myth as they connect the individual voice with cultural narrative. They are not only inheritors and interpreters of their own traditions, but borrowers of other traditions, as exemplified in Julia Kasdorf's *Sleeping Preacher*. In the title poem Kasdorf writes of her ancestors' fascination with an outsider's message caused them to destroy the family photographs.

. . . Our great-grandma saw him
swoon across the front pew
and preach against jewelry,
fancy dresses for women, and photographs.
That day she threw all the old daguerreotypes
in gilt and red cases, all the prints
of her parents on their wedding day,
of the milk wagon parked outside their barn,
and herself in high button shoes
into the cookstove. . . .
. . . She did not think of us,
only to save us, leaving nothing
for us to touch or see
except this stubborn will to believe.[28]

Kasdorf's poems create a new set of images to "replace" the lost photographs based on stories passed onto her from the community, as well as on her observations of what she has imbibed from living in close proximity to that community. One of those images, rising up powerfully

---

26. Hall, "Identity and Diaspora," 394.

27. Ibid, 395.

28. Julia Kasdorf, *Sleeping Preacher* (Pittsburgh: U. of Pittsburgh Press, 1992), 6.

to replace the lost photographs, is that of Bertha Peachey Spicher Sharpe, the strong woman who told Kasdorf many of the stories woven into *Sleeping Preacher* and whose vitality is evident in the flourishing of the morning glories in the poet's Brooklyn garden even after Bertha's death. Bertha's presence—as refracted through Kasdorf's imagination—serves as a corrective for the destructive effects of the sleeping preacher's instructions to burn the photo albums. Ultimately her presence overpowers that of the sleeping preacher as the volume concludes with "Morning_Glories": Bertha's memory is ineradicable as the seeds of the flowers Kasdorf attempts to weed from her city garden to clear enough space for tomatoes, the fruit at the center of so much of the domestic labor she writes about in the volume. While Kasdorf is not certain that tomatoes will thrive in her city garden, she knows that the plot will "come up all morning glories" next spring.

Certainly not all Mennonites destroyed their photographs. Unlike the Amish, most Mennonites have sanctioned the use of photography since its invention, especially for purposes of record-keeping. But that is not the point. Mennonite poetry is not to bear the burden of representing "the truth" about Mennonites. Rather, it must remain true to the poet's particular perspective. While most Mennonite communities were untouched by sleeping preachers, they appeared in various communities throughout the Midwest as well as in Big Valley. Kasdorf uses the sleeping preacher incident to suggest the missing images of her culture, as well as to warn against the desire to eradicate history, a temptation not only for charismatic leaders of extreme movements exemplified by a sleeping preacher, but also for contemporary Mennonites in conflict with their communities of origin. These images have a larger resonance for both Mennonite and non-Mennonite readers: What images of our past do we carry with us? What role has our community played in selecting those images for us? What is our role in shaping them? The poet's power as mythmaker enables her to recreate and juxtapose the images of the past in new combinations that set up tension and possibilities for dialogue—creating a past that "continues to speak to us" but that "no longer addresses us as a simple, factual 'past,' since our relation to it, like the child's relation to the mother, is always-already after the break."[29]

Sheri Hostetler's poem "Not of this World" evokes rural images drawn from her Swiss Mennonite farming community in Berlin, Ohio to create a myth of silence and passivity as it simultaneously pokes fun at the self-satisfied pride that sometimes underlies a life devoted to living out an ethic of austere simplicity and goodness:

I am like none of you. You must recognize

---

29. Hall, "Identity and Diaspora," 395.

deep in me how different I am. You're all
Wonder Bread and drive-ins. I am fertile
fields, head coverings, memories of martyrdom
like yesterday, hymns without organ. The
Bible whispers in my ear at night, it will
not keep still.

But my people do. *Die Stille im Lande.* We
never talk. Quietly we move, quietly the
fields are plowed, in quiet are the dishes
washed, the sheets pulled taut, silently the
hay flung high atop the wagons. Our horses
clip clop in a virtual vacuum. All around
us pins drop, and, still, we are still.

Nature loves our vacuum, blesses us with a
bounty you cannot imagine. Look at our barns,
they are filled with sweet hay, hay without
end, stacked fragrant, stacked sweet. We
do not talk but we smell the sweetness of
hay every day, oh stranger, you know not what
you are not.

I am like you. I talk with you, laugh
with you, make love with you, break bread
with you, I will even die with you. And my soul
will rest atop a haymow on Weaver Ridge while yours
goes to heaven.[30]

The silence of the community Hostetler describes, its embodiment in work — "our barns, . . . filled with sweet hay, hay without/ end, stacked fragrant, stacked sweet" — is questioned in the poem through the voice she has had to travel far away to discover in dialogue with those whose heads are filled with images of Wonder Bread. (Hostetler lives in Piedmont, California). Taken on a literal level, Hostetler's use of silence in this poem seems to contradict Kasdorf's image of the outspoken Bertha, vital and persistent as morning glories. One might ask whether Bertha could exist in a culture where, as in Hostetler's poem, "all around/us pins drop, and, still, we are still." But the symbolic, mythical silence of Hostetler's poem is really addressing the culture's self-satisfaction, its inability to question its own practices and traditions rather than describing its literal muteness. As a poem by a Mennonite poet, however, it paradoxically supplies the critique the lack of which it laments. And it does so by revealing the crossroads of cultures as the site

---

30. *Sojourner: A Woman's Forum* 13 (January 1994), 6.

where ethnic identity is articulated. For her portrait of the community's silence emerges only when the poet encounters an "other" with a different set of images that she imagines are "all/Wonder Bread and drive-ins."

In creating images of Mennonite ethnicity based on photograph-burning and silent farmers, one might ask: aren't Mennonite poets guilty of perpetuating the kinds of stereotypes I decried earlier in this essay? Similar charges were leveled against African American novelist and folklorist Zora Neale Hurston by Richard Wright, who felt that her novel *Their Eyes Were Watching God* perpetuated stereotypes of the "happy darky" in its evocation of an all-black Florida town that included dialect, tall tales and folk practices drawn from Hurston's rich experiences not only as a denizen of such a town but as an ethnographer of African American folklore. My answer is that poetry must be grounded in the local, the specific, the details of human experience, however various. The cultural pressure for the artist to create an "official" representation of his or her culture has never resulted in good art. Rather, the reader must come to understand the poet's discourse as a dialogue between the self and the particular, situated experience of his or her world — a discourse that can have a universal appeal, paradoxically, because it is grounded in the particularities of everyday experience. The more good poetry we have from Mennonite writers, the more poets seek out their own personal metaphors, the more various the images they create — collectively — the greater the riches they offer to the ongoing dialogue of cultural identity and self-understanding.

The poet's unofficial voice is one that encourages a paradoxical truth-telling, one that will enrich a community that willingly expands to embrace its challenges. It is a journey that can enlarge the sense of community for both poet and reader. As Sheri Hostetler writes:

At the time I began writing poetry, I was somewhat estranged from my Mennonite heritage, faith, and community. I had been running away from home for a long time; poetry made me stop and actually look at what I was running from. When I did, I saw red-winged blackbirds, furrowed fields, a clarifying simplicity, holiness. Religion means, literally, to "re-bind," to bring together what had once been whole. Poetry was a religious practice for me, then, in that it bound me back to my community, its stories, memories, and faith. . . . Poetry helped me to see that the Mennonite community was my community.[31]

---

31. From an essay written for the anthology in progress, *A Cappella: An Anthology of Mennonite Poetry in North America*, ed. Ann Hostetler.

THE SIGNIFYING MENNO:
ARCHETYPES FOR AUTHORS AND CRITICS

ERVIN BECK*

Abstract: One way to define the uniqueness of Mennonite literature is to identify its recurring archetypes. This article discusses ten archetypes, almost all of which have also been depicted in familiar visual images—testimony to the archetypes' importance in an otherwise image-shy Mennonite culture. Menno Simons, in his cultural roles of trickster deceiver and trickster subverter, is the dominant archetype. He serves Mennonite culture in the same way that Henry Louis Gates says the Yoruba divine trickster Esu-Elegbara illuminates the theory and criticism of African-American literature.

Most recent theoretical discussions of the nature of Mennonite literature have been concerned with the relationship between the writer and the community.[1] Insofar as these discussions have analyzed the writer's depiction in literary works of the Mennonite community, they have focused on the literature itself.[2] But more often they have been concerned with the relationship of the writer to the actual Mennonite community and have therefore emphasized moral and sociological concerns extrinsic to the literature itself. If Mennonite literature is to develop a tradition of literary criticism that is as good as the literature itself, then we need to consider more fully what might be the elements of content and style that distinguish Mennonite literature both from the

---

*Ervin Beck is Professor of English at Goshen College. He was the organizer of the Mennonite/s Writing in the U.S. conference held at Goshen College, October 23-26, 1997.

1. The classic, early statements are by John Ruth, *Mennonite Identity and Literary Art* (Scottdale, PA: Herald Press, 1978); Elmer Suderman, "Mennonites, the Mennonite Community and the Mennonite Writer," *Mennonite Life* 47 (Sept. 1992), 21-16; and Al Reimer, *Mennonite Literary Voices: Past and Present* (North Newton, KS: Bethel College, 1993), especially chapter 4, "To Whom Are the Voices Speaking?" Ruth urges Mennonite authors to write from the center of the community and articulate its best aspirations; Reimer says a Mennonite author must write from the margins of the community and speak prophetically to it; Suderman says it doesn't matter where the writer is located so long as good literature is the result. Papers at the conference Mennonite/s Writing in the U.S. that dealt directly with that issue were Hildi Froese Tiessen, "Beyond the Binary: Re-inscribing Cultural Identity (or the Locations of Culture) in the Literature of the Mennonites"; Ann Hostetler, "The unofficial voice: The Poetics of Cultural Identity and Contemporary U.S. Mennonite Poetry"; Jeff Gundy, "In Praise of Lurkers (Who Come Out to Speak)"; and Ben Hartman, "The Artist and the Community."

2. One of the best such analyses is Jeff Gundy, "Voice and History in Patrick Friesen," *The New Quarterly* 10 (Spring-Summer 1990), 138-49.

litereture of mainstream English culture and from the literature of other ethnic groups.[3] To that end, I will address the basic question of what distinctive archetypes we might expect to find in literature written by Mennonites, whether that literature depicts literal Mennonite experience or experience that is not overtly Mennonite.

As my title indicates, I take my model from *The Signifying Monkey: A Theory of African-American Literary Criticism* (1988) by Henry Louis Gates, Jr., which is the most creative and ambitious attempt thus far to define the uniqueness of an ethnic group's literary tradition—including content, genres, rhetoric and hermeneutic.[4] Although I will pursue a different and more limited concern—and in a less dazzling, more Mennonite-plain manner—I take my inspiration from Gates's statement:

> Each literary tradition, at least implicitly, contains within it an argument for how it can be read (xx).

and from his quotation of Paulin J. Hountondji, who said that African literature:

> must promote within African society itself a theoretical debate of its own that is capable of developing its themes and problems autonomously instead of remaining a remote appendix to European theoretical and scientific debate (xx).

Of course, Mennonite culture is inherently more "European," and certainly less separated by race from mainstream culture, than is African-American literature. Nevertheless, if we are indeed a distinct ethnic group—as we think we are, and as I will also demonstrate—then our theoretical literary concerns must match those of Gates and Hountondji. We must at least *begin* by assuming that both we and our literature are *different* and then set about speculating on the nature of those differences.

In trying to identify outstanding archetypes in Mennonite literature, I have limited my analysis to those archetypes that are embodied in more or less well known visual images from traditional Mennonite culture. If we assume that Mennonite theology has tended to be image-denying—even, at times, iconoclastic—then those relatively few images that we have created or adopted and passed down through generations must

---

3. Some studies that have tried to deal with inherent features of a Mennonite literature and art are Victor Duerksen, "In Search of a Mennonite Imagination," *Journal of Mennonite Studies* 2 (1984), 110-11; E. F. Dyck, "The Rhetoric of the Plain Style in Mennonite Writing," in Hildi Froese Tiessen, ed., *The New Quarterly* [Mennonite/s Writing in Canada issue] 10 (Spring-Summer 1990), 36-52; Jeff Gundy, "Humility in Mennonite Literature," *MQR* 63 (Jan. 1989), 5-29; Reinhild Janzen, "Conclusion: Thoughts on Mennonite Aesthetic Identity," in *Mennonite Furniture* (Intercourse, PA: Good Books, 1991), 201-8; and Hildi Froese Tiessen, "Mother Tongue as Shibboleth in the Literature of Canadian Mennonites," *Studies in Canadian Literature* 13 (1988), 175-83.

4. New York: Oxford U. Press, 1988.

embody experiences and ideas that are very important for us. In language, a speech community always creates a word to encapsulate complex, distinctive experiences and ideas that often arise in discussion. Hence our typical, specialized vocabulary of terms such as *Gelassenheit, Gemeinde, Hochmut, Demut, community, discipleship,* etc. How much more impressive is it, therefore, when our image-shy culture embodies crucial, recurring ideas and experiences in visual images. Such images give archetypes a virtually iconic status in our culture.

The first two archetype-embodying images — of Menno in the coach (Fig. 1) and of Menno in the molasses barrel (Fig. 2) — are the most fundamental ones, since they clearly establish the uniqueness of Mennonite ethnicity and also give literary creativity its Anabaptist sanction. Both of these images arise from folk legends told about Menno, and both clearly establish him as the archetypal trickster-figure for Mennonites. Therefore, even if we did not know that we are "ethnics,"[5] our folk tradition of Menno as the archetypal trickster would be adequate proof of our distinctive traditional culture, simply because most ethnic groups have such a trickster in their stories of origins. In being a trickster, Menno resembles the better known Anancy and Brer Rabbit in African-American culture as well as wily Coyote in American Indian lore. In religious ethnic traditions, he also resembles the rabbi trickster in Jewish lore; the dialect preacher-trickster in Swedish-American lore; and the missionary trickster in Mormon lore.[6]

Henry Louis Gates, Jr., of course, grounds his entire theory of African-American literature in the Yoruba divine trickster Esu-Elegbara and his African-American descendant "The Signifyin(g) Monkey." A brief list of characteristics of Esu-Elegbara, as identified by Gates, resonates with what we can, by analogy, see in Menno Simons, the founder of our faith community. Esu-Elegba is the creator of the universe (7), which results in many etiological, or "origins," tales being associated with his creative actions. He is also the "sole messenger of the gods" (6), who interprets

---

5. I find it very interesting that the *Harvard Encyclopedia of American Ethnic Groups* (Cambridge, MA: Belknap Press, 1980) does not regard Mennonites as constituting an ethnic group, although it does list the Old Order Amish and the Hutterites as ethnic groups (vi, etc.). I interpret that to mean that the editors regard religious faith as a lesser mark of ethnic distinctiveness than Mennonites do. The *Encyclopedia* lists many characteristics that, in various composite arrangements, contribute to distinctive ethnicities. Among those elements are whether or not a people regard themselves as different from others ("an internal sense of distinctiveness," vi), and whether they are, in turn, regarded as different by other people ("an external perception of distinctiveness," vi). I sense that Mennonites have traditionally regarded themselves to be very different from other people.

6. Ed Clay, "The Rabbi Trickster," *Journal of American Folklore* 77 (1964), 331-45; Larry Danielson, "The Dialect Trickster among the Kansas Swedes," *Indiana Folklore* 8 (1975), 39-59; William A. Wilson, "Trickster Tales and the Location of Cultural Boundaries: A Mormon Example," *Journal of American Folklore* 20 (1983), 55-66.

the will of the gods to humans and carries humans' desires to the gods. He guards the crossroads between the divine and the profane (6). As a "mutable figure" (6) of many shapes, manifestations and transformations, Osu-Elegbara resembles Menno, whose chameleon-like ability to evade the authorities who pursued him is legendary.[7] Tricksters like Esu-Elegba are also physically wounded creatures. Anancy, for instance, is a grotesque spider who lisps. Esu-Elegba and Menno even have identical physical deformities: Esu limps (6) and Menno was so lame that he eventually used a crutch.[8]

About the trickster-figure in folklore Roger Abrahams says that he is, at various times, "clown, fool, jokester, initiate, culture hero, even ogre."[9] Paul Radin more neatly dichotomizes the trickster's role, saying that he is "at one and the same time, creator and destroyer, giver and negator, he who dupes and who is always duped himself."[10] It is this latter dichotomy that Menno illustrates in his two distinctive trickster roles in Mennonite culture — in the stagecoach as clever, tricky, deceptive manipulator of an external threat; and in the molasses barrel as inept, foolish dupe or destroyer while interacting with people of his own community.[11]

The image of Menno in the stagecoach gives us a Menno who becomes a literal trickster through artful deception and manipulation of a situation (Fig. 1). The story concerns Menno in flight from authorities and sitting in the front outdoor seat of a stagecoach. In response to the sheriff's query as to whether Menno is in the coach, Menno leans down into the coach and asks, "Is Menno in the coach?" and then drives on, scot-free, when the people say that, no, Menno is not inside the coach.[12]

---

7. David Augsburger, "Menno Simons' Birthday Tales," *Festival Quarterly* (Winter 1996), 7-9, is a compilation and elaboration of eight different oral traditional narratives told about Menno by Mennonites. Six concern Menno's escape from his various pursuers.

8. Augsburger, "Menno Memory #5," quotes Menno as saying: "I ruined my hip leaping from a high window to escape . . ." (9).

9. "Trickster, the Outrageous Hero," in *Our Living Traditions: An Introduction to American Folklore*, ed. Tristram P. Coffin (New York: Basic Books, 1968), 171. Abrahams, who was a consultant to Gates, gives additional insight into trickster-figures in the "Introduction" to his *African Folktales: Traditional Stories of the Black World* (New York: Pantheon, 1983), 1-29.

10. *The Trickster: A Study in American Indian Mythology* (2nd ed.; New York: Basic Books, 1968), 171.

11. I have discussed Menno in these terms in the context of Mennonite oral narratives in "Mennonite Trickster Tales: True to Be Good," *MQR* 61 (Jan. 1987), 58-74, where I see him as the prototype of the plain-coat preacher trickster in contemporary Mennonite lore. In that discussion I postulate that Menno is a literal deceiver-trickster in his (and Mennonites') negotiations with non-Mennonites (exoteric lore); and a subverter-trickster in his negotiations with fellow Mennonites (esoteric lore).

12. The transcribed oral account that I published in the *MQR* essay cited above is undocumented there, but was told by J. C. Wenger — who himself was characterized as the plaincoat preacher-trickster in many Mennonite oral narratives.

FIG. 1—MENNO IN THE STAGECOACH = TRICKSTER AS DECEIVER [13]

In Dutch culture, this is the origin of the "Mennonite Lie," which means, according to historian J. G. de Hoop Scheffer:

13. "Menniste Leugen" [Mennonite Lie]. Drawing by T. Schaap-Stuurman for a Mennonite card game conceived by J. Siersma and sold by the Dutch National Federation of Mennonite Sisters in 1979.

To say a truth and to withhold a truth, and then especially to say half the truth and appear that the truth has been told completely; to evade the answer on a question and yet give the person who asks the impression that nothing is lacking in the answer — that is what non-Mennonites label with the term "Mennonite tricks."[14]

Mennonite creative writers and critics might find in this behavior by Menno a kind of sanction, at the historical source, of fiction and other creative, figurative expression — despite both Menno's own writing on truth-telling[15] and despite the Mennonite community's official emphasis on speaking only the plain truth.

In literature, this archetypal "Mennonite lie" is found in the conduct of, among many others, Dirk Pieter Smuel, Klaas de Praet and Adriaen Cornelisz in *Martyrs' Mirror;* in the verbal evasion of authorities by many ordinary early Anabaptists;[16] in the "liars and rascals" that give the title to Hildi Froese Tiessen's collection of Mennonite stories;[17] in the refugee-rescue stories told by Peter Dyck;[18] in the half-lie told in Moscow by David Epp, Sr., in *The Blue Mountains of China;* and especially in the conduct of David Epp, Jr., in the same book. In an elaborate ruse — a silent deception of neighboring Mennonite villages on the Siberian-Chinese border — David Epp leads his own Mennonite village in a brilliant escape across the river into freedom on a frigid night, thereby deceiving both the soviet authorities and the other Mennonite villages nearby. His willfully deceptive action nevertheless establishes a moral and political precedent for other heroic actions in the conclusion of the novel.

---

14. J. G. de Hoop Scheffer, "Mennisten-Streken," *Doopsgezinde Bijdragen* (Leeuwarden, 1868), 28.

15. *The Complete Writings of Menno Simons, c. 1496-1561,* trans. Leonard Verduin and ed. J. C. Wenger, with a biography by Harold S. Bender (Scottdale, PA: Herald Press, 1956), 521.

16. See, for example, John S. Oyer, "Nicodemites among Wurttemberg Anabaptists," *MQR* 71 (Oct. 1997), 487-514.

17. *Liars and Rascals* (Waterloo, ON: Univ. of Waterloo Press, 1989). In the "Introduction" to that collection of Mennonite short stories, Froese Tiessen cites novelist Jacob H. Janzen in 1946 as remembering when a fellow Mennonite called him a "liar" for writing fiction (xii) and recalls a time when another Mennonite referred to Rudy Wiebe as a "rascal" for writing fiction (xiii). She interprets these responses as representing "antipathy" or "antagonism" towards fiction and also proof that Mennonite culture has lacked "a nuanced understanding of the nature and value of literary culture" (xi). If that is true, it is only partly true, since in folk cultures the tale-teller is very often called a liar, not so much to pass moral judgment but, rather, to name the narrative convention in which the teller is working, i.e., fiction rather than legend. For instance, I once tape-recorded tales from a teller in a remote region of Belize. Throughout the session his wife stood in the doorway, covering her laughing mouth with her hand and exclaiming gleefully, "Liar! Liar!"

18. Peter J. Dyck, *Up from the Rubble* (Scottdale, PA: Herald Press, c. 1991); *Peter J. Dyck: Storyteller,* video, Shipshewana, IN, Menno-Hof, 1995, 168 min.

FIG. 2—MENNO IN THE MOLASSES BARREL = TRICKSTER AS
SUBVERTER [19]

---

19. "Mennist Zoet" [Mennonite Sweetness]. Drawing by T. Schaap-Stuurman for a
Mennonite card game conceived by J. Siersma and sold by the Dutch National Federation
of Mennonite Sisters in 1979.

The image of Menno in the molasses barrel emphasizes even more so the trickster's function of standing at the beginning of the creation of things — in this case, at the origins of Mennonite material culture. Menno fell into the barrel (Fig. 2) when he was standing on it while preaching in a barn. When authorities surrounded the barn, he panicked, slipped, broke the top and fell in. Children (some variants say women) licked the molasses off his trousers so he could flee without leaving a trail behind him. Dutch Mennonites tell this story to explain why Dutch Mennonites from that day forward have had a sweet tooth.[20]

Again, we find in this story a justification for Mennonite cultural practices that go beyond the merely theological, pious or practical. In using Menno to explain a cultural trait, the story takes a first step in justifying many other cultural practices that are not specifically encouraged in scriptural texts — perhaps also including literary creativity. In fact, if we look at sugar and sweets as luxury items that go beyond common, everyday necessity, then we might even find in the story a justification of literature that flirts with "art for art's sake," rather than a literature that merely exploits the more practical uses of words, such as in songs and prayers that promote the faith.

In literary texts, Menno in the molasses encourages us to look for Mennonite versions of the Jewish *schlemmeil*, or "unlucky bungler"[21] — although sometimes it is difficult to tell whether his (or the Mennonite's) bungling is actual foolishness or a crafty foolishness that constitutes a deliberate subversion and critique of cultural norms. In any event, Menno's best counterpart in recent literature is his own namesake Yasch Siemens (Siemens=Simons) in Armin Wiebe's hilarious book of stories *The Salvation of Yasch Siemens*. Yasch — like many other tricksters a marginalized person in his own community — is poor, unlucky (initially), unsophisticated and unsuccessful in terms of Gutental community norms. Significantly, the only early Anabaptist history he knows is of the *Naktlopers* who ran naked through the streets of Amsterdam when Anabaptists seized the city hall on May 10-11, 1535. Like them, Yasch Siemens' life and comments are remarkable subversions of conventional norms. Mennonite and other readers like him so much that Wiebe has

---

20. For a transcription of an oral version of this story by David Augsburger, see my "Mennonite Trickster Tales," *MQR*, 70. This, of course, is the kind of origins, or etiological, tale that is frequently associated with divine trickster figures. The story of Menno in the stagecoach can also be seen as an etiological tale, that is, as the prototype for, or origin of, the "Mennonite lie" and all other accounts of Mennonites as tricky deceivers. See my "Mennonite Origin Tales and Beliefs," *MQR* 64 (Jan. 1990), 32-48.

21. *Merriam-Webster New Collegiate Dictionary*, 9th ed. For a discussion of the *schlemmeil* in Jewish-American literature, see Allenn Guttmann, "Jewish Humor," in *The Comic Imagination in American Literature*, ed. Louis D. Rubin, Jr. (Rutgers: Rutgers U. Press, [1973]), 329-38.

written two sequels: *Murder in Gutental* about a bumbling private detective and *The Second Coming of Yeeat Shpanst* about an unpredictable politician. Other Mennonite subversive tricksters cut out of the same mould are Dallas Wiebe's Skyblue the Badass and perhaps Paul Hiebert's Sarah Binks. If we choose not to use the Yiddish term *schlemmeil*, we can name the Mennonite trickster-subverter by using vocabulary from our own dialects: either the Plautdeitsch *downix* (which Yasch Siemens is sometimes called in the novel) or the Pennsylvania-German *snickelfritz* or *nixnutz*, with the latter being found in both Plautdeitsch and Pennsylvania-German.

Other significant visual icons and literary archetypes, of course, come to us through *Martyrs' Mirror* and the familiar engravings by Jan Luyken.

FIG. 3—DIRK WILLEMS = SELF-SACRIFICE [22]

The Dirk Willems archetype may represent for us the Mennonite who so internalizes the Gospel of Love that he risks his life to save his enemy — only, in turn, to be imprisoned and killed once he reaches shore with the officer he has saved. This image of Dirk has so intrigued Mennonites in recent years that David Luthy of the Amish Historical

---

22. Dirk Willems Rescues His Pursuer. Etching by Jan Luyken for the 1685 edition of *Martyrs' Mirror* by Thielman van Braght. —John S. Oyer and Robert S. Kreider, *The Mirror of the Martyrs* (Intercourse, PA: Good Books, 1990), 24.

Library in Ontario has documented over 90 uses of this picture in printed sources from 1940 to 1994 — with 32 appearing from 1980 to 1989 and 42 from 1990-94, and no end in sight.[23]

The most famous representation of the Dirk Willems type in literature is undoubtedly Jacques the Anabaptist in Voltaire's *Candide*. Jacques risks his life in rescuing a menacing, drowning sailor, only to be ignored by that same sailor when Jacques himself falls into the ocean and drowns. Voltaire was amazingly prescient in epitomizing in his character one of the most cherished self-images held by Mennonites. James C. Juhnke's play *Dirk's Exodus* is a literal representation of this archetype. In other recent literature, David Epp, Jr., in *The Blue Mountains of China*, gives his life as a sacrifice for many by returning to his deserted village to await apprehension by the soviet police. He thereby makes up for the deception he used in saving his fellow villagers and also deflects upon himself, apparently, the punishment that the soviet authorities would otherwise have laid upon the Mennonite villagers that had remained in Russia.

FIG. 4—ANNEKEN HENDRIKS = THE MARTYR [24]

23. David Luthy, "Dirk Willems: His Noble Deed Lives On," *Family Life* (Feb. 1995), 19-22.

24. Anneken Hendriks Burned at the Stake. Etching by Jan Luyken for the 1685 edition of *Martyrs' Mirror* by Thieleman van Braght. —John S. Oyer and Robert S. Kreider, *The Mirror of the Martyrs* (Intercourse, PA), 24.

Ever since many of the original engravings by Luykens were purchased by American Mennonites in 1989, the images of individual martyrs told about in *Martyrs' Mirror* have increasingly captured Mennonites' attention and imagination. In particular, the image of Anneken Hendriks as martyr for her faith has become well known (Fig. 4). One reason, no doubt, is that it shows the equality in spiritual heroism that women shared with men in early Anabaptist times. Another subtextual reason may be because Anneken Hendricks also visualizes the suffering heroism of women in the later Mennonite community, which has been overwhelmingly patriarchal. Of course, all of the stories in *Martyrs' Mirror* more or less embody the martyr archetype. And we need to keep in mind that *Martyrs' Mirror* represents the largest body of narratives available to — but obviously neglected by — Mennonite literary critics.

Among women who accept their suffering lot in patriarchal Mennonite culture are all of the Mennonite women in *Peace Shall Destroy Many;* the speaker in Di Brandt's poems; Magda in Rosemary Nixon's story "The Essence of Mushroom Broth"; and many others. Exclusive of gender concerns, an obvious modern martyr — albeit self-chosen — is John R. Reimer in *The Blue Mountains of China*, who walks down the Transcanadian Highway bearing his literal cross in symbolic penance for the Vietnam War. His brother Samuel U. Reimer actually dies because of his radical faith.

Recently Julia Kasdorf has called our attention to the icon of the digger who appears in a landscape on the frontispiece of editions of *Martyrs' Mirror* from 1685 to 1990 (Fig. 5). The motto above him interprets his significance: "Work and Hope." Those few words brilliantly epitomize Mennonites' traditional preference for doing over being; for service over theologizing. And they also embody Mennonites' traditionally humble attitude toward the question of personal salvation, whereby it is arrogant to be sure of salvation and more suitably humble to merely "hope" in God's grace.

Of the Mennonite colonists in Paraguay in *The Blue Mountains of China*, Rudy Wiebe refers to their "thoughtless faith" and their propensity to "work and wait."[25] This attitude is best embodied in Frieda Friesen, one of the main unifying elements in that otherwise fragmented work. Her personal motto, "It does come all from God, strength and sickness, want and plenty,"[26] which she learned from her father, epitomizes the stoic acceptance of the difficulties in life that the icon also illustrates.

---

25. (Rpt. 1995; Toronto: McClellan and Stewart, 1970), 117, 121, respectively.
26. Ibid., 12, and often throughout the novel.

From 1812 to 1821 the "Anabaptist" almanac published by the J. Klopfenstein family of Mennonites in Belfort, France was universally used and admired in that country. Archetypally, the cover illustration embodies the idea of Mennonites and Amish as being "the quiet in the land," tilling their fields in an idyllic life in harmony with nature (Fig. 6). This French engraving continues the attitude toward Mennonites that was commonly found in the encyclopedias produced in the eighteenth century by the French *philosophes*. In the French Enlightenment,

Fig. 5—The Anabaptist Digger = "Work and Hope" [27]

---

[27] "Arbeite und hoffe" [Work and Hope]. —Thieleman J. van Braght, *Martyrs' Mirror* (Elkhart, IN: John F. Funk und Bruder, 1870), title page.

Mennonites became a local "Noble Savage" people worthy of Rousseau's most optimistic philosophy.[28] This attitude, of course, also informs the depiction of Jacques the Anabaptist by Voltaire, even though Voltaire made Jacques a Dutch urban businessman rather than an Anabaptist peasant like those who lived in the countryside near his home in Valdoie (near Belfort) and whom he personally admired.

FIG. 6—THE ANABAPTIST FARMER = NOBLE SAVAGE [29]

Today this archetype is most likely to appear in literature about Mennonites and Amish written by outsiders, such as Sue Bender's recent book *Plain and Simple: A Woman's Journey to the Amish*. However, it also

28. Anthony R. Epp, "Treatments of Anabaptists in Eighteenth Century French Reference Works," *MQR* 60 (April 1986), 165-79.

29. "Le Nouvel Anabaptiste, ou L'Agriculteur-Pratique [The New Anabaptist, or Practical Agriculture]. —J. Klopfenstein, *Le Nouvel Anabaptiste* No. 24 (Belfort: 1844), cover.

appears deliberately and fully developed in Joseph W. Yoder's *Rosanna of the Amish*, the Mennonite novel that has sold more copies than any other.

Fig. 7—The Hutterite Dovecote = Good Community [30]

The image of a large dovecote of many compartments was drawn of Hutterites in 1607 by some Jesuit critics who were worried about the way Hutterites were attracting new members. Although the intent of the Jesuits was satirical, by depicting Hutterite community as a dovecote swarming with life (albeit grotesque life) they actually acknowledged, at least implicitly, the strong appeal that Anabaptist community life had for many people. This image may stand for all depictions of Mennonite community found in Mennonite literature—ranging from the strict communitarianism of the Hutterites to the looser association of the Amish to the more individualistic Mennonites. In fact, I suspect that the image of community is the most ubiquitous archetype to be found in Mennonite literature and also the most useful one for getting at the heart of Mennonite literature.

Jeff Gundy's depiction and overt discussion of Mennonite community in *A Community of Memory: My Days with George and Clara* is an unusually positive example, but virtually all Mennonite literature deals to some extent with the possibilities and perils represented by such birdhouse living.

---

30. The Hutterite Dovecote. — Christopher Andreas, V*ier und Funffsig: Erhebliche Urfachen* ... (Ingolstadt: Andream Ungermener, 1607), frontispiece.

FIG. 8—THE ANABAPTIST CAGE = BAD COMMUNITY [31]

31. The Anabaptist Cages at Munster.—Piet Visser and Mary S. Sprunger, *Menno Simons: Places, Portraits and Progeny* (Altona, MAN: Friesens, 1996), fig. 7b, p. 27 (used there by permission of Esther van Weelden, Amsterdam).

The kingdom of the Anabaptists of Munster lasted from February 1534 to June 1535 and was brought to an end by the public execution of many militant Anabaptists, including their leader Jan van Leiden six months later. The bodies of the Anabaptist leaders were placed in cages and hoisted up St. Lambert's Church, where they were left to rot and be eaten by vultures (Fig. 8). Mennonites on heritage tours seek out these cages as grisly reminders of the tragic outcome of communitarianism that yields too much authority to the fanatic leadership of a few — usually patriarchal — leaders.

The cages serve as an icon to remind us of some of the more extreme cases of community-building, where enforced conformity leads to oppression and, sometimes, violence and death. One good literary case in point is the rigid community of Wapiti, established by Russian immigrants in western Canada under the tyrannical Deacon Block in Rudy Wiebe's *Peace Shall Destroy Many*. Samuel U. Reimer also

FIG. 9—MENNONITE SISTER = COY SEXUALITY [32]

32. "Menniste zusje" [Mennonite Sister]. Drawing by T. Schaap-Stuurman for a Mennonite card game conceived by J. Siersma and sold by the Dutch National Federation of Mennonite Sisters in 1979.

experiences the negative pressures of a more enlightened Mennonite community in *The Blue Mountains of China*, as does also Mika in Sandra Birdsell's *Night Travellers* and Andrea Doria's mother in Janet Kauffman's *Collaborators*. Warren Kliewer's *The Violators* is yet another example.

"Mennonite sister" (Fig. 9) has been a proverbial phrase and concept in Dutch culture ever since at least 1621 when Jan Jansz Starter composed a famous poem exposing her wiles. She is a "prudish, shy and serious Mennonite girl with double standards, who . . . is ultimately seduced."[33]   In more recent literature she cultivates a modest, cool exterior appearance but nevertheless harbors strong sexual drives that she can barely suppress.

Hazel in Merle Good's novel and film *Hazel's People* is of such a sexually ambivalent nature. A more subtle case is Anna Friesen at the well with Joe Hiebert in Paraguay in *The Blue Mountains of China*.

The method I use here — of finding culturally endorsed images and then identifying their archetypal fulfillments in Mennonite literature — may ultimately be of limited value in finding and identifying crucial archetypes. For instance, in my initial preparation of this essay I had not yet found an image to serve as an objective correlative for what I know to be one of the most ubiquitous archetypes in Mennonite literature, the village or kin community that wanders over the face of the earth seeking a "Promised Land" — as in Jeff Gundy's *A Community of Memory*, Rudy Wiebe's *The Blue Mountains of China*, Al Reimer's *My Harp Is Turned to Mourning* and Dallas Wiebe's *Our Asian Journey*.

However, even that archetype may now have its own image if the MLR edition of *Our Asian Journey* becomes widely enough known. . On its cover is a compelling watercolor painting by Peter Goetz of horse-drawn wagons pulling yet one more Mennonite community across forbidding landscape to a better place (Fig. 10).

---

33. Piet Visser, "Aspects of Social Criticism and Cultural Assimilation: The Mennonite Image in Literature and Self-Criticism of Literary Mennonites," in Alastair Hamilton, et al, eds., *From Martyr to Muppy* (Amsterdam: Amsterdam U. Press, 1994), 78. For an English translation of the poem, *Het menniste zusje* (The Mennonite Sister) by Jan Jansz Starter, see Irvin and Ava Horst, "Simplicity Laments Corrupted Manners," *Mennonite Life* 10 (1955), 129-31.

FIG. 10—THE CARAVAN = COMMUNITY ON THE MOVE [34]

CONCLUSION

If we take the claims of postmodernism seriously, it may at first glance seem hopelessly naive and retrogressive to define Mennonite literature according to archetypes. After all, archetypes are Platonic essences. And Northrop Frye, the most outstanding archetypal theorist and critic, has long ago been discredited for thinking that he had identified the universals of world literature and the unity of meaning to which they point. We now see that he mistook the European tradition for the world tradition, and that he found in his archetypes the Christian universalism that his life as Anglican priest had predisposed him to find. Similarly, the armchair anthropologists whose work has fed into archetypal criticism—Joseph Campbell, and Sir James Frazer before

34. "Asian Journey," watercolor by Peter Goetz (1997), Kitchener, ON; owned by Dallas Wiebe. Reproduced with permission.

him — violated all standards of modern comparative anthropology by taking rituals out of context, stripping them of their culture-specific meanings in order to construct meanings that their contemporaries needed: in Frazer's case, a neo-Christianity justified by death and resurrection rituals; in Campbell's case, a New Age synthesis.

Yet if we see in Frye, Campbell and Frazer once again the "social construction of knowledge," we must distinguish what they were doing with archetypes from what Mennonite critics might do with them. Frye and others mistakenly generalized about archetypes in regard to all people, in every place and every time. We can more modestly — and more persuasively — use archetypes as a hermeneutic tool within our own "interpretive community," knowing full well that they do not represent universal experience, but rather Mennonites' experience and knowledge as we/they have constructed it through almost 500 years of history. True, many individual archetypes — especially trickster — will resonate with other communities. But the combination of archetypes that make up the Mennonite psyche is different from that of any other group and creates the peculiar, emotional response to experience that many of us recognize as "Mennonite."

Archetypes will not go away, although their use and meaning may vary, depending upon whether we use them to prove the "essence" or the "contingency" of experience. In other words, if we use archetypes primarily in a monolithic way to claim that all Mennonite experience is the same, we will be falling into the syndrome that now discredits the work of Frazer, Frye and Campbell. But if we use archetypes in order to clarify the unique variant that each author creates out of Mennonite experience — the "signature" that Leslie Fiedler said a good writer impresses upon the archetype — then archetypes will serve us well in helping us find and understand the uniqueness of each work of Mennonite literature and the rich diversity of experience that it affirms.

THE STORYTELLER'S GIFT\THE GIFT OF STORY: NARRATIVE VOICES IN THE WRITING OF S. C. YODER

JANE HOSTETLER ROBINETT*

Abstract: The role of storytelling (personal narrative) in the work of Mennonite writer Sanford C. Yoder in *Down South America Way* (1943) and *Horse Trails along the Desert* (1954) shapes the narrative strategies and choices of the writer. Yoder's use of stories helped him deal with the constraints of writing within the Mennonite community and establish an understanding of the role and value of storytelling and the imagination. Yoder's books and his use of stories also helped to create a taste for narrative in the Mennonite reading public, which, in time, would make it possible for the larger Mennonite community to see the role of the writer of fiction as a valuable one.

As any Mennonite child who has grown up around a copy of the *Martyrs' Mirror* knows, personal stories have been recorded from the beginning of the Anabaptist movement. But as persecution grew in Europe and the educated leadership of the movement was lost, education and, therefore, written accounts grew more rare. Mennonites became in many senses, a hidden people whose stories were known only to themselves. Because of this, there has always been a strong oral tradition within the Mennonite community. Personal histories and stories were told and re-told and occasionally written down in lengthy genealogy books. But, with the exception of those who worked in missions, written accounts of individual experiences, especially those of Mennonites in the world at large, were relatively rare. When he began publishing in the 1940s, Sanford C. Yoder's narratives helped to create an interest in and an appetite for more stories, the untold stories of Mennonite lives, past and present.

Personal narrative, such as we find in Yoder's work, became the strategy which helped legitimize the imaginatively constructed narratives we designate as fiction. In addition, Yoder's personal narratives made room for, and privileged, the imagination, thus affirming its importance and value. By drawing on a firmly established oral tradition in the Mennonite community, and converting its techniques and texts into written form, Yoder drew readers into his

*Jane Hostetler Robinett is Associate Professor in the Department of Rhetoric and Writing Studies at San Diego State University, San Diego, California. She is a granddaughter of Sanford C. Yoder.

stories, thus inviting them to use their own imaginations to see in the mind's eye what they could never witness in daily life. A look at two of Yoder's books, *Down South America Way* (1943) and *Horse Trails Along the Desert* (1954), will illustrate his most important, and most overlooked, contribution to twentieth-century Mennonite writing: his use of personal narrative, his gift for story-telling.

The difficulties of legitimizing personal narrative for a Mennonite writing in the 1940s and 1950s are clearly demonstrated in Yoder's second book, *Down South America Way* (1943).[1] In 1919, at the behest of the Mennonite Board of Missions and Charities (MBCM), he had made a trip to Argentina to assist in opening the mission work in Latin America.[2] In 1940, again sponsored by the MBMC, he went first to Argentina and then on to Paraguay to visit the Mennonite colonies in the Chaco, recently established by the refugees who had fled from Russia and the terrible persecution they suffered there between 1929 and 1934. *Down South America Way* is a brief account of his trip and what he found there, "a small part of the story," as his preface points out, of the Mennonites in Argentina and Paraguay.

The purpose of the book was to "inspire interest in our neighbors who live in the land to the south," and the writer's intention is that out of his account would grow a better understanding of the problems of the "Argentine and Paraguayan churches and . . . a larger and more substantial support in prayer, in sympathy, and where needed, in material resources."[3] He was 61 when he made the trip, 64 by the time the book was published. A veteran of the pulpit and the lectern, his gift for story telling was already fully developed by the time he began his career as a writer.

Although careful to delineate his purpose as a serious one, he was too good a writer not to understand that he must not only inform but also entertain and engage his readers if he were to gain their sympathy and support for their far-off brethren. He was also clearly aware that he was a Mennonite abroad in the wide world, the eyes and ears of the folks at home. He had to find a narrative strategy that spoke for the official voice of the Mission Board, one that held to his announced purpose. He also had to create a strategy that gave him room to speak for himself, as a highly educated man and an accomplished traveler. In this book, Yoder

---

1. *For Conscience Sake*, his first book, an account of the Mennonite migrations out of Russia following the end of World War I, was published in 1940.

2. A brief written account of this trip exists in book form in Yoder's *The Days of My Years*. There may also be accounts of his visits there among Yoder's letters and papers in the Archives of the Mennonite Church at Goshen College.

3. Sanford C. Yoder, *Down South America Way* (Scottdale, PA.: Herald Press, 1943), preface.

maintained a neat balance between these two narrative modes, switching back and forth as he journeyed from New York to Brazil and on to Argentina and the Chaco, then back to New Orleans and home again. He is at his best when writing in his private voice, although he often cut that voice short in deference to the stated purpose of his text.

As the book opens, we set out on what he clearly meant for us to see as an adventure:

> At midnight of June 14, the *S.S. Uruguay*, a 33,000 ton liner of the United States Shipping Board, pushed away from her mooring and quietly sailed out of New York harbor into the sea...headed for South American ports . . . the next morning all traces of land were gone . . . [and] before evening the awnings were spread, deck chairs assigned, the swimming pool was opened, deck sports were arranged, and everything was set for the comfort, entertainment and welfare of the passengers during their nineteen-day voyage to the Southland (1).

This opening connects the narrative to one of the oldest and richest of story forms: the formula of the epic, the faring forth and return of the hero. True to form, the midnight departure out onto the open ocean is followed by an invocation of God in which the writer remembers God's admonition to the sea to stay within its bounds. This, in turn, is followed immediately by an invocation of the muse, in a quotation from George Gordon, Lord Byron:

> Man marks the earth with ruin — his control
> Stops with the shore: upon the watery plain
> The wrecks are all thy deeds. . . . (3)

The reference to the dangers of seafaring leads Yoder to remember that Byron's views are no longer true since the invention of "battleships and submarines, torpedoes and nautical mines"(9). That reminds the reader that this is June 1940, and with the world already at war, the sea is no longer a safe place for travelers, even those thousands of miles away from the land battles. Within the opening three paragraphs, Yoder has situated the reader firmly in the narrative mode of the epic adventure (which, we should note, was for thousands of years an oral form), invoking the protection of the gods and the power of the muse to assist him in telling his tale. Yoder was not a warrior going out to do battle, like Achilles or Theseus, nor would he claim the hero's title for himself. He was instead, a man of peace, and like Homer, a storyteller. But it is clear that he saw this journey in larger terms than those of simply going off on a fact-finding tour for the Mission Board. Reading these opening paragraphs, we know that we are going to share adventures and strange places, that we are setting out on a quest to find lost brothers and sisters, like Achilles or Theseus, nor would he claim the hero's title for himself. He was instead, a man of peace, and like Homer, a storyteller. But it is clear that he saw this journey in larger terms than those of simply going off on a fact-finding tour for the Mission Board. Reading these opening paragraphs, we know that we are going to share adventures and strange places, that we are setting out on a quest to find lost brothers and sisters, and we are reminded that setting out on the unknown road is always dangerous, especially in times of war.

When the ship crosses the equator, we are given an account of the "initiation of those who are going over the fabled line for the first time" by Father Neptune, an event which the writer also noted "frequently becomes an inglorious affair," a small masterpiece of understatement (6). Nevertheless, the scene was too interesting for him to exclude. First, passengers were called into Neptune's court at pool side, to answer for their conduct and Neptune imposed appropriate sentences on them. The sentences were carried out by the members of his court, and "all the victims finally ended up in the swimming pool" and were eventually given a "diploma certifying to their fitness as worthy mariners" (6). Yoder included the full text of the diploma, but before we imagine the dignified college president and representative of the Mission Board being tossed into the pool, we need to remember that this is an account of his *second* trip to South America.

Later on, when the ship put into port in Rio, he was enthusiastic about the beauty of the city and its surroundings. As we might expect of any traveler, he took a drive to the top of Corcovado to visit the great statue of Christ that watches over the city. But he also visited the same little Catholic chapel he had visited twenty years earlier, which was "now in a bad state of repair," a suggestive observation which points to a similar spiritual condition among the citizenry (12). Here is the public voice of the minister, interested in and concerned for the spiritual life of the country he was exploring. But before the contemporary reader is tempted to impute to the writer a note of smugness about the superiority of American life, Yoder makes an extraordinary observation. He noted that in this country the "racial barriers have crumbled here, and the races not only intermingle but intermarry as well" and that he finds these interesting mixed-blood people "loveable," and "very courteous and polite." He was aware that there were problems here too. "We are told," he says, thereby perhaps casting a shade of doubt on the veracity of the statement to follow, "that underneath the outer gloss is too often a moral corruption that is appalling" (13). His train of thought seems play to the party line of the Mission Board, the idea of a great mass of the misguided heathen in foreign parts. But what follows is an abrupt departure from that line:

> Twenty years ago I felt that on the whole we people of the United States had something to say to these folks, but *now I do not think so.* We have plenty of sin hidden under the cloak of respectability and sometimes under the pretense of piety. . . . [4]

Clearly, those twenty years as a pastor, bishop and college president had given Yoder insight and understanding which precluded self-righteous attitudes and misplaced pride. His humility and compassion set him apart from Mennonite travel writers of narrower understanding and experience.

Through all of this, he played the role of introducing his little-traveled Mennonite audience to the wide and interesting world, all the while presenting it through the familiar screen of Mennonite ideals and concerns, tempered, as we have seen, by his compassion and understanding of the non-Mennonite. He not only visited the Catholic chapel in Rio; he also visited the outdoor cafes and window-shopped along the beautiful and worldly Avenida Branco. There is a constant alternation between his descriptions of the beauty of the countries and the poverty found there, the good he found in the people and the religious indifference and moral laxity he saw. As we have witnessed, in regard to the Brazilians, he makes a number of observances that reveal both his thoughtful humanity and his acceptance of the cultures he encountered. In Argentina, he noted the beautiful homes of the rich, but reported that "the homes of the poor are *poor*," with no windows and dirt or rough brick floors.

His emphasis on the extent of the poverty he found here is not, however, an indication of a tendency to cross-cultural patronization. Having come from a poor family himself, he knew well what poverty looked like in the United States and meant his readers to understand that even our poor may be better housed than the people he met here. And as with his remarks on the Brazilians, he followed his observation immediately with a caution to his readers not to feel self-righteous. Although these people live in dwellings far below the average American ones:

> . . . why need people judge others by their own standards? After all, life and happiness does not consist of the abundance of things

---

4. Italics mine.

which one possesses and 'to be content with such things as we have' is a Biblical virtue that most of us have not acquired (41).

Here both the public voice of the minister and the private voice of the traveler/writer join forces to prevent readers from distancing themselves from these far-off folks whom Yoder clearly did not see as foreigners and heathens, but as poor people struggling to make homes and lives for themselves and their families. By using economic identifiers ("poor") rather than national, class or religious ones, he invoked experiences his readers were familiar with, and thereby erased the line between American Mennonite readers and slum dwellers in Argentina by appealing to the common economic struggles and humanity they share.

Even though roughly two-thirds of the book is devoted to the official visits he made in Argentina and Paraguay to the little congregations and missions and colonies of Mennonite folk, it is the private voice of the traveler and his ability to characterize the local that carry the reader into the book. In one chapter, "With the Redeemed in Argentina," he met an old man whose faith and strength of character in the face of personal disaster, seemed to strike a chord of admiration in him. "Here at the outskirts of the city," he writes, "lives an old brother ninety-three years old . . . one of the old frontiersmen . . . [who] saw his daughter disemboweled by an enraged, drunken husband and within a few weeks he buried his wife, who was prostrate with grief" (47). When he visited Bragado, blind Dona Carmen sent him a "cluster of large lilies" from the garden she still kept, lilies which must have reminded the writer of those in his wife's garden at home. When he went to visit the man who was the first Mennonite pastor in Argentina, and with whom he had stayed twenty years earlier, he remembered that on his first visit he was struck with very well-behaved children and the "quiet, composed manner" of the mother with her large family. The second incident he recalled was a special menu planned for his visit, centered on a couple of ostrich eggs. The whole family joined their father outside the house at the well to see the eggs opened, when, to everyone's dismay, the egg "exploded and filled the air with fumes that drove us all to cover"(58). As usual, in telling the story Yoder uses pronouns that make it clear he includes himself as one of the family. He shares his stories with his readers as he had shared the experience with others involved in the incident; he does not separate himself from the Brazilians, Argentinians or Paraguayans he met. That participatory attitude, in turn, does not allow readers to separate themselves from either the events or the people in the story.

On a trip out onto the Pampa with the pastor of the little church at America, he met an old couple who "lived together for years, raised their family, had grandchildren and great-grandchildren before they took their nuptial vows"(60). He passed no judgement on this couple; instead he noted that living together was a common custom, perhaps fostered by the fact that the laws of Argentina forbade divorce. What was unusual and admirable here, he pointed out, was that through reading the scriptures they had decided, in their old age, to be married. He added, for the Mennonites at home, that they were "not Christians but are interested and took all our admonitions and counsels kindly," and left open the possibility that they "may yet find their way home to God"(60). The portraits of those he met and the events he witnessed and took part in constitute the kind of embedded personal narratives that give this book substance and texture.

One of the most interesting examples of his use of oral narrative is the story of yerba mate. By this time he was on the border of Paraguay, traveling up the Rio Paraguaya. As the ship made its way upriver past occasional crocodiles sleeping on sand bars, he remembered a story he had been told:

> Long ago, so the story goes, when Paraguay was young and its population sparse, a monk was grazing his goats on the open spaces. The debilitating, languid climate brought their vitality down until they hardly had enough energy . . . to nibble the grass that grew round them. But he observed that after having browsed upon the leaves of certain shrubs, his flock was greatly exhilarated and become more active and alert and frisked and frolicked, as good goats should; even sedate old billy forgot his dignity and gamboled like a kid. Curious of the strange effect of this plant, the herdsman began to chew its leaves, and to his surprise, he found that his energy rose and he partook of the spirit of his goats. When word of the unusual behavior of his erring subordinate came to the ears of the bishop, he sought to ascertain the cause and when introduced to the leaves of the offending shrub, he, too was seized with the same exalted paroxysm and indulged in the antics that were considered far beneath the dignity of his noble position. And so the effect of yerba mate was discovered. . . . (82)

A bishop himself at the time, Yoder was clearly amused by this little story. But perhaps the most interesting thing for readers is that Yoder went on to point out that the same story was told of the discovery of coffee plants and thus, perhaps, needed authentication. As a scholar, and as a Mennonite, he was aware that tales of origins like this one, no matter how charming and funny, were not acceptable explanations, but must be confirmed by the sober and factual narratives of science. But when he set out to confirm the story, he changed his mind. He deliberately refused to consult encyclopedias or other factual texts to authenticate the story because:

> . . . those unromantic and matter-of-fact authorities would surely say that this story, though beautiful, is not true and the use of mate had a very prosaic beginning. Hence, I choose to be ignorant rather than wise, for I prefer to carry with me a vision of gamboling goats and kids exhilarated by the leaves of this innocent tree, and of rollicking monks and cavorting bishops who first felt the effects of the plant that has now become the famed beverage of the Latin American world (92).

This is a declaration of independence not only for the writer himself, but also for all would-be Mennonite writers of fictions which are "not true" but which embody a multiplicity of truths. It is also a deliberate and public valorization of the imaginative and playful, even when it turns its attentions to the actions of religious leaders. Yoder's position within the Mennonite community gave real weight to this deliberate choice of the richness of the fictional over the limitations of the merely factual.

As Yoder traveled deeper into Paraguay and the Chaco, dozens and dozens of anecdotes illustrate his mastery of narrative and his eye for salient detail. He alternates between public and private voices, and the rhythms of the alternations give the narrative a kind of movement which propels the reader along the road with him. In Asuncion one afternoon, he observed a religious procession, and "by taking a shortcut through crooked alleys and across plazas," he arrived at the great cathedral in time to get a place to stand near the alter while high mass was being celebrated (94). A Mennonite minister among "the crowd that jammed the building" at a Catholic mass is not what Mennonite readers in the mid-1950s might expect, but there he was, and consequently there we are too, enjoying a scene the writer evidently found impressive. He visited the girls' orphanage at Las Palmas, outside of Asuncion. To get there, he and his companion had to take the streetcar, which he preferred to the crowded bus that "jolts and bounces across the rough street." On the way, he recounted the experience his companion had had on such a bus trip when he nearly fell into the lap of a lady "occupying the seat close to the one he was aiming at, and drew from an observant army officer [riding the bus] the remark, 'He would make a poor parachutist if he can't make a better landing than that'" (94).

Always following accounts like these, he returns to his public voice, the voice of the teacher, minister and scholar. While his private voice is attuned to the unfolding richness of the natural world he saw around him, and to the people he met and events he witnessed, his public voice gives his readers accounts of the historical, architectural, geographical and climatological detail, and of sermons preached and songs sung, of meetings held and the financial, educational and other problems of the little communities, and the faith, work and lives of the Mennonite folk he had been sent to visit. In addition, his private voice attests to his own belief and faith and records an occasional admonition to the readers to see the world and its peoples from a wider and more compassionate point of view. When he speaks in his private voice, we learn of his stay in the Jacob Seimens' home in the Chaco, and the details of his room, from the roses on his night stand to the drinks made from the "blossoms of a tree that grew in the forest," the recipe for the plaster that coats the houses (milk and eggs), accounts of delicious breakfasts, of "getting a very satisfactory haircut of the household variety," of "mosquitoes that turn the hour into a nightmare" and of a very late night conversation he had with a young German "night prowler" who gave him "some startling information regarding the German Bund and its activities in Paraguay" and who seemed to have a lot of information about smugglers and their activities (119, 131, 134).

Throughout *Down South America Way*, this rich blend of private and public voices carries us along, but it also leaves us with a yearning for a fuller account of those stories that Yoder truncates in deference to his public purpose. Fortunately, this private narrative voice finds its full expression in *Horse Trails Along the Desert* (1954), an account of the three years that Yoder, then 26, and his wife Emma, 22, and their year-old son Myron spent homesteading on what was the last piece of homestead land opened up by the U.S. government. This book won Yoder national recognition and election to the International Mark Twain Society and the Eugene Field Society. Here, Yoder leaves the double-voiced narrative and the constraints of reporting for the Mission Board and tells his own stories. However, even here, an official justification for these lively personal narratives was apparently felt necessary and is provided on the inside blurb of the book jacket by Herald Press:

> This is a good book to read when the evening calls for relaxation . . . through his personal experience the author leads the reader to a deep appreciation of the Scripture.[5]

This is somewhat at odds with chapter titles like "The Call of the West," "Knights of the Jingling Spur," "Riding for Rustlers," "Outlaw Hogs" and "A Runaway on the Columbia." This time the justification for story-reading and story-telling comes from his publishers and not from Yoder,

---

5. Sanford C. Yoder, *Horse Trails along the Desert*, (Scottdale, PA: Herald Press, 1954), from the dustjacket.

whose unapologetic childhood reading included accounts of General Phil Sheridan's cavalry, the Dalton boys and the James brothers.[6]

Yoder feels no need to justify his stories of homesteading in the desert of western Washington around the turn of the century. He defends the sagebrush country in which he chose to live and will not allow anyone to disparage what he clearly considers to be the best years of his life. By casting these narratives, his oral stories, into written form, Yoder gives not only to his children and grandchildren, to whom the book is dedicated, but also to the Mennonite community itself the accounts of the experiences which shaped and defined his life, character and faith. In fact, the existence of these stories in written form privileges them in a way that oral transmission can not. Unlike cultural oral narratives, which are widely known and widely repeated, personal oral narratives are quite likely to disappear with the death of the transmitter or teller. Yoder's decision to commit these stories to writing is clear evidence of his awareness that they are too important to allow to vanish from the collective memory of his family and his community.

In many of the stories, he reflects on how events of this period deepened and broadened his spiritual life, which was rooted in the teachings, moral tenants and spiritual understandings of the Amish and Mennonite churches. But equally important is the fact that these experiences took place outside the confines of the Mennonite community and away from the structure and customs of a close-knit, churchgoing society. In his opening chapter he described the life and the country they lived in and made their position clear: "Churches, such as there were, were twenty miles away: consequently attendance was out of the question"(7). However, even in such thinly-settled country, Sundays remained special days for them, and they made Sundays special days for their widely-scattered neighbors:

> Since we were the only outfit that was equipped with wagons, work stock, and saddle horses, we got to the railroad more frequently than did the other settlers. When we went, we brought mail and supplies for the community. Sunday was the time when they came to our place to get their letters and papers and to exchange such news as there was (7).

Later on, a former missionary and his wife took up a claim adjacent to theirs and during their "eight months' residence we spent many happy Sundays together," sometimes holding church services "for such as

6. The Daltons and the James brothers (Frank and Jesse) were both famous outlaw gangs of the frontier west.

78

cared to come" (2). Though he made no apology for this lack of church attendance, it is also clear that he knew his readers would need an explanation.

The opening narrative move in the book, like the opening in *Down South America Way*, evokes the same familiar and much loved form: the archetypal hero tales of myth, epic and fairy tales, those journeys undertaken for adventure and fortune which lead the hero into strange countries, hardship, danger, suffering, and reward him with the achievement of strength, compassion, humility, courage and wisdom. *Horse Trails* opens with an account of one of Yoder's boyhood heroes, his older cousin, Phil Yoder, whose father's family had moved from Iowa, where S.C. Yoder grew up, out to the open range north and east of Cheyenne, Wyoming, in the mid-nineteenth century. There they had stock ranches. Phil was born and raised on that unfenced range land, and occasionally he would come back to Iowa, accompanying carloads of horses to be sold there. He stayed with his relatives and his appearance always caused a stir, especially among the plainly-dressed Amish boys like Sanford and his identical twin brother, Sam:

> His high-heeled boots and what is known now as a ten-gallon hat, tight-fitting trousers and highly colored silk muffler made him a striking and picturesque figure which stirred the blood of the youngsters who saw him (2).

Here is the hero come back to his ancestral homeland from wild country, dressed in strange costume. But even more important than his exotic appearance Yoder tells us, were his stories of the range wars between cattlemen and sheepmen, of round-ups, of ". . . his long freighting trips to Cheyenne when he camped at night beside his wagon and sometimes slept in the snow. . . ." Those stories, Yoder writes, stirred up "the spirit of adventure within me from which I never fully recovered. . . ." (2)

Those oral tales may also have served as one of his earliest models for narrative, and this book, designated a "collection of reminiscences" by the book jacket, clearly takes its structure more from oral tradition than from written forms. Like the storyteller he is, Yoder uses a written structure which is less concerned with observing linear conventionalities than it is with focusing on character, incident and event. He uses some of the same devices found in oral narrative: repetition, recursion and commentary, drawing his material both from his own experiences and from oral stories told to him by others during his homesteading years. He begins by giving us a broad overview of the experience and then settles into telling stories, a technique that gives the reader multiple points of entry into the text. This makes it possible for us to return to favorite incidents again and again without losing the narrative thread, just as told tales are heard over and over without losing their power or interest. Essential to the unfolding narratives are numerous portraits of the desert folk:

> Among them was Abe Harder, a Linotype operator and a lawyer, but mostly a hobo. He took up a claim with the intention of raising chickens, but when everything had happened that usually comes to pass when a lawyer bestows his practice upon poultry . . . he had only one fowl left—a Blue Andalusian rooster which he named Andy. . . . The last time he came he was leading—or carrying— Andy across the weary distance that lay between our place and his. Upon leaving, he turned him over to us whereupon he soon found his way into the frying pan (7).

There are other portraits as well, a listing reminiscent in some ways of Homer's catalog of ships and heroes in the *Iliad*. Among them are George and Mary Guthrie, former missionaries to India; Buckaroo Brown, a "lone wolf" wrangler, who worked for the Bracket H outfit and became a close friend of the Yoders, and with whom the writer rode for rustlers and rounded up wild horses; Johnnie Tincup, a half-Chickasaw who bossed the cowboys for the Running W ranch; Henry Gable, the horseman who owned and ran the Bracket H, and whose horses were known far and wide for their quality; White Bluff Charley, of the Nez Perce people; Chief Joseph, whom Yoder greatly admired and to whom he dedicated a long chapter; John Gibson, a half-Cherokee "one of the best friends I had," Yoder writes, but who, for all that, "was not above taking advantage of a person in a horse trade" (167). Not all of the important characters in the book are human. There is a detailed account of the roundup of wild horses and of how he acquired Babe, his "beautiful chestnut sorrel mare, a three-year-old, with silver mane and tail and white stockings on her hind legs that reached to her knees, and white anklets on her forelegs"(17). There is the long-legged, fleet-footed Roany, Buckaroo Brown's favorite horse, and the three bands of wild horses who have never been caught, chief among them the Wild Gooses and the black stallion who leads them.

The book is filled with the kinds of adventures and dangers that all hero tales anticipate. There is deceit and deception. When Yoder and the two men who accompanied him (his younger brother, Elmer, and his wife's brother, George) "[step] off the Northern Pacific train that early April morning" they were "hardly off the platform until a real estate agent spotted us and followed us to a restaurant across the street from the depot," eager to have first chance at selling these innocent newcomers on a land deal (13). Fortunately, they got some good advice from an old settler and, at least for the moment, avoid being swindled. A year later, however, Yoder, like many a hero before him, forgot his early lesson. He began to look for homestead land, and found a wonderful quarter section of land on the south slope of the Horseheaven Hills. He located the owner and made the necessary arrangements to file a claim on the land. Together, they rode the sixty-five miles to the Federal Land Office at Cleveland, where he formally filed his claim and took possession of the land. But his elation at acquiring his claim was short-lived. The land he had paid for and filed claim on was disputed territory. The railroad, which claimed rights to all even-numbered sections and all land within twenty miles of the road itself, had been given an extension of its land rights, and Yoder's claim, it turned out after the case had been adjudicated, belonged to the railroad. It also turned out that the people involved in the sale—the landowner, his new friends, and even the Federal Land Officer at Cleveland all knew of the dispute and all failed to tell him the truth. So the land he thought he owned disappeared into the maw of the railroad, and so did the first money he had earned and saved.

There are dangerous adventures on the road: when they sold their house in Prosser, Washington and got ready to move out onto their holdings on Sunflower Flat, Yoder went ahead with their household possessions loaded onto his freighting wagon. He had been told by the old hands that he could reach Big Rattlesnake Spring easily by dark. But sunset found him high up at the summit of the mountains. From there he could see "away off to the east and far below" him the green patch that he had to reach "in order to find feed and water and a camping place for the night" (36). And there was more trouble ahead:

> The descent on the steep, rocky slopes was worse than I had anticipated. There were places where from my seat I looked down hundreds of feet to the floor of coulees and valleys. At times I drove with the lines wrapped around my arms or in my teeth, while I hung on the brake lever with both hands and pulled with all my might, and yet the wagon pushed up on the team until it looked as though the whole outfit might go over the embankment and land in a heap on the rocks far below (36).

Once he got down into the canyons, darkness set in. For a moment Yoder hesitated in the dark mazes of the gorges and considered camping dry. But he knew that his team had to have water. The trail grew dim and hard to follow in the rocky country, but he lighted his way through the coulees with matches. Up on top of the mesas, the sagebrush guided him. Tired and discouraged and "almost faithless in anything that man had told" him, he could find no comfort and encouragement.

81

Didn't people tell me that I could easily make the Big Rattlesnake Spring by dark? And here it was, long after sunset, and I was, nobody knew how far from my destination. Didn't people tell me that the road was good? And here for hours I had bounced up and down in my wagon, and walked and stumbled, then bounced again until my body was sore, my temper was hanging by a thread, my faith was shaken and my confidence shattered . . . when I saw the little junipers along the hillsides, I was reminded of what Elijah did in the day when his confidence in men was low and I was about to give up too (38).

The double darkness of night and discouragement was suddenly broken by the sight of a tree against the sky line. In this country, our writer knew (but tells us, in case we don't), trees grew only near springs or streams or along irrigation ditches. He drove on, and when his team suddenly came up against a fence, he knew that he had reached his destination. He opened the gate and "step[ped] into water to [his] ankles." "Never," he writes, "since I was a little boy, playing in the puddles along the road, have I been so happy to have my shoes full of water" (38). Later on, while he rested his team at the last watering place before the Columbia River, watching the little desert birds among the cool shadows of the trees and shrubs, and the range horses drinking at the spring, he remembered Psalm 104:10-12:

He sendeth the springs into the valleys,
Which run among the hills.
They give drink to every beast of the field:
The wild asses quench their thirst,
By them shall the fowls of the heaven have their habitation,
Which sing among the branches.

The biblical texts shine with life for him; he sees in them a living reflection of his daily reality, and as we read his stories, those old texts also take on new life for us. Here is the storyteller who draws myth into daily life, for whom God (or the gods, as they were for Homer, and for the tribal storytellers of oral cultures everywhere) is alive and breathing, as close to us as the water we drink. The oral tradition is present in these stories not only in the techniques or narrative strategies which Yoder chooses, but also in his mindset and vision of the world. His links to oral tradition connect both writer and reader not only with the personal, cultural and historical past, but also with ancestral and mythic roots. Here is a writer who sees his life as linked to the living presence of the Creator, an idea literally as old as the desert hills he rides across.

The task of storytellers is, was and always will be a fundamentally moral one: to remind listeners and readers that their lives are connected

82

to many other lives, and beyond that, to the life of the Creator, and to examine the implications and consequences of the presence or absence of those connections. Yoder succeeds admirably in all of these things in *Horse Trails Along the Desert*. His stories read like fiction, and to the extent that they have been selected out of many, many more that he might have told, re-created (as stories are with every telling) and ordered, they are fictions. By assuming the mask of the storyteller, he took a long step toward validating the worth of imaginative creations for a Mennonite community at mid-century. Because these stories come from a man whose public life was dedicated to the Mennonite community, the idea that there is real value in such creations was heard. By recounting his experiences far away from the Mennonite community and the Mennonite church, he also made it clear that much can be gained from living outside the community. *Horse Trails Along the Desert* not only fulfills the promise of the embedded personal narratives in *Down South America Way*, but also underscores for aspiring writers the idea that leaving the Mennonite community does not mean abandoning the faith. In addition, it points out that a Mennonite writer's subject matter need not be confined to the Mennonite community. Yoder's stories, whether embedded in larger texts as in *Down South America Way*, or fully told, as in *Horse Trails Along the Desert*, and his gift for storytelling and story-making helped blaze a trail for the Mennonite writers who have followed him.

THE SILENCE OF VICTIM, STORY-TELLER AND CHURCH IN *LIGHT FROM HEAVEN*: A SOCIAL COMMENTARY

PHOEBE BEACHY WILEY*

Abstract: In 1946, some years after the death of the actual "Annie" Armstrong, Christmas Carol Kauffman wrote *Light from Heaven*, the fictionalized story of the abused mother and her children, in the hope that their story would comfort and encourage other victims of abuse. In Annie's lifetime as well as when Kauffman wrote the story, the permanence of marriage was a given in the Mennonite church. In addition, the church placed considerable emphasis on submission for women. This paper examines Annie's response to the abuse, the author's attitude to that response, and the reaction of well-known Mennonite men to the novel. The responses of all concerned follow logically from the twin emphases of submission for women and the permanence of marriage.

Most novelists state that any resemblance of their characters to persons living or dead is purely coincidental. Not so, Christmas Carol Kauffman, one of the best-selling Mennonite authors of the 1950s and 1960s, chose to fictionalize the stories of actual individuals who had overcome adversity of one kind or another with "the help of God and God's people."[1] One of those novels, *Light from Heaven*, has had an astonishingly long life in print. The novel debuted in 1947 as a serial in *The Youth's Christian Companion*, a weekly publication with a circulation of over 28,000, a few months before Herald Press published it in book form. Over 3000 copies of the book sold in the first six weeks, and Herald Press reprinted it four times between 1948 and 1966. Hardcover sales had reached almost 15,000 copies in 1965 when Moody Press began publishing it in paperback. Fifty years after its appearance in book form, it is still available in paperback.

The novel tells the story of Annie Armstrong, whose husband psychologically abused her and physically and psychologically abused their children, and of her oldest son Joseph, Annie's only confidant even in his childhood. It emphasizes her unceasing prayers for herself, her children and her husband as she tried to mitigate the negative effects of

---

*Phoebe Wiley is Director of the Writing Center and teaches critical reading, orientation and Women's Studies courses at Frostburg State University, Frostburg, Maryland.

1. Though Kauffman made this statement in 1966, long after the publication of *Light from Heaven*, she used the same criterion for all her novels. —Letter to a Rev. Bartlett, April 18, 1966, Christmas Carol Kauffman Collection, Hist. Mss 1-497, 1/8, Archives of the Mennonite Church, Goshen, IN.

his abuse. Throughout her marriage Annie never broke her silence, and she encouraged her three children to maintain silence as well.

As a young reader, I accepted Annie's silence without question, though I marveled at her endurance, the strength and comfort she derived from her spiritual life, her determination to remain a loving wife in spite of years of abuse, and the effect of her prayers on her children. When I reread the book during dissertation research, I discovered that the book is full of silence, not just Annie's, but Kauffman's as well. Although the novel tells the story of one woman who "chose" to remain silent in an abusive situation, the silence seems also to be a social commentary on Mennonite emphases of the time, including the permanence of marriage and the need for wives to be in submission, for when I researched responses to Kauffman's treatment of Annie, I discovered silence in the larger church as well.

The novel, set in the early part of the twentieth century, offers several possible reasons for Annie's silence. First, Annie's husband Bennet removed her physically from her parents' community in the East and took her to the Midwest, which prevented Annie's parents from learning anything about Bennet except what Annie chose to tell them. Second, Annie's pride, mixed with a fear of pity, kept her lips sealed. Very early in the novel Kauffman shows the reader how important saving face was for Annie. She wrote, "Little did [Annie's] friends and neighbors realize the aching void in her young heart. Annie would die before she'd tell anyone she had been disappointed."[2] Annie obviously wanted to avoid becoming an object of pity or gossip to her neighbors; and allowing them to assume her to be a happily married woman gave her at least a semblance of control over her life.

Through the years, as disappointment and grief gnawed at her vitals, Annie maintained her stoic silence, even when Bennet abused Joseph (and later the other children):

> Annie didn't care to [tell] that her little son had to work as hard as other boys twice his age. She didn't care to tell that he was a child who got many cruel whippings from his father until his eyes sparkled at anyone who treated him kindly. She didn't want to tell that she herself was so hungry for love that she alone lavished all her affection on him. Annie Armstrong wasn't a woman to tell such things to anyone, and so no one knew. . . . Why should she tell these things? (52).

Annie clearly preferred maintaining her pride to looking for a confidant, perhaps because even the most trustworthy friend could offer no solution, since divorce was out of the question; pastors of the time had

---

2. Christmas Carol Kauffman, *Light from Heaven* (Scottdale, PA: Herald Press, 1948), 7.

no training in counseling; and apparently no one writing in church publications had yet admitted that problems existed in Mennonite families. In addition, both published and unpublished writings of the time placed great emphasis on a wife's duty to submit, and they remained almost completely silent about the husband's responsibility to love his wife.

Thus, even if Annie's pride had permitted her to confide in friends about her situation, the societal climate around her might well have dissuaded her. As it was, Annie confided only in Joseph, even when the doctor discovered a heart condition that Annie believed would shortly take her life: "For over eleven years now I've been living with a broken heart. . . . My mother never knew before she died what I went through. None of my friends know all this unless they'll soon wonder why I always wear the same old dresses" (78).

Shame for the abuse she could not end mingled with Annie's pride and fear of pity. Years later, during Joseph's courtship of Delores, Annie wondered fearfully what would happen if Delores discovered the truth about the Armstrong family. When she learned that Dolores had already learned a bit from Joseph's Aunt Sara, she asked immediately what Sara knew, then wondered, "How can I ever face people again?" (354). She expressed great relief when Joseph promised to tell no one that his father forced him to move out for dating Delores (who could not expect a large inheritance): "Oh, I'm so glad if you won't tell. I hate this so" (353). As had been true many times through the years, Annie was ashamed of Bennet's unchristian behavior, but her pride outweighed any desire she may have had to expose him.

One final reason for Annie's stoic endurance may have been her belief in the church's teaching on submission. As a submissive wife, she "shook with anguish" when Bennet beat four-year-old Joseph despite her protestations that Joseph had not lied—"with every blow her own body suffered torture with his" (41)—but she made no physical effort to stop him, either then or during other beatings through the years. Nor did she defend herself when Bennet ordered her to stop peddling eggs and baked goods in town to earn money (her underwear was literally in shreds). Instead she told Joseph, "He thinks I've done wrong to make so many friends behind his back. *Maybe I should have asked him first*" (132).[3] Despite the fact that she still needed money, she obeyed Bennet's orders.

When Bennet wrapped cinders in straw and brown paper as his children's only Christmas present a number of years later, Annie told the children that what Bennet did was "awful," but added,

---

3. Emphasis added.

Let's never tell a single soul. Let's all love Father anyway, and let's try to figure out how we can do something real nice for him sometime. *That makes me much happier, for then I know God never takes his eyes off of us, even in the dark, when I keep such thoughts in my hear* (182).[4]

Clearly Annie believed she was doing the right thing by being a submissive wife, for, no matter what Bennet did, she remained silent and responded with love, kindness and respect—behavior she obviously believed won God's approval.

Only once did Annie openly rebel. When the Armstrongs moved west and the school teacher offered Joseph a Christmas gift, he asked for stamps, something Bennet had refused him. Bennet learned of the gift when cousin Freddie replied to Joseph's letter. When Bennet jumped up to strike Joseph, as he had done many times before, Annie stopped him:

Something she didn't realize she possessed rose up within her in defense of her boy who was now almost a man. In the past years Joseph had received too many punishings which had been laid upon him unjustly and sometimes even knavishly. If the child had been given a hearing in court they would have been pronounced unwarrantable. . . . How could [Bennet] stand there and accuse his son of not being a Christian when he displayed such a violation of the laws of Christian conduct himself? How could a lawbreaker rightfully punish another? Annie couldn't stand it. She stood up very straight and looked Bennet square in both eyes. She rebelled this time (162-63).

It seems odd that, after standing by helpless many times before, Annie openly rebelled in only this one instance, when Joseph was almost grown—unless she did so because she feared Joseph would strike back at his father. Though Annie had done what she could to lessen the abuse through the years—sometimes by not telling Bennet everything, as in the case of the stamps Joseph received from the teacher; sometimes by remonstrating; always by encouraging her children to try their best to be obedient and loving—she had never before defied him openly.

Annie never considered leaving Bennet, but when her health failed she attempted to protect the woman she assumed would be her successor after her death, telling Joseph that if Bennet fell in love with someone else, he should "[t]ell her just how your father has treated me and give her fair warning. I wouldn't want another woman to be fooled as I was. I feel it's my duty to give her this message" (79-80). Given the church's teaching on marriage and her acceptance of that teaching,

---

4. Emphasis added.

Annie could not end her own suffering, but she wanted no other woman to suffer as she had. Kauffman wrote:

> Were it not for the fact that [Annie] enjoyed her daily communion with God, the disappointments and griefs of life would have completely overwhelmed [her]. Her personal devotion to God, that moment-by-moment witness-bearing of Spirit with spirit which has sustained many a weary soul that otherwise would be daily terrified by the events of life, gave calmness to her. Annie Stokes Armstrong lived through her trials calmly, believingly, and in her soul God whispered daily His low sweet amen of peace. . . (395).

Kauffman apparently approved fully of Annie's behavior, as did Annie's children, though Annie's silent acceptance left her with literally no help except God's. When Delores told Joseph before their marriage what she had learned from his Aunt Sara, Joseph told her that his Aunt Sara knew very little: "Mother kept all her sorrows to herself. She confided in me only when she thought she was going to die. . . . *We've tried all our lives to shield Father*" (351).[5] The last statement is startling. The silence of Annie and the children would naturally shield Bennet, as well as prevent gossip about the family and save face for Annie. However, it seems a strange thing for the family to do–deliberately *encouraging* people's belief that Bennet's public appearance (regular church attendance, singing and even public prayer) matched his private behavior — unless Annie believed that by so doing she "reverenced" Bennet and thus followed God's will.

So strongly did Annie impress on her children the need for silence that they maintained it even after Bennet's death. After Bennet's funeral Lowell said, "I never could make myself tell Hilda [his wife] everything. What's the use?" Virginia echoed him, and Joseph said, "Delores, of course, knows how it went before we were married, and afterwards. But if Mother could keep her sorrows to herself, why shouldn't we?" (451). Obviously someone talked or Kauffman would have been unable to tell the story. But the spirit of silence was maintained, for Kauffman never revealed the identity of the real family, despite repeated requests.[6]

The novel gives plausible reasons for Annie's silence; a look at what was happening in the broader Mennonite community shows other possible reasons for the silence of both Annie and Kauffman. Daniel

---

5. Emphasis added.

6. Nothing in the correspondence indicates that anyone suggested a different solution for Annie. Instead, correspondents wanted to know the identity of the real Armstrong family. Some even insisted they knew them. C. F. Yake wrote a disclaimer in response to one family's request: "The family of William Jennings wishes to have it stated that Joseph Armstrong in *Light from Heaven* is not their father. Beyond this no further statement will be made by author, editor, or publisher." – Yake, "Rumors," *Gospel Herald*, May 4, 1948, 413.

Kauffman wrote in his 1898 *Manual of Bible Doctrines* that love should unite couples more closely than law. Although he admitted that in a loveless marriage "union by law becomes a galling yoke," he offered no help to someone like Annie, who had accepted Bennet at face value and found out only after her marriage that his appearance was a facade. Instead, Kauffman wrote about the sanctity of marriage, a "holy institution . . . designed to maintain the purity of the human family," and the evils of divorce.[7] He wrote that marriages should be permanent, no matter how unhappy, and added: "True, it would work a hardship on some people; but people ought to bear the burdens which they themselves have shouldered."[8] Daniel Kauffman's wide influence, and the voices of men who agreed with him, would affect Mennonite women and men for many decades.

Church papers carried further messages emphasizing women's submissive role both at home and in the church, and unpublished papers echoed them: a woman stepped "out of her proper place" if she attempted to "give counsel to men. . . . She shall meekly submit to the man in the Lord";[9] the woman who read the Bible and proposed to obey it was "bound to acknowledge the headship of her husband or father";[10] a woman's lot may be harder than man's "to show us and all mankind the exceeding sinfulness of sin, or how bad it was for the woman to eat of the forbidden fruit first and by her example and words lead men [sic] to eat also";[11] a woman's *"dignity consists in obeying her head, man"*;[12] "dominion over the woman is committed to the man because of Adam's prior creation" and because of "her responsibility in the fall."[13]

Year after year from 1914 to 1955[14] *Gospel Herald* articles on women's conduct outnumbered articles addressed to men, sometimes by as much as twelve to one (in 1940). The average number during that period was 4.5 articles addressed to women for every one addressed to men. Many of the articles emphasized submission. During that time period, only *one*

---

7. Daniel Kauffman, *Manual of Bible Doctrines* (Elkhart, IN: Mennonite Publishing Co., 1898), 181.

8. Ibid.

9. J. S. Shoemaker, "Query Department," *Herald of Truth*, Sept. 22, 1904, 308.

10. "Woman's Emancipation or Degradation–Which?" *Gospel Herald*, Nov. 11, 1920, 646.

11. Pius Hostetler, "Prayer Head Covering and Woman's Subjection," *Herald of Truth*, Aug. 15, 1902, 242.

12. Harold S. Bender, "An Exegesis of I Corinthians 11: 1-16," unpublished paper. Theological Seminary c. 1922, Mennonite Historical Library, Goshen, IN. Emphasis added.

13. Mahlon Hess, "The Devotional Head-Covering: An Exegetical Study of I Corinthians 11:2-16," bachelor's thesis, Eastern Mennonite School, 1941, 17, 24. Mennonite Historical Library, Goshen, IN.

14. In the years divisible by five, with the addition of 1914.

article stressed the need for husbands to love their wives as Christ loved the church. In 1930 J. S. Ressler wrote:

> That there is need of this admonition of Paul to husbands is evident, for it is repeated a number of times in different New Testament letters. That there is need of reminding husbands of their duty in this respect in our present time is very apparent to anyone who has lived a score or two of years in almost any community.[15]

Ressler's reminder to men was buried under an emphasis on submission, and it would take another three decades before church papers paid serious attention to problems in Mennonite families. In 1960 Orval Shoemaker wrote that Mennonites had put up a front of denying that Mennonite families had problems; he saw authoritarianism as a common problem and noted that much abuse could occur in homes where the husband viewed himself as the head or ruler of his family. He speculated that some people might avoid mentioning their problems because they knew of no one who could help, and that others, who assumed Christians should not have such problems, were ashamed to ask for help. Annie Armstrong likely fit both categories, for Mennonite women had no forum for such issues until the birth of the Peace Section Task Force on Women in Church and Society in 1973,[16] and it would be another fourteen years before an entire issue of *The Women's Concerns Report* was devoted to spousal abuse. Even in 1987, speaking out was difficult. One woman wrote: "The church only made me feel more inadequate because of its emphasis on family stability and church participation. My pride would not allow me to admit or speak of the problems in my home."[17]

Another woman, who did break her silence, wrote:

> When I was a member of the Mennonite church it did not have any sanctions against spouse abuse nor did I expect much support as a victim. People told me to pray for him; they told me not to do things to make him angry, that I should try harder to make the marriage work. I don't recall that anyone ever told my husband not to hit me.[18]

Annie died many years before this woman told her story, but it is likely Annie would have received the same advice that this anonymous woman did had she asked for help. The permanence of marriage was taken for granted, like the number of hours in a day, and Annie would likely have heard something to the effect of: "You made your bed. Now

---

15. J. A. Ressler, "Husbands, Love your Wives," *Gospel Herald*, Dec. 25, 1930, 822.

16. Now *Women's Concerns Report*.

17. "Raised on Forgiveness," *Women's Concerns Report* (Sept.-Oct. 1987), 7-8.

18. "Mennonite Roots," *Women's Concerns Report* (Sept.-Oct. 1987), 12-13.

lie in it." Kauffman wrote the story years after Annie's death, but she obviously approved of Annie's behavior, which she praised both in the book itself and in her preface.

When Kauffman wrote *Light from Heaven* in 1946, the doctrinal era of the Mennonite church, under the influence of Daniel Kauffman, had ended, but its influence certainly had not.[19] Mennonite wives and children in abusive situations were expected to endure. Divorce was out of the question, as Kauffman was well aware when she wrote *Light from Heaven*, and the preface gives no indication that she questioned the status quo in any way. She told readers:

> The tragic story of this boy and the tremendous influence his praying mother had on his life gripped my soul. Having two boys of my own, I was deeply touched. I immediately asked God to make it possible for this story to be published so that other young men and boys who have, or have the memory of, a mother's prayers will appreciate what a blessing is theirs (ix).

Kauffman may have been implying that boys who recognized their good fortune would not become abusers, but nowhere did she make an explicit statement. She dedicated the book "To every young boy and To every young man Who has or has had, A Praying Mother." She added: "To every Joseph—to every Annie—to every Lowell and Virginia, my heart goes out in true concern and sympathy. May this sad but true story somehow give you a little comfort and courage" (ix-x). Kauffman knew the importance of prayer, both from personal experience and from her work in a city mission some ten years before she wrote *Light from Heaven*, for she worked with children who had no stability at home. She noted that children often arrived an hour before services began in their eagerness to escape their "poor homes, and cursing drunken fathers, and come to a place where there is order and peace."[20]

Perhaps because of what she had seen during her work at the mission, Kauffman directly addressed other victims of abuse in her preface, but she made no appeal to the Bennets who might read the book, nor did she offer any course of action to the abused women and children in her audience. Given the climate in the Mennonite church at the time, it is perfectly logical that Kauffman offered no solutions to the victims, but it seems odd that she made no appeal to current or future Bennets, considering the preface in *Search to Belong*, a 1963 novel in which

---

19. See Leonard Gross, "The Doctrinal Era of the Mennonite Church," *MQR* 60 (Jan. 1986), 83-103.

20. Christmas Carol Kauffman, "Echoes from the Mission Hall," quoted in Alta Mae Erb, *Studies in Mennonite City Missions* (Scottdale, PA: Herald Press, 1937), 180.

Kauffman addressed five audiences. She wrote the novel in the hope that it would:

> 1. Encourage foster children to respect and honor their foster parents. 2. Encourage foster parents to understand, love, and respect the adopted child. 3. Assure children of unfortunate circumstances that they can overcome every obstacle. . . . 4. Remind workers in children's homes of the lasting impression they make on the children they work with. 5. Help the general reader understand the needs of the foster child.[21]

Does the difference in prefaces result from a difference in the author's maturity, or does the topic itself shape Kauffman's response? I suspect the latter. The permanence of marriage was simply assumed in the Mennonite church, and Kauffman did not question it. Having seen the effect of abuse on children when neither parent was a Christian, Kauffman was eager to tell the story of a praying mother and the positive effect on her children. The importance of prayer, then, was what she chose to emphasize.

Instead of directly addressing the Bennets, as she did the victims, Kauffman explained in the novel and in the preface *why* she described Bennet's behavior: "These things [descriptions of Bennet's cruelty] are anything but pleasant to relate, but in order that the characters of this story be understood, they are given."[22] In the preface she stated that it would have been "impossible" to "depict adequately the misery and soul struggles" Joseph suffered had she not shown something of Bennet's character.[23] Though Kauffman obviously exposed Bennet, that was not her purpose for describing his character. She told readers, "I was quite taken aback when someone asked if the motive for writing this story was to reveal hypocrites. That would be my last motive" (ix). Instead, Kauffman praised Annie's silent endurance — "What woman could have understood him as well, and been willing to endure what she did without complaining?"[24] — and emphasized Annie's behavior: "so characteristic of true Christian motherhood" (ix).

Like the author, the well-known Mennonite men who read the book prior to its publication in book form accepted Annie's silence without comment. Paul Erb, who became editor of *Gospel Herald* in 1944, was "delighted with the story," found Kauffman's characterization of Bennet and Joseph well done, and called it "religious without being preachy."[25]

---

21. Christmas Carol Kauffman, *Search to Belong* (Scottdale, PA: Herald Press, 1963), vii.

22. Kauffman, *Light from Heaven*, 96.

23. Ibid., ix.

24. Ibid., 93.

25. Christmas Carol Kauffman Collection, Hist. Mss 1-497, 1/8, Archives of the

The several questions he raised had to do with factual accuracy about minor details (the spelling of the doctor's name, for example). In a letter to Kauffman during the serialization of the book, C. F. Yake passed on "a word of appreciation from someone who covered the church quite extensively. He reports unusual interest in . . . 'Light from Heaven,' and assures us of the deep appreciation of our readers for it."[26] In another letter to Kauffman, Yake expressed pleasure that readers appreciated the "splendid story now running. . . . Everywhere there is a tremendous amount of interest in this story, and we feel certain that it is doing a great amount of good to a large number of readers."[27] A letter from Kauffman to Yake during the serialization had almost the same words: "I trust that the story will continue to carry its message and life's lesson I intended it to do. It no doubt has similarities to many persons [sic] experiences."[28] J. C. Wenger found "the misery of the hero Joseph . . . rather intense and sustained, if not practically unrelieved" (he said nothing about Annie's misery). He also found the ending of the book weak, noting that "Sister Kauffman should add one more chapter and let Joseph blossom out as a faithful and effective minister,"[29] advise which Kauffman took to heart. On the whole, though, Wenger found it "*a very effective story,*" which he found "most gripping".[30]

In the introduction to the novel Yake stated that Kauffman's "characters portray devoted spiritual living on the one hand and extremely selfish and self-righteous living on the other." He pointed out the "conspicuous contrast" between the two, said Kauffman's novel teaches "forcibly great and noble lessons from life," and added: "The lessons in life to be learned will prove valuable helps in Christian living."[31] Yake did not include specifics on the lessons, but if one accepts Annie and Joseph as the role models Kauffman intended, presumably abused wives were to pray and endure, honor their husbands, and teach their children to do the same. Perhaps one can also assume that the Bennets should reform, but Yake did not make that clear.

Kauffman knew abuse occurred in other Christian families, for she wrote in her preface: "It is surprising the number of letters of confidence which have come to my desk since this story started as a serial . . . telling of other Bennet Armstrongs still living."[32] Yake, too, knew of abuse, for

Mennonite Church, Goshen, IN.—Letters to Kauffman, March 9 and May 26, 1946.

26. Ibid., letter dated Nov. 26, 1947.

27. Ibid., letter dated Jan. 29, 1948.

28. Ibid., letter dated April 23, 1948.

29. Ibid., letter to Paul Erb, Feb.17, 1948.

30. Ibid., Emphasis added in the original.

31. Kauffman, *Light from Heaven*, xi.

32. Ibid., ix.

in response to requests for the identity of the real Bennet and Joseph Armstrong, he wrote to readers of *Gospel Herald*: "Our readers should remember that obviously there are quite a number of Bennet Armstrongs living today, and that the important thing about the story is to benefit by the lessons which it teaches,"[33] not, he implied, to be concerned with the identity of the novel's villain and hero. Again, though Yake may have wished the Bennets of the church would take Kauffman's message to heart, he did not address them directly nor specify what lessons should be learned. Only one author did so. In a 1948 *Gospel Herald* editorial devoted to the question, "Does Bennet Still Live?" the author (presumably Paul Erb) wrote:

> It is disconcerting and humiliating, to say the least, to discover that there are among us many Bennets, gripping, tyrannical, selfish husbands and fathers who make the lives of wife and children a fearful misery. One girl writes that her father beats his children cruelly and has called them and their mother every conceivable evil name, and yet insists that his sins are all under the blood. . . .[34]

The author noted that other "devoted, patient wives . . . must endure the agony that Mrs. Armstrong knew."[35] It was for these "Bennets," he wrote, that the Apostle Paul wrote the command for husbands to love their wives and "provoke not [their] children to anger." He ended the editorial with the hope that God would "use Sister Kauffman's narrative to comfort the sad heart of many an Annie, to encourage many a crushed Joseph, and *to awaken and reform many a sinning Bennet. May Bennetism be not once more named among us.*"[36]

The editorial goes a step beyond the preface and introduction in its hope that "many a sinning Bennet" may be reformed, but the unspoken emphasis on submission remains, for this author, too, could hope only for "comfort" for such wives and encouragement for the "crushed" Josephs. Perhaps writers like this editorialist would have spoken to a Bennet if they had known him, perhaps not. Certainly no one spoke to Annie's husband, though at least one pastor saw past his facade, as Joseph learned much later:

> "I wasn't altogether blind when you lived here."
> "You saw?"
> Brother Collins laughed very, very softly. It was a sympathetic, understanding laugh, however.

---

33. C. F. Yake, "Rumors," *Gospel Herald*, May 4, 1948, 413.
34. Editorial, *Gospel Herald*, April 6, 1948, 315.
35. Ibid.
36. Ibid., Emphasis added.

"I never told," Joseph said. "Mama never told. How could you tell?"

"Reading character comes by experience, I guess," Brother Collins said (435-36).

Given the church's emphasis on submission during Annie's lifetime and beyond, Brother Collins' silence is understandable, if not admirable. So is Kauffman's, and certainly Annie's. However, I find it telling that during the height of the novel's popularity, only one person, the *Gospel Herald* editorialist, directly addressed the men like Bennet who made the lives of their wives and children so miserable.

Twenty-two years later, in 1970, Norman Shenk wrote that "an over emphasis upon 'wives submit' without a consistent positive unselfish emphasis on 'husbands love' may be partially responsible for church problems."[37] I believe that the heavy emphasis on submission for wives and the near silence on husbands loving their wives, along with the emphasis on the permanency of marriage, made for many, many "Annies" in the Mennonite church. These Annies were silenced by the silence surrounding abuse, by their pride, by their fear of pity, and by their sense of guilt or failure. Such Annies likely contributed to the popularity and long life of *Light from Heaven* because they did, as Kauffman hoped, derive comfort and courage from Annie Armstrong's story. Annie Armstrong's story was not unique, nor was her solution — her silent endurance. *Light from Heaven,* read in the light of Mennonite writing contemporary with it, provides a window into the troubling social and religious mores of the time.

---

37. Norman G. Shenk, "Women's Liberation," *Gospel Herald*, Dec. 8, 1970, 1010-11.

GRAVEN IMAGES AND THE (RE)PRESENTATION
OF AMISH TRAUMA

DANIEL W. LEHMAN*

Abstract: Two recent narratives about crime and trauma in Amish communities provide the occasion to think about what authors and readers mean when they create and consume texts variously as fact or fiction. When writers depict events that also have form outside the text, readers inevitably measure that text — whether classified as fiction or nonfiction — against what they know of the same lives and events in history. In this way of reading, truth — while perhaps never quite certain — always matters. Concentrating on several texts that particularly concern Anabaptist communities, and grounding the discussion in religious convictions (for example, the prohibition of oaths and/or photographs) that have affected our thinking about truth and representation, can show how the notion of "implication" can provoke careful attention to the ethical and interactive dimensions of writing and reading historically based narrative.

Some of the Amish community were very upset; they did not understand that the writing of a novel is not to be exactly what happened in the event. The book is not to be really true, but is to be as the author sees it. It is not untrue; it is a novel.

> —Correspondence from a Mennonite neighbor of the Amish of Kishacoquillas (Big) Valley in Pennsylvania after the publication of Ted Wojtasik's historical novel *No Strange Fire* (Herald Press, 1996).

ABC News didn't seem to be interested in the truth. We had arranged for them to interview an Amish bishop and several brothers, but when the news crews arrived, the ABC news producer didn't bring any note pads, didn't take any notes. It was like they had already decided the story they were going to present and weren't going to be bothered by the truth.

> —Comments from an Ohio State University rural sociologist who specializes in Amish life after the February 1997 airing of an ABC-News "20/20" segment on child abuse in Amish communities.

Two recent narratives about crime and trauma in Amish communities provide the occasion to think about what authors and readers mean when they create and consume texts variously as fact or fiction. Some

---

* Daniel W. Lehman is Professor of English at Ashland University, Ashland, Ohio.

readers might describe each of the two reactions presented in the head quotes of this paper as "naïve." For example, a traditional critic who adopts Aristotle's generic boundaries for texts ("the historian narrates events that have actually happened, whereas the poet writes about things as they might possibly occur"[1]) would dismiss the reaction by at least several members of Big Valley's Amish community. To that critic, the fictional narrative presents an imaginative world contained within the covers of a book and therefore is not to be judged by the facts of external life. On the other hand, a contemporary critic might dismiss the critique of the truth value of ABC's nonfictional "20/20" narrative as hopelessly nostalgic: as trying to reassert some standard of original truth and uncontaminated text in a poststructuralist age where facts cannot be experienced except through competing narratives. As Lydia Neufeld Harder wrote in a recent essay in *Mennonite Quarterly Review*, "every description of reality is finally hermeneutical and rhetorical. The notion of complete objectivity is becoming more and more suspect. We have begun to doubt that the self is capable of apprehending reality in a direct, unmediated way."[2]

This essay offers yet another way of looking at this problem: when writers depict events that also have form outside the text, readers inevitably measure that text — whether classified as fiction or nonfiction — against what they know of the same lives and events in history. In this way of reading, truth — while perhaps never quite certain — always matters. This tension between text and outside experience creates readers and writers who are "implicated" — an adjective that means deeply involved in or even incriminated by history and narrative and that complicates more tidy notions of "implied" readers and authors. In this approach, neither of the foregoing reactions to the two narratives about trauma in the Amish community would be inappropriate as a starting point for critical discussion. By concentrating on several texts that particularly concern Anabaptist communities and by grounding the discussion in religious convictions (for example, the prohibition of oaths and/or photographs) that have affected our thinking about truth and representation, I hope to show that this notion of implication can provoke careful attention to the ethical and interactive dimensions of writing and reading historically based narrative.

---

1. Aristotle, "Poetics," in *The Critical Tradition*, ed. David H. Richter (New York: St. Martin's, 1989), 48.

2. Lydia Neufeld Harder, "Postmodern Suspicion and Imagination: Therapy for Mennonite Hermeneutic Communities." *MQR* 71 (April, 1997), 270.

No Strange Fire and the Ethics of Representation

No Strange Fire is a novel based on actual events—the burning of six Amish barns in the Big Valley area of Pennsylvania in March 1992. Although Ted Wojtasik tells his readers that his novel is "a work of imagination, though loosely based on an historical event,"[3] the Amish are right to understand that many readers of this sensitive and intriguing book will be swayed by its depiction of their valley and their trauma and that they thus have a stake in their own representation. First, their theology and practice does not admit differing senses of truth. The prohibition of oath-taking outlined, for example, in *The Truth in Word and Work: A Statement of Faith by Ministers and Brethren of Amish Churches in Holmes County, Ohio, and Related Areas* makes truth unequivocal: "Because Christians already have a high regard for the truth, they do not accept the worldly system which has a time of being 'especially truthful.'"[4] Second, the world's desire to consume the exotic culture of the Amish through pictorial and narrative representation raises issues for the Amish of what they consider sinful pride and idolatry. Meanwhile, the Anabaptist friends and neighbors of the Amish find themselves in the often contradictory posture of seeking to guard the privacy of the Amish while, perhaps unwittingly, helping to erode that privacy by seeking to interpret the lives of the Amish for the larger community. While non-Anabaptists who do not understand Amish belief might see these traumatic events affecting only particular individuals, Amish and Mennonites tend to see them as community traumas that raise fundamental questions about the way believers present themselves to those outside their communities.

Indeed, Mennonite historian John E. Sharp, quoted by Herald Press on the book's back cover, joins these issues by claiming both the novel's superior version of truth and its superior access to the inner life of the Amish: "The media flashed images of highly traditional Big Valley Amish around the world," Sharp says of the sorts of 20/20-style narratives we will explore later, "yet no one has been able to cross their porches and open their doors like novelist Ted Wojtasik has done. His pen probes the heart and soul of Amish families who suffer losses of barns, animals, family, and *privacy*."[5] Sharp's assertion, while a laudable tribute to this laudable book, reveals an interesting inner contradiction: Wojtasik probes the hearts and souls of his subjects, crosses their porches and opens their doors, all to tell the world the story of their loss of

---

3. Ted Wojtasik, *No Strange Fire* (Scottdale, PA: Mennonite Publishing House, 1996), 399.

4. Paton Yoder, "The Amish View of the State," in *The Amish and the State*, ed. Donald B. Kraybill (Baltimore: Johns Hopkins U. Press, 1993), 51.

5. Wojtasik, *No Strange Fire*, back cover. Emphasis added.

privacy? My intention here is not to collapse Wojtasik's project with that of ABC News nor to claim in some clever deconstruction that both texts are equally exploitative and fallacious. Instead, I want to demonstrate how a text that represents previously existing events—in a way much less typical of a fictional text not closely linked to historical characters—always implicates its writers and producers, and how it forces them to own up to the manner by which they gain access to the thoughts, the conversations and the lives of their subjects.

Wojtasik and his publishers are careful to lay that foundation, relating how the author lived and worked among the Amish, how he "woke at dawn to milk cows, knelt with families for morning prayers, ate in Amish kitchens, pitched hay, rode in buggies, loaded milk cans, . . . watched Amish women bake, roamed through fields of grain."[6] Even given some hyperbole in this description, a reader of *No Strange Fire* cannot fail to recognize its author's commitment to erasing many of the boundaries between himself and his subjects in preparation for his task so that he could understand their ways of structuring reality as well as the stories that provide meaning to their lives. There seems to be a mutuality at work here, a give and take in which both Wojtasik and the Nebraska Amish of Big Valley are able to see something of themselves through the eyes of the other.

As Julia Kasdorf suggested in her analysis of the work of Russian theorist M. M. Bakhtin, "An other, looking with concentrated attention, can 'consummate' you—make you whole—know you as you cannot know yourself through knowledge gained from that person's distanced perspective."[7] But the flip side of that equation is that the other then gains power over your identity through representation, over some part of your "you," in the manner that I have described as implication. Some members of the Amish community can resist being made victims in the transaction merely by refusing to concern themselves with the way they are depicted. But others—both in the Big Valley and in the Holmes County cases I am discussing—do recognize that the depiction of their lives for mere consumption can threaten their identities.

The Amish readers who object to *No Strange Fire*'s genre-bending fictivity may be responding as much to that power as they are to its factual rearrangement. The well known objection by the Amish to photographic representation normally is explained as "a way of suppressing pride."[8] But that explanation, while important, scarcely

---

6. Ibid., 400.

7. Julia Kasdorf, "Bakhtin, Boundaries and Bodies," *MQR* 71 (April, 1997), 175.

8. Donald B. Kraybill, *The Riddle of Amish Culture* (Baltimore: Johns Hopkins U. Press, 1989), 34.

answers the force of the Second Commandment that underlies the prohibition: "Thou shalt not make unto thee any graven image, or any likeness of any thing that is in heaven above, or that is in the earth beneath, or that is in the water under the earth. Thou shalt not bow down thyself to them, nor serve them; for I the Lord thy God am a jealous God . . ." (Ex. 20: 4-5). The commandment sets up representation as a contest between a God who is jealous of divine creative power and subjects who are tempted not only to replicate that creation but to celebrate their power to mimic God.

FACTUAL REPRESENTATION AS CONTEST

In terms of the implicated text, the contest is between a creator and a created—a struggle to define the terms of meaning and the manner by which human subjects are presented to the world. "[O]nce I feel myself observed by the lens, everything changes," says Roland Barthes of photography in terms we can explicitly apply to subjects who know they will be or have been captured by historical narrative.

> I constitute myself in the process of 'posing,' I instantaneously make another body for myself, I transform myself in advance into an image. This transformation is an active one: I feel that the photograph creates my body or mortifies it according to its caprice.[9]

The recognition that a photograph might cause one to transform oneself into an image is what raises the issue of graven images or idolatry.

And photographer John Berger goes a step further, establishing the relationship between the instantaneous photograph and the narratives that grow up around it to contain it and to give it meaning. These narratives provide the stage of the representation that undermines identity. "All photographs are ambiguous," Berger says. "All photographs have been taken out of a continuity. If the event is a public event, this continuity is history; if it is personal, the continuity, which has been broken, is a life story."[10] Elsewhere, Berger contends that this ambiguity normally is masked by the insertion of photographs into other texts, particularly by the words chosen for captions or for accompanying descriptions, "which explain, less or more truthfully, the pictured events."[11]

A reporter's notes, a historian's decision to create a particular scene out of the many facts available to her, a historical novelist's decision to read minds or to be omnipresent or to manipulate point of view, even a

---

9. Roland Barthes, *Camera Lucida* (New York: Noonday, 1981), 10-11.

10. John Berger, "Appearances," in *Another Way of Telling*, eds. John Berger and Jean Mohr (New York: Pantheon, 1982), 91.

11. Ibid., 128.

network's decision to inject a scene of wailing children into a highly scripted news magazine show — these are the writer's efforts to assert factual authority and to deny the ambiguity inherent when facts are wrestled from continuity.

But to grant this sort of ambiguity is never to say, as do some contemporary critics, that all fact-based narratives are equally unstable and that the events underlying representation are, by consequence, essentially meaningless. An example of such a reader would be Phyllis Frus, whose otherwise helpful *The Politics and Poetics of Journalistic Narrative* asserts that "arguing over which parts a writer 'got right' in terms of accuracy is a hopeless exercise because we have no primary or original text to compare later versions to."[12] I certainly will grant Frus's desire not to return to some sort of safe empirical realm wherein the genre police upon finding error or an imaginative author would consign a narrative to "fiction" and declare it irrelevant to history. But I will not grant her accompanying conclusion that arguing about accuracy is a hopeless exercise.

FACTUAL AUTHORITY IN THE CASE OF ABC'S "20/20"

Matters of accuracy, though slippery and seldom proven, are anything but irrelevant, as I hope to show by discussing the "20/20" report about child abuse in the Holmes and Wayne county Amish community. In this discussion, I reflect the position taken by Jane Tompkins in her effort to engage competing nonfiction accounts of Native American captivity. Tompkins wonders if it matters if the smell of singed flesh in a nonfiction narrative is merely representational or if it takes place in history. Pain becomes an ethical consideration, Tompkins concludes, asserting that

> arguments about 'what happened' have to proceed much as they did before post-structuralism broke in with all its talk about language-based reality and culturally produced knowledge. Reasons must be given, evidence adduced, authorities cited, analogies drawn. . . . If the accounts don't fit together neatly, that is not a reason for rejecting them all.[13]

Media scholar John J. Pauly suggests a standard of research that merges close textual as well as close social analysis in processing nonfictional claims. He recommends that the text be studied for the

12. Phyllis Frus, *The Politics and Poetics of Journalistic Narrative* (Cambridge: Cambridge U. Press, 1994), 229.

13. Jane Tompkins, "'Indians': Textuality, Morality, and the Problem of History," in *"Race," Writing and Difference,* ed. Henry Louis Gates, Jr. (Chicago: U. of Chicago Press, 1985), 76.

circumstances of its writing and its publication or broadcast, as well as for the way the "reporting process implicates writer, subjects, and readers in relationships beyond a text."[14] Applying that standard to the ABC News "20/20" report on alleged abuse among the Amish of Ohio's Holmes County both refutes the assertions of some contemporary critics that it is futile to check facts outside the text and also shows how subjects construed by nonfictional representation interact with actual subjects outside the boundaries of texts.

Aired first on Feb. 21, 1997 and rebroadcast on July 27, the report, "The Secret Life of the Amish," centered on dramatic footage of a Holmes County sheriff's deputy helping ex-Swartzentruber Amish deacon Paul Edwards regain custody of his two younger children, Emery, 5, and Anna, 4 from his estranged wife, who is still a member of the Swartzentruber community. During the scene in which the children were taken from their mother—a scene that anchor Hugh Downs touted before and after a commercial break as "a dramatic showdown between two worlds" and "a heartbreaking confrontation between a husband who broke the rules and the wife he left behind"[15]—ABC camera operators circled the buggy as the children wailed and their mother pleaded for her children.

The footage was folded into a report during which reporter Deborah Roberts asserted that "20/20 found case after case of former Amish who described childhoods filled with everyday physical punishment." As proof, Roberts offered two unidentified Amish women who said they had been sexually abused by relatives and three other former Amish members—Ruth Bontrager, a 16-year-old Amish runaway from Wisconsin; David Yoder, an Ohio truck driver who left the church; and an unidentified "former Amish woman" from an unspecified location— who alleged that they had been whipped or physically abused. Roberts interviewed Holmes County psychologist Elvin Coblentz, who said he was concerned that Amish people tend to "brush it [sexual abuse] under the carpet," and Holmes county law enforcement officials, who said they were "unaware of abuses within the Amish groups in their area." Roberts said Amish church leaders declined on-camera interviews "since their religion frowns on photographs," but she said they "do not condone beatings, and they have no knowledge of sexual abuse within their groups."[16]

---

14. John J. Pauly, "The Politics of New Journalism," in *Literary Journalism in the Twentieth Century*, ed. Norman Sims (Oxford: Oxford U. Press, 1990), 112.

15. "The Secret Life of the Amish" from "20/20," prod. Ene Riisna (ABC News, Feb. 21, 1997 and July 27, 1997).

16. Ibid.

Despite the seriousness of the charges, the various allegations and denials contained within the report paled as drama beside the harrowing footage of the two Edwards youngsters taken from their mother, footage which "20/20" placed at the center of the report that aired during the February sweeps month in which the ratings of local television stations are measured.

A close look at ABC's reporting methodology reveals that the network was less than candid about the seriousness of its efforts to balance the story as well as the way in which it gained access to Edwards' story. For example, although Roberts admitted that, on one of Edwards' searches for his children, "we agreed to help with his expenses and followed him on the road,"[17] the network did not say how much it paid Edwards or for what duration they were in his company. In a recent conversation, George M. Kreps, an associate professor of sociology at Ohio State University's Agricultural Technical Institute in Wooster, Ohio, said he believed the reporting essentially began and ended with Edwards and that "20/20" was determined to air the show once it had the dramatic footage of the children taken from the buggy.[18]

Kreps said he arranged for an interview between "20/20" associate producer Frank Mastropolo and the Amish bishop and elders who preside over the Holmes and Wayne county communities around which the allegations centered. Held on December 15, 1996, about two months before the report aired, the interview consisted of a two-and-a-half hour question and answer session, Kreps said. "ABC asked a lot of questions such as, 'Isn't it true there is abuse' or 'Isn't it true that the bishops try to cover this up?'" the Ohio State sociologist recalled. He said the bishop and other Amish elders told Mastropolo that they first try to resolve disputes within the community but would go to authorities if they believed that crimes had been committed.

"I should have known right then that ABC was not serious about these interviews," Kreps said, adding that not only did the producers not bring notepads, but "in fact, they borrowed what paper they used from us after they got there." The sociologist said his last pre-show contact with ABC was two days before airing when Mastropolo called and asked him, "Isn't it true that more and more Amish are leaving?" to which Kreps responded that while overall numbers in the Amish community are growing, the rate of those leaving has remained constant at 15% since his department first began to measure Amish population in 1965. That interchange apparently was partly the source of ABC's unattributed conclusion that —"abuse is a problem that's driving a growing *number* of

---

17. Ibid.
18. George M. Kreps, telephone interview, Oct. 6, 1997.

members away"[19]—despite no evidence of increase in the *percentage* of those leaving. Kreps concludes,

> We are fairly sure that they had filmed 99% of the report by October 15, including all the footage where the children were taken from the buggy. The corn is green in all the footage and it would not have been green when they came to us for our help in contacting the Amish community. They had the report they wanted to do before they ever talked to us.[20]

Indeed, ABC's decision to circle their cameras around the wailing children and to center their report on these dramatic photos illustrates the way that media representation builds capital by satisfying viewers' desire for forbidden or spectacular images. Much of the drama of the scene builds from the viewers' guilty desire to eavesdrop on the mother's actual reaction to having her children taken from her. From the relative safety of their living rooms, viewers can tap into "reality" shows where they can see conflict, bodies in pain or pleasure, or even actual death without risking their own safety. ABC's decision to air this footage at the heart of its "20/20" magazine show, to tout the footage going into and emerging from commercial break, to air the show during sweeps month when local ratings are measured, and to rebroadcast it five months later all demonstrate the way that the powerful scene produces profits. Even the various attempts to "balance" the show by featuring such experts as Donald Kraybill, Wilmer Otto or Maynard Knepp on the late news in various localities afforded ABC a way to entice viewers to stick with their stations until they could be counted for the sweeps that set advertising rates for profitable local news shows.

Despite all this network news gathering, *Wooster Daily Record* reporter Eric Johnson, in a comprehensive article published February 20, 1997, reported that ABC News had not contacted the children services administrator for the Holmes County Department of Human Services nor the executive director of the Wayne County Children Services Board in preparing their report on child abuse. Psychologist Elvin Coblentz, who had been depicted in the report sharing his concern about sexual abuse, showed the *Daily Record* a copy of a letter he sent to the "20/20" producers, which said in part, "Please stop this story of falsehoods about the Amish!"[21] And Wayne Weaver, an emergency room doctor at a Millersburg hospital who was raised in the Amish community, said that none of his hour-long interview with a "20/20" producer was used for

---

19. Riisna, "Secret Life of the Amish."

20. Kreps, telephone interview.

21. Eric Johnson, "Tone of '20/20' report on Amish disturbing," Wooster *Daily Record*, Feb. 20, 1997, 1.

the show, despite his detailed explanation of how shunning actually works and his expertise on the incidences (or lack of incidences) of abuse in the Amish community. Saying he believed his interview was not aired because his conclusions contradicted ABC's opinions, Weaver concluded, "They can do everything they want to do, create any impression they want to, just by exclusion."[22]

REDEEMING NARRATIVE RESPONSIBILITY

These competing stories about ABC News malfeasance, naturally, are also narratives to which listeners or readers might also attribute more or less credibility. This exchange of narrative indeterminacy is enough to make some critics abandon attempts to classify narrative as either factual or fictional. For example, in her recent study of historical fiction, *The Character of Truth*, Naomi Jacobs asserts:

> Facts not only can be manipulated but are inherently futile and false; any testimony about the past is a lie because nothing anyone can remember about the past is equal to the totality of the past. Even honest attempts to tell the truth will fail, because all knowledge is incomplete, all perceptions slanted. And even if we could know "what really happened," we would only know events that were shaped by specific perceptions, sometimes irrational, sometimes subconscious, of History itself.[23]

While such assertions are intended to subvert the putative equation of historical text with truth and fictional text with falsity, they set up other sorts of absolutes that seem equally ill-advised. New binary oppositions pit unequivocal truth against unequivocal falsity, assuming the latter because the former is impossible. Yet I would contend that not all manipulated facts are equally false; not all testimony about the past is equally futile; not all honest attempts to tell the truth are identically failed. Some knowledge is more incomplete than other knowledge; some perceptions are more slanted than others.

Ted Wojtasik's decision to live among the Nebraska Amish of the Big Valley and to attempt to understand the lives of the people before depicting them in narrative stands in relatively sharp contrast to ABC News' hurriedly staged interviews where, by most accounts, little give and take actually occurred. And while both the novel and the television show used occasions of suffering to market the story of the Amish to

22. Christine L. Pratt, "Holmes residents voice opinions of '20/20' broadcast," Wooster *Daily Record*, Feb. 25, 1997, 1.

23. Naomi Jacobs, *The Character of Truth: Historical Figures in Contemporary Fiction* (Carbondale: Southern Illinois University Press, 1990), 179-80.

outside consumers, it is clear that ABC News exploited the photographic representation of suffering much more directly. Ultimately, it is easy to see that the conventional distinctions between fiction and nonfiction matter rather less than the relationships between producer/author, subject and viewer/reader and the amount of exploitation that these relationships exhibit.

Certainly, there is no "objective" stance outside history and culture from which we can sort these confusing claims with certainty. My readings will be flawed and culturally produced, as will be others. But paying specific attention to specific types of assertions and narrative power relationships can teach us about the way truth matters as well as the differing responses that authors, subjects and readers might have to those texts. Given the evidence that many journalists and viewers or readers are eager to consume a simplistic version of Amish culture, it is important for exploitative representation to be resisted by careful attention to the manner by which such representations intersect actual lives and cause pain. From this perspective we can begin to build an ethics of reading, writing and representation more in keeping with our commitment to truth and community.

A LONG DRY SAFARI

CARROLL D. YODER[*]

Abstract: As we follow a reluctant Thomas Martin during a hunting trip in the opening scene of *A Long Dry Season* by Omar Eby, we are introduced to the unifying archetype of the novel, an African safari. Long associated with wealthy expatriates, geographical beauty, danger and uncertainty, the safari functions as an ambivalent symbol, revealing both exterior and interior impediments that would sabotage the protagonist's desperate attempt to remain true to his mission in a postcolonial era. Five safaris in Part I explore complicity with a colonialist past, love of the land, failures of the institutional church, personal annihilation, and the death of youthful idealism. They culminate in a "safari" to Mombasa when Martin, a veteran Anglican missionary, seeks out his estranged wife. He has finally realized that it is God's grace mediated through a woman, not the accomplishment of his mission, which brings safety and true salvation.

By the time Omar Eby's novel *A Long Dry Season* appeared in 1988, I found myself apologizing for my dusty old dissertation that was eventually resurrected and published as *White Shadows: A Dialectical View of the French African Novel* (1991). I had used "Black Orpheus," an essay by Jean-Paul Sartre, to sample more than one hundred years of French African literature. Sartre's dialectical explanation of white supremacy made it too easy to place novels written by expatriates and Africans into three categories: thesis, antithesis and synthesis. I had agreed with Albert Memmi that "no European within the colonial situation can escape his role of usurper. In order to accept himself, he must either leave the colonies or else in some way legitimize his privileges."[1] Following the logic of my own predictable analysis, Eby's novel deserved purgatory if not outer darkness because of the missionary hero's fervent pursuit of his mission in a postcolonial era.

Indeed, the dramatic tension that sustains the narrative in *A Long Dry Season* grows out of Thomas Martin's desperate defense of his mission. Are the best efforts of this well meaning expatriate destined to fail? Do power and privilege as well as Thomas' resentment of his wife corrupt

*Carroll D. Yoder is Professor of French at Eastern Mennonite University, Harrisonburg, Virginia.

1. Carroll D. Yoder, *White Shadows: A Dialectical View of the French African Novel* (Washington: Three Continents Press, 1991), 99.

the fruit of his superhuman endeavors? To answer those questions the discerning reader would do well to examine closely five different "safaris" found in Part I of the novel: a hunting trip, a solitary detour through a game park, a Sunday excursion, a funeral and a trip to a mountain. These various safaris function as the central, ambivalent symbol of Eby's work, provide insight into Thomas' character and serve as harbingers of the final, most important safari at the end of the novel.

The hunting trip in the opening pages of the novel reminds us of Africa's rendezvous with the West. We find artificial, foreign elements normally associated with the safari: an African guide treated with condescension, an illegal kill, violence and deceit. Little wonder that Thomas tries to put distance between himself and Peters, the young agronomist who kills a water buck and lies about it. Far too sensitive and perceptive to identify willingly with colonialism, Thomas rejects both colonialism and neocolonialism with its promise of technological progress. Eby makes that point most graphically through the use of symbols: a broken clock, a cistern "broken and without water" and an orange "bitter with wildness."[2]

"So. . . ." With that first word Eby catches our attention: "So in the morning before daylight they drove away from the church-farm and headed for the high country" (11). The "thus" or "therefore" meaning of "so" suggests that we are missing information about the drive into the high country; things are not as simple as they would appear on the surface. A flashback reveals tension between the main character Thomas Martin and his wife Maxine. In spite of his distaste for hunting and his wife's frank disapproval, Thomas has reluctantly accepted a safari invitation—"caught between being rude to the men and taking a day out of their long weekend together with his family" (12). Another "so" brings us back to the excursion: "So in the early Saturday morning, just after sunrise, they came out into the high country and drove quietly across the tractless grass" (14). If Thomas accompanies the party into the high country, it is because of his passivity and his natural tendency to please others.

Or, on second thought, can one explain his behavior so easily? Although Thomas prefers binoculars to guns, he also loves the land. More than passivity accounts for his journey into high country where he studies "the distant light and shadows for movement" (15) and shares a water flask with the doctor. The opening safari exposes the legacy of colonialism, and it also shows that Thomas cannot escape a certain

---

2. Omar Eby, *A Long Dry Season* (Intercourse, PA : Good Books, 1988), 73.

complicity with the past. Daily he must reckon with the consequences of the Western adventure in Africa.

The first safari introduces us to several unsavory characters—Peters, Ogot and his Peace Corps girlfriend. In their personal relationships they symbolize the hypocrisy of neocolonialism, showing no respect for themselves or others. Peters punishes his houseboy for stealing and treats Ogot with contempt, but has no qualms about the illegal shooting of a water buffalo. Ogot betrays the faith and traditions of his people by trying to arrange an abortion for his girlfriend. The moral laxity, insensitivity and slovenly appearance of his fellow Americans arouse a fierce anger within Thomas. He is no less upset by Ogot because the latter's behavior reflects upon his father Mzee Jeremiah, a close friend and collaborator with Thomas in the work of the church. The proposed abortion reminds him of his own desire for a son, of the awful curse that childlessness represents for the African people. As second generation expatriates and an African Christian, the three implicitly threaten the future of Thomas' own mission.

Later Thomas allows his anger to express itself with surprising ferocity in an airline office when he meets Peters, Esta and Ogot and realizes that the barren woman who attracts him now serves as a mistress to the two men. He vomits out a "poisonous truth," accusing Peters of being a "cancer on the face of Christ's ministry" (174). The fragility of his own moral equilibrium accounts for the intensity of his hatred and explains the ambivalence found in the term "poisonous truth."

Many of the first Europeans in Africa showed little respect for the people they encountered but drew inspiration from the magnificent land of a wild and beautiful continent. While Thomas rejects the injustice of colonialism and identifies closely with the African peasants, he finds himself in love with the land—a love that he is reluctant to admit to himself but is revealed in a second "safari."

A flashback sketches a slow drive through a game reserve and shows how he indulges in his own solitary safari—a rite that he must practice in secret (21). The journey provides him with esthetic pleasure, for the giraffe cows recall "painted nursery room toys" (20) and the silence produces a kind of paradox—evoking his earthiness (his kinship to the mute animals) while confirming his immortality. The detour through the game reserve contrasts with his urgent sense of mission—a dogged devotion to his people, made all the more persistent by the mistakes of the past. "He was at peace here, yet strangely full of guilt" (21). Thomas judges himself harshly, feels conflict between his silent pleasure, savored alone, and his mission; he mourns Maxine's inability to enjoy African landscapes. Devoted as he is to his mission, the side excursion through the park has both refreshed and troubled his soul. The game park interlude contrasts with the ugliness of the urban night that follows, a "small levy against the day's indulgence in solitude and silence" (22).

The following morning he encounters two American tourists Jason and Arlene, stranded by the side of the road while on their own safari. Thomas despises their artificiality (manicured toes, polished boots, canned peaches, lemon-scented paper washcloth, porcelain cups). And yet those symbols of comfort and cultural insensitivity remind him of Maxine's fondness for beauty. He accepts the fruit and admits his love of the land.

Jason responds with a quote from Hemingway, evoking other safaris: "I had loved country all my life; the country was always better than the people" (27). Thomas' reaction to the Hemingway quote provides insight into his character. A "dark flood" pounded in his veins and "something cruel and fresh as the sudden air through a window" (27) fell into the space between the three persons. Why cruel? Why fresh? Although the conflict between Thomas and Maxine seems to oppose people to art, we realize that Thomas is more involved with the esthetic pleasures of the safari than he would care to admit. He has gained a new, disturbing awareness of himself. How else does one explain his lack of courage to read Hemingway when he says, "I don't think I could read it now. I don't have much courage" (28).

Further evidence of Thomas' lack of ease follows Jason's question about his work. He identifies himself as a teacher, which is a half-truth that avoids reference to his real mission—one born in humility, lacking an elaborate support system and aiming to restore "broken people, not cisterns" (74). Many of the incidents in the novel document his patience as he struggles to help those who need him, but he refuses to reveal his missionary calling to the American tourists because of pride and self-condemnation: "You are not fit to be a missionary" (28).

To understand his sense of mission one must place it within the context of African countries following independence when the expatriate presence tended to go in two different directions. On the one hand, non-governmental agencies such as Mennonite Central Committee cooperated with the local church in providing technological assistance in education, health and agricultural development. When Thomas yields to the temptation of a white lie, he identifies with that more acceptable type of work. On the other hand, many of the longterm missionaries who remained sought to assume servant roles by transferring leadership positions to the Africans and sacrificing the material comforts of home.

A Long Dry Safari

At his commissioning service Thomas had heard an "old saint" say, "If you are a good missionary you will become homeless — forever an alien. Never again fully American, yet never fully African" (199). Thomas clearly believes that the way of the cross is found in the loss of self as one cares for others, as one dies "to ambition, to selfish love of success, to the fame of an expanding program" (199). The inspiration for this journey provides a contrast to the traditional safari, complete with all the pleasures of home and designed to entertain the participants.

An element of danger figures in both the first safari story and the flashback safari. Thomas hides his fear that a rhino or buffalo might come charging out of the bush, and the doctor disapproves of Peters' hunting tactics because the buffalo are "too dangerous an animal for one to hunt alone" (16). Part of Hemingway's fascination with the safari came from his need to prove his masculinity and to defy death. Although Thomas' remark to the American couple, "Have a safe safari, and watch out for the rhino" (28), is offered lightly, it introduces us to a central theme of the novel — safety. At the end of Part II Thomas will puzzle, "But safe from what?" (122).

Following the "real" safari on Saturday, Thomas and Maxine pack up the Land-Rover for "a day's safari" (37) to attend a rural church at Kwoyo. Their non-heroic excursion represents Thomas' kind of safari, a day of small rewards and plenty of irritating frustrations — more like chasing rabbits than stalking big game. As the first two safaris provided insight into Thomas' feelings about the land and its people, so this third one shows how human imperfections tarnish the vision of a church triumphant. Eby emphasizes the symbolic importance of that trip by repeating the use of the word "safari" seven times (37, 51, 52, 56 and 57).

Just as the priest Father Drumont in Mongo Beti's *The Poor Christ of Bomba* learns during a journey into the interior that his mission among the Tala people fell far short of its original goals, so Thomas is exposed to a litany of little disappointments. The Sunday market keeps believers away from worship. Pastor Otieno, who had once traveled to North America, assimilates only the worst traits of Western Christianity. The vitality of a bare-breasted dancing girl along the road seems to mock the lack of imagination found in the church services. And finally a flat tire and a missing jack bring the day to an appropriate, ironic end.

A more disturbing incident occurs later that evening when Thomas decides to confront the mechanic Musa in order to deal in biblical fashion with his own problem of anger. He fails miserably, for ironically the suspicion of an adulterous liaison between nurse Paisley and Musa only rekindles his anger. Later, when he complains to Mzee Jeremiah, the old pastor muddies the ethical waters even more. We learn that

Christian white men are obsessed by adultery but forget that anger is an even worse sin, for "'he who sows discord among the brothers is worse than an infidel'" (53). The pragmatic implications of Mzee's words of wisdom cast their own shadow when he chides Thomas: "Your counsel on this matter is not wise. Not only do we need Musa, but also Miss Paisley and her good work among the rural clinics" (54).

More situational irony develops as Thomas and the Mzee discuss anger and adultery. Esta listens, giggles, drops a crochet hook and swings her breasts "like heavy over-sized pears" (54). Thomas' concern about sexual immorality reflects his own still-hidden desires for Esta. The exploitative relationships between whites and Africans involving Ogot, Musa, Peters, the Peace Corps girl, nurse Paisley and Esta anger him because they confirm the fragility of his own mission to serve people instead of promoting material progress. And his attraction to Esta seems to grow out of an unconscious desire to accomplish his mission by "saving" an African woman from the greatest of all curses, childlessness, while preserving his own identity through the birth of a son. Sexual conquest, a perversion of Thomas' mission, suggests a short cut to racial understanding, motivated by easy desire and facilitated by a lack of responsibility.

As noted above, Thomas' rejection of the colonial safari associated with violence, comfort and duplicity in favor of a love of the African people reveals his defensiveness toward his own mission and more involvement with the past sins and consequences of colonialism than he cares to admit. The game park excursion suggests that esthetic reasons, not only people, motivate his mission. The Sunday safari highlights practical problems, showing some small victories but also documenting the inevitable compromises that erode the spirit of the missionary.

Two more safaris completing Part I of the novel set the stage for an analysis of Thomas' interior journey. These last two safaris—a funeral service and a trip to the mountain with Colins—are linked thematically by a reference to a broken cistern and a confrontation with death itself.

The fourth safari, a funeral voyage that Thomas makes alone without his wife and fellow Christians, goes beyond the pettiness of cultural misunderstandings, cheapened ceremonies and backsliding believers. The village appears deserted, silent. "The land slept mute and unstirring . . ."(59). The gravediggers sing an ancient song in a language they no longer can speak as they prepare the grave for a young man whose burial is witnessed by his grandfather.

In this visit Eby begins a transition from a kind of hunting expedition with its trophies of newborn believers (Thomas' sense of mission to the African people) to a journey inward, which embodies a search for safety and salvation. It is easy for Thomas to renounce colonialism, sensitive as he is to the plight of the African people. His natural generosity and strong sense of integrity place him on the side of the oppressed; he reserves his anger for those who "sin" against their own people and he seems content to serve as an humble laborer in God's vineyard. But the journey into his own heart is another matter. That safari provides neither material comfort nor a sure sense of mission while it probes his relationship with God.

Throughout the novel Thomas struggles hard to find the courage and strength to maintain his equilibrium. In many ways he resembles a super missionary, even stirring feelings of envy among his fellow whites. Not only is he a pastor, teacher and natural administrator with mechanical skills; he also understands African culture, respects his elders, knows the value of solitude, loves his family and appreciates the spiritual resources found in community, especially during his time of illness. His personal accomplishments are matched only by his ability to identify shortcomings within others and himself. Much of the drama in the story grows out of the slow unraveling of Thomas' sense of mission in spite of his best efforts. The task he has accepted goes beyond what is humanly possible to achieve.

At the funeral Thomas senses a desolation that he himself fears to admit. The old grandfather touches on the tragedy of a young man dying: "Now are the waters of his youth poured out; now is he empty like a broken cistern. We grieve when the young die, but there is some lifting of the sadness, for here already is the young man's seed sprung, his boy child" (63). The old man's words of despair and consolation are those that Thomas himself wants to appropriate, for he desires a son to ensure his immortality should his own mission fail. Although there is a difference between the two kinds of hope — the one African, thankful for unbroken rituals, the call of the soil, the promise of new seed; the other Western, a Christian faith in the hope of the resurrection — both provide mutual encouragement. "Why do you wash the body?" Thomas asks the old man and answers the question for him in his mind: "The washing of the dead springs from a primordial reverence and intimacy with the land too indistinct to shape one's own intellect" (65). The interior safari towards death, couched in terms of reverence and intimacy for the land, points toward a resolution of the conflict between love of people or love of land.

The reference to a broken cistern recalls the message of the mountain, a message sufficiently disturbing to send Thomas in the opposite direction on a road "that would lead him to a revelation" (60). He spends the eve of this fifth and final safari of Part I with Colins and his wife. On the way to their home he lends a tool to an old man whose bicycle tire needs fixing. That simple act raises yet another doubt about his mission: maybe the old man "did not need this white man but only his tools" (67).

The conversation between Thomas and his friends that evening explores further the possible failure of the Western experience in Africa, but the real reason for the safari emerges after the mountain climb. That next day he finds the courage to share a deep, personal fear with his friend. On the mountain a wild orange tree and a broken cistern witness to the dream of a lonely German soldier who, Thomas imagines, was "to man faithfully this small station, understanding the significance of its insignificance" (73).

The trip to the mountain represents a positive, courageous stage in Thomas' interior journey. His triumphal cry, "I will restore broken people, not cisterns; I will plant young men and women, not orchards. And the showers of blessings will return, and they will break the long dry season!" (74) appears at first glance to be a positive affirmation of his mission. Has Thomas found his way, regained his vision at the end of Part I?

But while he reaffirms his vision he hears "foreboding whispers of the mountain" (74), a sign that all is not well. He has not yet accepted the implications of the German boy's tragedy. That young idealist had also believed sincerely in the nobility of his military mission destined to become a lost cause. Even the colonial enterprise enlisted men of vision who believed in their task of bringing water and fruit to a dry and thirsty land. At a symbolic level Thomas the missionary shares more than he wants to admit with the soldier whose mission was to develop and defend the territory for his Fatherland. The clear contrast between saving broken people and building cisterns is not as easy to maintain as it would appear. Furthermore, one could argue that the healing of broken people assumes an even greater arrogance than does that of introducing technological progress, especially in Africa where people are valued more than things. Colins understands Thomas' dilemma when he observes, "Trying to perfect the beautiful . . ." (104).

In *Contemplative Prayer* Thomas Merton asserts that full maturity of the spiritual life cannot be reached unless we first pass beyond the dread, anguish, trouble and fear that necessarily accompany the inner crisis of "spiritual death" in which we finally abandon our attachment to our exterior self.[3] Thomas resists the abandonment to the exterior self through most of the book. His insight and dedication, which make him such an effective missionary, serve paradoxically to render his own salvation all the more difficult, for grace comes to those who need it the

_____

3. Thomas Merton, *Contemplative Prayer* (New York: Doubleday, 1969), 110.

most. Thomas sacrifices himself willingly over and over, but cannot face the thought that he should perhaps give up his mission, his own African safari, for the sake of his wife who cannot adjust to life abroad. It is interesting to note that our first premonition of Maxine's departure, an event which eventually provides a glimmer of grace, comes as an off-hand reference to a safari of her own.

We receive the first faint hints of Thomas' salvation when he takes time to detour through the game park, shares a ritual at a funeral and then later shows Colins the mountain. Although these journeys arouse feelings of guilt, each grows out of his own need and initiative. The guilt in the game park seems misplaced when we know that the "day's indulgence and solitude" has assuaged an "old hunger and this sacred thirst" (22) and made it possible for Thomas to put up with the miseries of a small town hotel, where he seeks a blessing to counter the "inevitable decay of life" (23).

Silence, solitude and beauty form a contrast to the balancing act that makes up his usual missionary activity, for which he feels so personally responsible. On the mountain he is able to share a deep-seated fear — that of annihilation. How could God's servant perish if his vision is one of humble hope, if he builds "for eternity a Kingdom not made with hands?" (74). He holds onto his vision "stubbornly," using the survival of his mission as a stay against death itself. The mistaken association of mission and salvation is made explicit at the end of Part II when Maxine, deflecting his desire for a son, reminds him that "a man's soul is safe" (122).

The journey towards wholeness takes a strange turn in Part III when a three-day delay sets the stage for an "urban renewal," quite unexpected for Thomas who awaits impatiently his return to the bush. Asked by the Bishop to preach in the cathedral, he protests, "I have no message from the Lord—" (127), but then consents. The sight of a crippled boy's face with its "expression of infinite puzzlement" raises the "age-old questions about the meaning of temples of the Lord in the land of the poor" (130). But the boy's hope, the voice of the organ and the choir's proclamation of God's word opens Thomas' heart to water images that contrast with those of the land, of the long dry season: "And the ocean was delight and sorrow, petty meanness and love outpouring, intermingled with penitence and thanksgiving and forgiveness and praise" (131). As his own efforts crumble away, he experiences a mystical unity: "We are all of us together carried in the one world-womb" (131).

The worst is yet to come upon his return. No restoration follows his anointing of Mzee Jeremiah, Maxine deserts him, the church is implicated in poaching, the Bishop's healing service turns into a circus.

The water imagery of the cathedral has become "disease and misery rising and flooding him like a great wave, the water of annihilation drowning him among the refuse of humanity" (195).

But failure and humiliation finally set the stage for a sixth and final "safe safari" (208) when he embarks upon a trip to Mombasa in search of Maxine—willing to abandon his mission to save his marriage. At the railway station he listens for the sea, remembering how it had earlier "spoken of peace and of something eternal awaiting him" (209). Wearing a fresh safari suit, he encounters Jason and Arlene on "another safari" (212). He lies to the couple, cutting off any complicity with their luxury safari by air along the east coast of Africa.

In the end, Thomas has accepted the Bishop's truth: "Your marriage is more important to you than your mission to us" (208). He has recognized the failure of his vision, returned to Maxine, "safe in her arms" (216). He has now realized that safety comes through the abandonment of self— not through superhuman efforts to preserve a mission, noble as it may be. Truth breaks through; the person whom Thomas had seen as a threat to the accomplishment of God's will in his life has become the bearer of divine grace. By leaving her husband Maxine has deepened his spiritual crisis and brought an end to Thomas' perfectionistic quest to justify his existence through his own good works.

Thus the final safari resolves the conflicts posed in the five safaris of Part I. Thomas' dismissal of the American tourists signals his refusal to compromise with the legacy of colonialism. Away from her husband at the beach, Maxine of her own free will begins to paint African landscapes that had previously overwhelmed her. In her paintings Thomas discovers a mutual love of the land, now accepting it without coercion or guilt. Eby's ambivalent ending (we are not sure that Maxine will be able to endure life in the bush) goes beyond the old question of "missionary go home, your church is a failure" that emerged during the Sunday safari. The trip to Mombasa means that Thomas can pack his bags if necessary, for he no longer equates his mission with his salvation. The grace that comes through a woman frees him from the fear of annihilation expressed at the funeral and in other parts of the novel. The irony that undermined his vow to "restore broken people, not cisterns" has been erased by his commitment to his wife, the broken person closest to him. Thus the promise of rains at the end of parts I and II finally comes to full fruition in a safari blessed by "the fall of distant rains which marked the end of a long, dry season" (216).

CONSTRUCTING NARRATIVE: AN INTRODUCTION TO DALLAS WIEBE AND *OUR ASIAN JOURNEY*

PAUL TIESSEN*

Abstract: When Dallas Wiebe's *Our Asian Journey* began to appear in excerpted form in 1989, a new and specifically Mennonite literary world which could offer that project a place had begun to take form in the United States. At the same time, Wiebe's stature as an established writer, his fairly traditional Mennonite background to the end of his undergraduate years at Bethel College in the early 1950s and his commitment to re-tell a historically established Mennonite story in his most impressive work to date make him an ideal figure to give that literary world a particular historic depth. After acknowledging Wiebe's place as a Mennonite writer within a developing tradition, the essay turns in the second half to a consideration of some of Wiebe's thematic and stylistic interests in his earlier work, not explicitly Mennonite, and their manifestation in *Our Asian Journey.*

In the more than forty years that he has published poetry and fiction, Dallas Wiebe, though born and raised in Kansas as a Mennonite, has not often been called a "Mennonite" writer. For a long time there was little on the surface of his work to identify it as Mennonite, and there were still only hints of any reading community that might want to explore it in such terms. By 1989, however, when he was looking for a publisher for his novel *Our Asian Journey*, there were people and institutions ready to begin constructing a kind of narrative that would lead to Wiebe's place as one of the "elder statesmen" at the large and impressive gathering of writers, readers and critics in 1997 at the Mennonite/s Writing in the U.S. conference hosted by Goshen College. It was *Our Asian Journey* — based mainly on documents of an 1880s episode involving groups of Mennonites moving eastward from south Russia to Turkestan to await there the return of the Lord — that helped to change things. This apocalyptic novel about people reading the Book of Revelation as literal narrative managed to catch the attention of Mennonite historians, who for generations have been important cultural gate-keepers and guides among Mennonites.

---

*Paul Tiessen is Professor of English and Film Studies at Wilfrid Laurier University, Waterloo, Ontario.

When he began writing *Our Asian Journey* in 1975, Wiebe could not envision a Mennonite audience for his work. He imagined for it a general literary audience like those he had been addressing with the help of small presses in the previous twenty years. This period began in 1956 and included his novel *Skyblue the Badass* (1969), a work characteristic of virtually all of his writing, filled as it is (to quote from the original dustjacket) with a "dazzling world of verbal pyrotechnics, . . . a world of allusion, insight, symbolism and cerebration."[1]

Historian James C. Juhnke provided Mennonite readers, and Wiebe, with the first public sign—the first "authorizing signal"—that Wiebe might have a place among them. Juhnke's announcement came when he published the final chapter (Chapter 7) of *Our Asian Journey* in a 1989 issue of *Mennonite Life*.[2] Juhnke was editor of this journal, which is based at Bethel College, where Wiebe had been an undergraduate in the late 1940s and early 1950s and where historians in those days had so pointedly turned their backs on the "Asian journey" episode of the 1880s that Wiebe's interest in it was immediately piqued.[3] Juhnke, who saw in Wiebe's novel a challenge to Christian readers, offered these words to pave the way for the new work:

> Dallas Wiebe, Professor of English at the University of Cincinnati, has written a novel about one of the most fascinating events of all Mennonite history—the trek of Russian Mennonites into Central Asia to meet the Lord. . . . We have all assumed that participants of this failed venture came out with embarrassment and disillusionment. How does this elderly Joseph Toevs [in whose voice the final chapter is narrated], apparent victim of Christ's failure to return on schedule, earn the right to sing a hymn of praise to God at the end of his life? Is our own praise of God pale by comparison, given our inability to harbor such radical hopes?[4]

---

1. Dallas Wiebe has published six books: *Skyblue the Badass* (New York: Doubleday-Paris Review Editions, 1969); three books of short stories: *The Transparent Eye-ball* (1982), *Going to the Mountain* (1988), and *Skyblue's Essays* (1995), all published in Providence, Rhode Island by Burning Deck Press; *The Kansas Poems* (Cincinnati: Cincinnati Poetry Review Press, 1987); and *Our Asian Journey* (Waterloo, Ontario: MLR Editions Canada, 1997).

2. Dallas Wiebe, "Our Asian Journey: [Laodicea]," *Mennonite Life* 44 (Dec. 1989), 16-21.

3. The "author" who speaks within *Our Asian Journey* tells of his experience with Mennonite historians in Chapter 2 of the novel. See especially the burlesque-like discussion on pages 38-52. Chapter 2 was the second of the three sections of *Our Asian Journey* published before the appearance of the entire work in 1997; see Dallas Wiebe, "II. Smyrna Friday, December 21, 1879 (o.s.), Lysanderhoh," *The New Quarterly* 10 (Spring/Summer 1990), 90-117. This special issue of *The New Quarterly* was guest-edited by Hildi Froese Tiessen, in anticipation of the Mennonite/s Writing in Canada conference held at Conrad Grebel College in 1990. For the third section of *Our Asian Journey* to appear in print, see note 5.

4. James C. Juhnke, "In this Issue," *Mennonite Life* 44 (Dec. 1989), [2].

Dallas Wiebe and Our Asian Journey

In 1993 yet another section of *Our Asian Journey* (part of Chapter 4) appeared,[5] again in *Mennonite Life*, this time hosted by the Arts Issue editor, poet Raylene Hinz-Penner. She saw in Wiebe the origins of a tradition, and labeled him "the Mennonite pioneer in creative writing in the United States," winner of such prestigious awards as the Pushcart Prize (1979) and the Aga Khan fiction award from the *Paris Review* (1978).[6]

In a 1995 issue of *Mennonite Life*, playwright, director and actor Warren Kliewer referred to Wiebe's avant-garde style in a review of *Skyblue's Essays,* and called Wiebe the "James Joyce" of what Kliewer correctly perceived had become an identifiable Mennonite literary movement in the U.S.[7] In 1997, anticipating the publication of the whole of *Our Asian Journey* on the eve of the Mennonite/s Writing in the U.S. conference, Jeff Gundy, himself a prominent Mennonite poet, teacher and critic, identified Wiebe as one of Mennonite writers' "elder statesmen" and characterized *Our Asian Journey* as an "impressive" novel.[8] In the *Mennonite Weekly Review* the writer and poet Elaine Sommers Rich referred to *Our Asian Journey* as a "magnificent piece of work."[9] In August 1997 Wiebe was invited to read a section of *Our Asian Journey* in a Sunday service from the pulpit at Bethel College Mennonite Church. Did anyone that Sunday recall Jeff Gundy's observation that twenty-eight years earlier Wiebe's *Skyblue the Badass,* his "semi-autobiographical *Bildungsroman,*" had dealt "memorably if caustically with [Wiebe's] Kansas boyhood and subsequent flight from the Mennonite community. . . "?[10]

Wiebe has come to endorse the importance of a Mennonite literary community for his work. In a 1993 interview with Hinz-Penner, Wiebe cautiously acknowledged what had been occurring amongst readers and writers for some time:

> Let's put it this way; when working on *Our Asian Journey* I thought the audience would be a non-Mennonite audience. Now I realize that probably only Mennonites will understand what it's all about. . . . Maybe then I ought to call myself a 'Mennonite writer.' It may be the only way I'll find an audience for my book.[11]

---

5. Dallas Wiebe, "Our Asian Journey: Thyatira," *Mennonite Life* 48 (Dec. 1993), 6-14.

6. Raylene Hinz-Penner, "In this Issue," *Mennonite Life* 48 (Dec. 1993), [2].

7. Warren Kliewer, [Review of Dallas Wiebe's *Skyblue's Essays*], *Mennonite Life* 50 (Dec. 1995), 38.

8. Jeff Gundy, "U.S. Mennonite Poetry and Poets: Beyond Dr. Johnson's Dog," *MQR* 71 (Oct. 1997), 20-21.

9. Elaine Sommers Rich, "Our Asian Journey," *Mennonite Weekly Review*, Sept. 4, 1997, 9.

10. Jeff Gundy, "U.S. Mennonite Poetry and Poets," 21.

11. Dallas Wiebe, "Interview," *Mennonite Life* 48 (Dec. 1993), 5.

Of course, things are not really that simple. Mennonites (like anyone else) will have to work harder than Wiebe suggests if they want to understand "what it's all about." In *Our Asian Journey* the literary conventions of piety and prayer meet head-on those of postmodernism, or at least Wiebe's send-up of postmodernism. Indeed, Chapter 2 of the novel warns the reader of these very things, with the narrator there self-consciously installing himself in the text and making sure that the reader/writer relationship will remain lively, just as the relationships between piety and postmodernism remain fluid in *Our Asian Journey*. It is either postmodernism, or a parody of the fashion for postmodernism that Wiebe seems to evoke when, in the 1993 interview with Hinz-Penner, he defines a Mennonite reader as one who can accept the idea "that there is nothing mutually contradictory between milking cows and belief in God. As Joseph Toevs finds out, buying your wife a new pair of shoes is not condemning your soul."[12]

Wiebe is a long-established master of irony and parody. Throughout his career he has taught his readers to be wary about the surfaces of texts, for they are sometimes cover-ups. Certainly Joseph Toevs's closing song of praise in *Our Asian Journey* is as likely to move us as it moved Juhnke, but what are we to make of its lines which give thanks to God not only for deliverance from the great plagues of the past but also for *Mohn-Kuchen* (poppy-seed cake)? Joseph Toevs provides the first-person point of view not only in the final but also in the first and middle of the seven chapters, chapters comprising fully two-thirds of this 449-page work. In the chapters that frame the novel we hear Toevs's first-person reflection upon his life as he looks back in 1921 from the vantage point of his 81 years. And in the 264-page middle chapter we read Toevs's diary of his trip from Russia to central Asia, begun in 1880 when he was 41 and continuing until 1885, when he arrived in Kansas. For long stretches — especially in Toevs's diary entries, which constitute a kind of vast inner monologue (but also in the two letters which make up Chapters 5 and 6) — the novel actually maintains a fairly resolute suppression of irony, and instead offers a lyrical defense of its own tendency toward the poetry of language and dream and Christian pilgrimage. In Toevs's words in Chapter 4 Wiebe seems to set aside many of the ambivalences of parodic and satiric clowning and give way to a text replete with the oft-sonorous, oft-simple language of the church. Still, what *are* we to make of an epic novel that after 449 pages leads us to its final amen with this sentence: "I thank our wonderful and gracious God who by his

---

12. Ibid.

directions and guidance brought me to this land flowing with hay and potatoes" (449)?[13]

Wiebe—the parodist, the trickster, the comic deconstructionist who rails in work after work against dominant idiom, ideology, myth— definitely is present within the voice of the gentle pastor, in its "by cracky" asides (440), in its outrageous, comic logic:

> Maybe the surest sign that there is eternal life is that as I come to the great death my visions are so constant and intense that not even Portzeltje, Gorovei, Vereniky, Piroscky, Borscht or Mohn-Kuchen can still them (441-42).

in its frequent and sometimes incongruous lists:

> I've received my catechism, baptism, ordination, my call, my latter days. I've raised a family. I've taken a great journey for my soul's sake. I've plowed my ground and harvested my crops. I've planted many trees. I've spoken the word of God and tended my sheep. I've purchased a new pair of shoes from Sears and Roebuck each year for Sarah. What else can I feel, think, or say now that I'm at the end of my pilgrimage on this earth? (442-43).

and in its Prufrockian search for an audience for his story, a story he already (if unwittingly) has told in the poetry of Chapter 4 and for which he wants to substitute the conventionally mandatory but guaranteed-to-be-boring *A Short Sketch of My Life As It Reveals the Direction and Guidance of a Wonderful and Gracious God.*

Clearly, Wiebe gives us two texts in one; indeed, he often gives us more than two, as voice, language, narrative—multiple discursive codes—share sometimes an uneasy and only provisional relationship. His text/reader relationship, like his figure/ground relationship, is never entirely stable. Even the richest layers of nostalgia are delicately interrogated, as is the impact on Mennonite believers of the Book of Revelation. Wiebe the prankster—making merry, winking at us—ever pushes his work over the edge and onto postmodernism's unstable ground, and so undoes any single reading of the story overall.

In many ways *Our Asian Journey* is a parable about interpretation, and ownership, of story. It addresses directly (most explicitly in Chapter 2) questions about the sources of narrative legitimacy, about the naturalization of dominant or master narratives. Mennonite institutions have been vigilant, even aggressive, about getting the story "right"; indeed, narrative is at the heart of their enterprise, as it should be. Taking religious and institutional language at its word, this novel

---

13. References to *Our Asian Journey* will be identified by page number placed within the essay and, in the case of some references to Chapter 4, by date of diary entry.

addresses the ways in which certain Mennonite fictions and Mennonite realities can be overlaid. It examines ways in which someone borne on the crest of a story—even someone like preacher Toevs—can be silenced or marginalized or paralyzed by the operation of that story and its extensions—prayer, creed, sermon, sacred text—within his or her own society. Thus, an enlightened and enlightening outsider in the novel, Gerhard Christian Wiebe, is justly cautious about being put-upon and giving too-ready assent to the temptations of an apocalyptic tale claiming divine origin: "No angel has been sent to me to thunder in my ear. No voice has spoken to me out of a burning bush" (53).

From the beginning of his writing career in the 1950s, many of Wiebe's works have been notoriously transgressive with respect to technique and theme alike, violating the logic of narrative realism and subverting the integrity of literary convention. Each text/world sets up a logic of its own, a value system that is not openly informed nor explicitly interrogated in any obvious way by a "norm" operating outside the immediate Wiebesque universe. Clichés and the conventions of language run amuck, sometimes bizarrely so; they seem not to be tempered by customary rules for storytelling. The individual word is often wrenched out of its customary place. In his ludic cultural probing, Wiebe is a kind of comic Brechtian, making normal the abnormal, simultaneously defamiliarizing and naturalizing text/audience relations, making deformations conform to the tough, sometimes "hard-boiled" logic that each story provides.

Indeed, it is a peculiar trait of Wiebe's work, and a strength, that he dares simply to assert a self-contained world of extremes with uncompromising intensity. He manages to get away with positing or proposing seemingly arbitrary but quite densely textured conditions and mythic lineaments, separating us from our usual run of everyday emotions but leading us into the momentum of a new and hitherto unused set of emotions. He creates literary worlds that might remind us at times of the absurd world of Samuel Beckett, though Wiebe's sometimes seem to have even less of a familiar center. Yet they are worlds that, through repetition of ritual and gesture, however minimalist, develop a predictable interior structure of their own, so that the characters in them can gain some control over, and even sometimes small victories in, their lives. Readers familiar with Wiebe's stories might recall the decrepit movie theater offering a kind of sheltering family-home in "Omega I," or the wicker laundry basket offering solace to the famous writer's living and breathing torso in "Night Flight to Stockholm." Or the counter-narrative that joyously develops in "Skyblue's Essay on Confession," when the protagonist becomes "state shepherd" for Ohio. In such stories, family romance meets a banal, or hilarious, or monstrous, absurdism. And the tonal variations—from a cryptic cynicism palpably evident in "Obituary" to the dogged stubbornness (itself undercutting pompous cultural posturings) in "The Fairy Feller's Master Stroke" to the multi-layered comic monologue in "At the Rotonde"—enrich the range of satire and parody.[14] Yet these are, in the end, works that contain a surprisingly humanistic subtext.

It seems paradoxical that along with the provisional quality in the realms inhabited by people in Wiebe's stories there is a striking palpability and wholeness. In *Our Asian Journey* the Mennonite world is simply there, blossoming forth, filled with a robust matter-of-factness, and at the same time a strong foreignness. Who would believe the hyperbolic logic of an epic pilgrimage from Russia to central Asia based on words torn from a few texts? Can the telegram from the governor general of Turkestan, Constantine Petrovich von Kaufman, described in Toevs's March 11, 1880 entry, really be taken as a sign so momentous that 200 Mennonite families give up a way of life over it? Surely the gibberish of the leader—his seemingly indecipherable language running for many paragraphs in Chapter 3—cannot inspire such international travels by a whole community. But for Wiebe these seemingly artificial developments can be taken for granted, need little defense. Their logic speaks out through the diaries at the center of this work, and seems not to need our sophisticated help. This is the kind of world Wiebe likes to write about; it flows from realism to postmodernism, absurdism to magic realism, epic history to autobiography.

For Wiebe the story of *Our Asian Journey* is quite simply there as story, and needs no further justification. That it has been a suppressed narrative, a story out of step with the establishment's master narrative, only makes him more interested in it. Wiebe, in effect, is arguing against a politics or rhetoric of coercion when it comes to the story of any social group, and his works overall testify to his guerrilla-like resistance to any rigidity or narrowness of dominating dogma and to his defense of the vulnerable and the disenfranchised. This particular story is a story waiting, as it were, for Wiebe to offer it as performance. The specifically Mennonite pilgrimage within the story is the pilgrimage also of everyman/woman, and Wiebe's performance of this Mennonite work, complete with a Mennonite author written into the text, demonstrates a

---

14. In this necessarily brief introduction to Wiebe's work, I have not offered extended description of any of it. Readers will find that these six stories were published as follows: "At the Rotonde," "Night Flight to Stockholm," "Omega I" and "The Fairy Feller's Master Stroke" in *Going to the Mountain*, on pages 27-36, 37-50, 60-98, and 162-72, respectively; "Skyblue's Essay on Confession," in *Skyblue's Essays*, 17-20; "Obituary," in *The Transparent Eye-ball*, 87-114.

place for the Mennonite story in the pluralistic zone of the contemporary literary world.

Our Asian Journey is both a lament for and a celebration of a Mennonite micro-universe. It is a reminder of poetry that is easily suppressed, and of the possibility of recovering valuable meaning even from Mennonites' discarded and rejected stories or counter-stories. Joseph Toevs, at the center of the novel, embodies what for Wiebe are some of its contradictions. Toevs does not know how to understand his great achievement in having constructed the 264-page narrative that makes up the powerful heart of this novel—his diary in Chapter 4. But readers can tell that he has become more a poet who has gained enormous vision than a preacher who has found any kind of audience. Filtering through Toevs's diary lies a deep sense of mystery, art and beauty that reaches beyond, though also includes and absorbs, the rational and material world. Notice the haiku-like poignancy in lyrical entries such as those of February 18, 1881; October 4, 1882; October 25, 1882; July 25, 1883; March 22, 1884, to locate just a few. Toevs's diary represents a minimalist architectonics of simple, flat, declarative sentences, interwoven with simple prayers (e.g. March 22, 1884). Notice the gentle personableness toward all God's creatures, yet the distancing that comes from his seeing young females in the stereotypical and sentimentalized terminology of a D. W. Griffith: "the Albrecht Girl" (211), "the Unruh girl" (213). For us Toevs becomes, in the end, not the "Kansas dirt farmer" his neighbors observe late in his life, but a man whose pilgrimage reads like the map of a great poem.

Joseph Toevs's very last words, which are also the closing words of the novel, actually offer a moment in the text that seems to resolve its playful contradictions. After his final song of praise to God, Toevs utters his oft-repeated prayer: "Even so, come, Lord Jesus" (449). Here, in the simple beauty of so much fervor and faith, Wiebe seems to let the text break the bounds of its own ironies; the preacher/poet's deep piety seems to overwhelm the postmodern writer's play with narrative artifice. And for all the doubts that have come along in Toevs's pilgrimage of faith, Wiebe seems, in the end, to let a deep longing, a knowledge of a serene and true peace, prevail. It is a knowledge that resonates also at the foundation of other of Wiebe's stories. Indeed, *Our Asian Journey* is a novel that both confirms and enlarges much of Wiebe's work. And in the other work by this "elder statesman," we may find also new ways of reading *Our Asian Journey*, for it is work that signals Wiebe's preparedness for his task here.

VOICES OF FAITH IN *BLUE MOUNTAINS OF CHINA* AND *A COMMUNITY OF MEMORY*

EDNA FROESE*

Abstract: Both *Blue Mountains of China* and *A Community of Memory* consist of short stories that together depict the familiar master narrative of the Mennonite exodus (Russian Mennonites and Swiss Mennonites, respectively) from European homelands to new land in the Americas. A comparative focus on the role of the storyteller within each text reveals important differences between Wiebe's and Gundy's definitions of community and their understandings of the function of the individual within those communities. The initially invisible narrator of *Blue Mountains of China* emerges as a character near the end of the novel, but only to become one more individual voice in a deliberately chosen community of faith, hence no more authoritative than any other voice. The increasingly visible and self-conscious narrator of *A Community of Memory* finally states a tentative affirmation of a community that is more given than chosen.

At first glance the task of comparing a Canadian novel about Russian Mennonites with an American creative nonfiction text about Swiss Mennonites seems rather daunting. True, both texts explore the broader Mennonite effort to find a place in which to worship and live in peace — and, incidentally, to prosper. Beyond that very general similarity, however, Rudy Wiebe's *Blue Mountains of China* and Jeff Gundy's *A Community of Memory* differ radically in their narrative methods. Nevertheless, I will attempt a limited comparison focused on the peculiar stance of the storyteller in each text. For the problems the reader encounters with that storyteller reveal much about the kind of Mennonite community the reader — Mennonite and non-Mennonite — is invited to consider.[1]

At first it is hard to find an obvious, or even implied, narrator in *Blue Mountains*. Chapter 1 gives us the voice of Frieda Friesen, comfortably

---

* Edna Froese is a Sessional Lecturer of English at St. Thomas More College, University of Saskatchewan, Saskatoon.

1. The "invitation" I speak of here refers to the experience the reader shares with the implied author during the reading of the text, not to any explicit or implicit invitation to join an actual community. Given the focus on community in contrast to individualism in both Wiebe and Gundy, the reading of these texts means not only the usual identification with key characters, but also a temporary experience of community. See Wayne Booth's *The Company We Keep* (Berkeley: U. of California Press, 1988) for detailed discussion of what Booth calls a "friendship" between reader and implied author.

and piously recalling her life for her great-grandchildren. But Chapter 2 tosses us abruptly into the tortured mind of young Jakob Friesen V as he vainly inserts childhood prayers for purity into the moral and social chaos of a Russian Mennonite village forcibly turned communist. Except for the four chapters given to Frieda Friesen, every chapter gives us another group of characters, another setting, another narrative stance. Each chapter begins in medias res and ceases while still "on the way" as is emphasized by the title of the final chapter. No omniscient narrator, no transitions help us create a meaningful whole out of these brief immersions into intensely personal, frustratingly incomplete struggles to translate faith and community into new contexts.

Not until the final Chapter 13 does someone emerge to collect all these narrative fragments into one basket. When young John Reimer first appears in the text as a crazy Mennonite walking across Canada, carrying a wooden cross, his symbolic freight is all too obvious. Rather improbably, several characters from previous chapters, mostly lapsed Mennonites, gather around Reimer in a ditch near Calgary. They turn out to be either related to one another or connected to the same Russian village of origin: the ethnic community is re-established despite their best efforts to forget Low German. In the ensuing conversations the question every main character in the book has grappled with surfaces again, this time explicitly: What does it mean to be a Mennonite in the world?

Reimer's sermon in reply to that question—which he hears as "What does it mean to be a Christian?"—echoes what Wiebe has written or said in other places. In an interview with Donald Cameron, Wiebe stated, "To be an Anabaptist is to be a radical follower of the person of Jesus Christ—that's really what it's about—and Jesus Christ had no use for the social and political structures of his day; he came to *supplant* them."[2] That sounds very much like John Reimer's insistence that to be a Christ-follower is to live radically, to begin "a revolution for social justice," not to set up "a church that can never change no matter where on earth or in what century it is, a church that's never as important to us as living, as eating, as making our pile."[3] Reimer thus criticizes both the rigid—and distinctly ethnic—traditionalism of those Mennonite characters who are not present because they are in carefully separated colonies in Paraguay, and the comfortably assimilated Mennonites seated with him. Reimer's succinct advice to the self-centered, incognito Mennonite, Elizabeth Cereno, "hate your life. Just a little, more" (259), summarizes verbally

2. Donald Cameron, *Conversations with Canadian Novelists*, Part 2 (Toronto: Macmillan, 1973), 148.

3. Rudy Wiebe, *The Blue Mountains of China* (Toronto: McClelland & Stewart, 1970), 257.

and directly what Wiebe has implied throughout the novel, through a dominant motif of "nothing" and through his subtle approval of certain self-negating actions. Reimer thus appears to be the voice of the implied author, Wiebe's alter ego—the prophet on the edge of the community, calling it to account.

The problem is that as a character John Reimer is unconvincing. After the religious uncertainty and the subjectivity of previous chapters, Reimer's wholly externalized certainty is too easy.[4] And to see him as merely a voice-over for the author finally explaining the right way to be Mennonite in the world is to impugn Wiebe's integrity and ability as a novelist. If, however, we pay attention to the kind of community that Wiebe depicts throughout and invites his readers to participate in,[5] Reimer's role takes on a surprising significance.

The structure of the novel itself makes the reader part of an Anabaptist-like process of discernment that is always provisional, always "on the way," always dependent upon other participants.[6] Because the implied author withholds immediate and explicit judgment on any of the ways of being Mennonite explored in each chapter, it is only the juxtaposition of chapters and the comparison of individual choices that make possible any evaluation of the versions of truth that individuals or specific communities insist upon. All the voices of faith, even those that question received tradition, must be heard.

And one of those voices is the voice of the implied author before he pretends to emerge as John Reimer. For while he does not explicitly evaluate the ways of being Mennonite that he depicts throughout the novel, he most certainly directs the process of discernment through the

---

4. See Ina Ferris, "Religious Vision and Fictional Form: Rudy Wiebe's *The Blue Mountains of China*," in *A Voice in the Land*, ed. W. J. Keith (Edmonton: NeWest Press, 1981), 88-96, for a critical discussion, and dismissal, of Reimer's credibility. Magdalene Redekop's "Translated into the Past: Language in *The Blue Mountains of China*," in *A Voice in the Land*, 97-123, is more aware of the dynamics of Mennonite community and hence gives a more useful reading of Reimer's role in the novel, but still notes Reimer's problematic character.

5. The complex structure of the novel and the frequent introduction of new characters, often with similar names, lead all readers to become temporary Russian Mennonites, experiencing similar dislocations from context to context and the resultant frantic search for anything familiar. In my dissertation, "To Write or To Belong: The Dilemma of Canadian Mennonite Story-Tellers," (Diss. U. of Saskatchewan, 1996), I examine in greater detail the reader's experience of loss of community and regaining of community in the novel.

6. It could be argued that such a process of discernment is also occurring among critics, especially in the ongoing argument about the importance of individualism in *Blue Mountains* and the role of John Reimer.

consequences he gives to specific actions, especially those that demonstrate the two kinds of nothingness in this novel. Those characters who choose to benefit only themselves rather than the community, who perpetually ask, "What is that to get ahead?" (252) eventually betray family members or discover that mere wealth finally "helps nothing" and gives no inner peace. Those characters who selflessly "forget about getting ahead, . . . about trying to be useful" (269), who recognize that Jesus "never gives you a thing to hold in your hand" (272), and who choose to obey the voice of God even though it calls them to do what will seemingly "help nothing," ultimately achieve an inner peace and make it possible for other Mennonites to do likewise.

None of these choices occurs in isolation. These sacrificial actions, clearly approved by the implied author, are either enabled by a community prepared to follow the teachings of Christ or thwarted by a community that has relegated those teachings to a Sunday recitation. Moreover, these crucial choices, in turn, help to determine the kind of community out of which others will make further choices. David Epp, for example, can leave his family in China and go back to Russia to certain death because he knows the community will take care of his family. That decision later influences his son to spend his life with the Ayerooas in South America. Samuel Reimer, in Canada a generation later, cannot obey God and go to Vietnam to preach peace because his community is too materialistically minded to care for his family. His children will live off the huge insurance policy he buys in his last days of cynical despair.

John Reimer, having given away his share of his brother's insurance, also demonstrates seemingly pointless selflessness, but not quite the way we might expect. Certainly carrying a wooden cross along the highway is "nothing to get ahead" as many Mennonites would define it. And his sermonizing is almost as ineffectual. Most readers are grateful when a policeman cuts his sermon short. What I find most compelling in Reimer, however, is that through him Wiebe himself makes a narrative choice that risks accomplishing nothing. Having allowed Reimer to become his prophet-spokesman who can make explicit an ideal Anabaptist community, Wiebe at the same time makes Reimer's authority suspect. The voluntarily chosen and thus always vulnerable and changing community of faith that Wiebe has been defining throughout the novel is ultimately not created or sustained through authoritative preaching, such as Reimer's, but through living. Hence, Reimer, unconvincing to begin with, is easily overshadowed by the unflinching honesty of Jakob Friesen IV, once a selfish kulak, now a man marked by suffering, who claims he "believes nothing." It is this man, not Reimer with all his answers, who most aptly concludes Wiebe's discussion of nothing with,

"It is nothing to drink alone when two are by the fire" (263). Having drunk to that truth, John Reimer and Jakob Friesen share the bread and continue to ask troubling questions. Reimer thus becomes simply one more voice in this textual *Beratung* (church meeting), this communal discernment of how to live out faith. Unfortunately, too many readers, more accustomed to focus on the individual, miss that dimension and see Reimer primarily as a "self-defined John the Anabaptist"[7] or "a willed figure who is unable to animate the imagination."[8]

The narrator in Jeff Gundy's *A Community of Memory* does not so efface himself or disguise himself as a fictional character in order to repudiate himself. But then *A Community of Memory* is not a novel, and the "characters" are not fictional characters but actual family members. Surrounded by photographs and diaries, church records and personal letters, and a cloud of witnesses who still remember the people he writes about, Gundy becomes the scribe for those "voices . . . that wanted to speak, that took on lives of their own," that were "reconciled to their dying but not to letting their stories die out."[9] He, the "teaching poet," the "relativistic modern-day academic" (xiv), as he describes himself, is now also the explorer and chronicler of his own family history.

Lest he be accused of pridefulness by his own people and of arrogant misuse of power by his fellow relativistic academics, Gundy presents himself as a very humble storyteller. His preface ends on a note of apology: "What is here is not complete, not satisfactory, not to be trusted, but it's what I, with the help of all these others living and dead, have been able to do" (xvi). He also knows quite well that he has the power "to twist and change and warp the words [he] writes about [George and Clara, his great-grandparents] any way [his] whims lead" (101). To negate that power, Gundy frequently reminds his readers of it, warning them not to take what he has written as absolute truth: "As much as possible [these stories] describe what 'really' happened, patched and filled and stretched where the details are lost or the narrative seemed to demand some invention" (xv). In the coda, he reiterates, "I haven't told it right, I haven't told 'the truth,' much less the whole truth. I've known too much or too little all along the way" (155). Humility here

---

7. Redekop, "Translated into the Past," 115.

8. Ferris, "Religious Vision and Fictional Form," 95.

9. Jeff Gundy, *A Community of Memory* (Urbana: U. of Illinois Press, 1996), xv.

means refusing to claim absolute veracity or to misuse the role of storyteller.

It also means a tentative stance toward the truth-claims embedded in the stories he tells. Unlike the implied author of *Blue Mountains of China* who refused to engage in explicit dialogue with characters, letting them state their version of truth with conviction, the implied author of *A Community of Memory* never ceases to engage in dialogue with the family voices he hears, and eventually with himself as he interrogates those voices. Some of his questions are speculations about his sources: "All this seems too romantic for the John Struhbar I know—but then how well do I know him?" (12). Some questions are directed to his sources: "Was it all really so fine or is that your code for a day when everything just went wrong, the pancakes were burned and the liver wasn't fresh?" (107). More questions are addressed simultaneously to the reader and to himself: "Should all this matter? What should it mean?" (48). The persistence of such questions addressed to those who cannot answer creates a subtle suspicion of all imagined replies, as if judgment itself can always be only partial and provisional. His very telling of these stories, Gundy insists, "is guilty and compromised in all the usual ways" (155).

Tentatively and humbly as this narrator begins, however, he gradually becomes ever more prominent in the text. The closer he gets to George and Clara, the ostensible focus of the chronological structure, the more frequently he enters the narratives, thus drawing attention to himself and to his acts of remembering and writing. These italicized sections—which frequently provide additional facts, name sources, and explain the wider political context—also describe the narrator's own emotions as he drives through ancestral lands or contrasts his relative prosperity and worldliness with the experiences of his pioneering forebears. Even as he acknowledges that their lives will "persist and echo down through the spiralling years . . . long after [he] is gone," he returns our attention to his own process of examining memories and weighing belief and unbelief (89).

In the final long chapter on George and Clara, his presence in the text eventually overshadows the stories he relates. Long before he confesses, "It's my story as much or more than anyone else's, no matter how much I might protest" (155), most readers will have already noticed that. Gundy the writer is the real center of this text, the one with whom sustained reader identification is possible. His initial humble uncertainty about telling these stories right has given place to a firm defense of his "community of memory" against the skepticism and individualism he encounters in the "more skeptical circles of contemporary theory" (137). While he concedes to Revell (and other postmodern critics he quotes) that communities "are capable of great viciousness," Gundy insists that "self-defensive individuality" is more likely to engender viciousness (137).

The community that Gundy, like some of Wiebe's characters, refuses to reject despite its potential narrowness, is not, however, the same kind of community that Wiebe depicts. This is a community that is given more than chosen. Along with the "material security of [his] youth," Gundy has inherited "the vision . . . of how people might actually live together in something approaching harmony" (120). In submitting willingly to "the accident of [his birth]," and in deciding to "[further] the life of the tribe" (156, 154), he becomes very like the subjects of his stories.

Though the first-person narrators of each chapter are clearly identified individuals whose position on the family tree is duly noted, their function as individuals is less important than their relationship with the church community, whether that be primarily the immediate family, or a larger group of Mennonites. Taken as a group, including even the recalcitrant Joseph Joder whose unorthodox views on salvation provoked repeated threats of excommunication, all these narrators speak with the same diffidence about the minimal importance of their small choices, the same quiet focus on the business at hand (whether putting in the crop or baptizing another group of young people), and the same grateful celebration of whatever simple pleasures come their way. They all live out a faithful obedience to God, according "to their lights." These people are all very like George Gundy, who "saw himself as part of a community, however minor and marginal and fallen it was, and knew that what he did mattered to others, if only a few" (138). All demonstrate degrees of *Gelassenheit*, the submission of the individual to the will of God and the church. What contributions they make to changes within the community are less emphasized than their contribution to continuity.

Although the stories include bitter quarrels in the church and inner conflicts over accepting the edicts of the church, the tone remains muted, with the certain knowledge that the church and community and family will continue in much the same form whether one brother or sister rebels or not. Dramatic as the changes in farming techniques and living standards actually are, they seem only cosmetic. The community remains as a given.

Herein lies a key difference between *A Community of Memory* and *Blue Mountains of China*. Through the complex narrative process, Wiebe invites his readers both to experience the painful dislocation of Russian Mennonites and to participate in their always problematic discussions of what it means to be a Mennonite in the community and in the world. And *Mennonite* carries at least the possibility of being something other than an ethnic identity. Though the briefly re-established ethnic connections do provide familial warmth, they also revive memories of betrayal and selfishness. It means nothing to speak Low German and discover relatives, if you have not also chosen to seek Jesus' kind of nothing, which means the denial of self for a larger vision of a dynamic, godly community. That kind of nothing may ask you to give up both family and Low German.

A Community of Memory, on the other hand, reaffirms memories and ethnic connections and makes those an integral part of the faith and the nature of the community. As Gundy notes, "I don't know . . . that what we believe is more than slightly a matter of choice. . . . [G]iven another set of ancestors I would certainly not be writing this particular book nor claiming this set of allegiances" (154). Such a "diffident" position on belief is consistent with the humble stance he has assumed throughout, but its effect is to create a distance between his non-Swiss Mennonite readers and the community he depicts. We can identify with the storyteller in his process of recovering and evaluating family memories, but our experience of his community of memories will be a limited one. Unlike the wider Christian community Wiebe seeks to define beyond ethnic parameters, Gundy's community depends on ethnicity and a shared history. If this community is not already the reader's community, it is easier to focus on the tales of pioneering struggle or to identify simply with the relativistic postmodern persona of the storyteller who, humble as he is, nevertheless foregrounds his individual search for meaningful community.

It is possible to argue, however, that Gundy the storyteller demonstrates the same ultimate subordination to the community that John Reimer does. Just as Reimer is reduced to another voice in a voluntarily chosen community of faith—at least in the minds of readers prepared to grapple with the perpetual dialogue between individual and community in the Russian Mennonite tradition—so Gundy, after playing devil's advocate with his questions, nevertheless acknowledges that his Swiss Mennonite community of memory has made him who he is. The difficulty in both texts is that unless you are already part of the communities they depict, you are all too likely to focus on the storyteller, the poseur, and miss his vital relationship to his community of faith, whether that community is chosen—as it is for Wiebe—or given—as it is for Gundy.

EMBODIED VOICES, IMPRISONED BODIES: WOMEN AND WORDS IN JANET KAUFFMAN'S *COLLABORATORS*

JESSICA W. LAPP*

Abstract. A continuing challenge for women writers and literary critics is to discover strong female characters who challenge past representations of women and explore the complexities of female experience. This is a particularly difficult task in literature by and about Mennonites, which in the past has rarely developed fully rounded female characters. This essay considers how Janet Kauffman's novel *Collaborators* (1986) develops powerful Mennonite women characters who model current feminist theories about women's emancipation through the appropriation of language. Though read by its reviewers as a novel about the separation of daughter from mother, Kauffman's novel ultimately recognizes how language, and stories in particular, enable us to build connections with others, breaking through traditional hierarchies to establish new communities based on collaboration rather than opposition.

"Words, infiltrators, transport a human weaponry—machetes, bombs, cyanide, firecrackers bound to go off—it is like that."

—Janet Kauffman in *Collaborators*

In a 1985 essay on the Mennonite woman in Russian Mennonite literature Katie Funk Wiebe notes that women characters tend to serve as a "'profound presence', rather than as articulate thinking persons." Thus they may "appear intellectually dull, spiritually unawakened, devoid of the joy of creative expression and thought."[1] Had Wiebe been able to expand her study and include a novel published the following year, Janet Kauffman's *Collaborators*,[2] she would have found an antidote to these earlier portrayals of female characters. Kauffman's novel develops energetic and creative Mennonite women characters who recognize the explosive potential of language and desire to use language—even wield it as a tool or a weapon—to escape the prisons they occupy voluntarily and involuntarily. In *Collaborators* the central female characters creatively

---

*Jessica W. Lapp teaches part-time in the English Department at Central Michigan University and is completing her dissertation in American literature through the English Department at the University of Notre Dame.

1. Katie Funk Wiebe, "The Mennonite Woman in Mennonite Fiction" in *Visions and Realities: Essays, Poems and Fiction Dealing with Mennonite Issues*, ed. Harry Loewen and Al Reimer (Winnipeg: Hyperion, 1985), 232, 235.

2. Janet Kauffman, *Collaborators* (Saint Paul, MN: Graywolf Press, 1986).

appropriate language in order to free themselves from the constricted definitions of a patriarchal culture and to create themselves anew, not as isolated oppositional figures but as collaborators within a community including both women and men.

Kauffman's novel fits within a developing field of women's writing, especially in the model provided by French philosopher and dramatist Hélène Cixous of a literature which refutes the traditional values imposed by society on women and on men. Part of the post-structuralist critique of Western philosophical systems, Cixous' writing emphasizes the damage done by the binary oppositions through which one aspect of society is valued while its "opposite" is devalued. In "Sorties" she lists these, one after another: man/woman, mind/body, culture/nature, etc.[3] These oppositions historically have limited women; biology was destiny and women were relegated to the "profound presences" of reproductive bodies without spirit, without mind. In "The Laugh of the Medusa" Cixous calls for women to write, for she identifies writing as a means of joining these oppositions, of uniting mind and body intrinsically in the physical/intellectual/emotional act of putting pen to paper (or fingers to keyboards). Historically, language has been appropriated by males for their own interests, and through language they have "demarcated" women; now women must claim that language back in order to "regain" themselves. Cixous challenges women to "write through their bodies" in order to break through all that divides them from themselves and from each other. "Let's get away from the dialectic," she notes, suggesting that only by refusing to join in an oppositional value system—one based on either patriarchal or matriarchal claims—can one create a just and equitable society.[4] She replaces the either/or of male versus female, of mind versus body, with the both/and of male and female, mind and body. What Cixous calls for, in fact, is collaboration. And Kauffman's novel represents one way to produce this new kind of writing.

Kauffman sets her novel on a tobacco farm in Lancaster County, Pennsylvania during the 1960s. Divided into four sections, the novel opens with a short chapter identifying the initial adversarial nature of the relationship between Andrea Doria, the narrator, and her mother, for Andrea notes: "My mother lied to me about everything" (3). Then we meet her mother, a titan in a red swimsuit who masters the waves, tobacco farming, other men and her own daughter. Through recounting her memories, Andrea's mother teaches Andrea about the life of a woman—of menstruation, the threat of rape, of physical love, and about

3. Hélène Cixous, "Sorties," in *The Hélène Cixous Reader*, ed. Susan Sellers (New York: Routledge, 1994), 35-46.

4. Hélène Cixous, "The Laugh of the Medusa" in *Critical Theory Since 1965*, ed. Hazard Adams and Leroy Searle (Tallahassee: Florida State U. Press, 1986), 312-18.

her quarrel with God — the unbridgeable gap between human and divine compassion and emotion which prevents her mother from wholeheartedly joining the Mennonite community. When Andrea is twelve her mother has a stroke and their relationship changes dramatically, for now Andrea must become the dominant figure, helping to run the household and teaching her mother to talk and walk again. Overwhelmed by her mother's outrageous personality through her first twelve years, Andrea now is overwhelmed by the absence of outrage and creates her own toward the stranger who is and is not her mother, who is frail and forgetful and conventional. Her mother's friend Ruth, a scholar of French literature, emerges to serve both as a link to keep Andrea bound to her mother, despite the dramatic change in her personality, and as a new tutor for Andrea in the art of growing up as a woman.

Through the two main characters, Andrea Doria and her mother, and the character of Ruth, who enters later in the novel, Kauffman focuses on language as the most significant tool in developing the self, especially the female self. Though many reviewers have read the novel as the story of the slow and painful separation of mother and daughter, the merged selves that must separate as the younger woman grows to maturity,[5] the action of the novel ultimately represents a coming together of mother and daughter. The structure of the novel suggests that Andrea writes from the position of an adult looking back onto her childhood, attempting to understand her mother and herself through the process of writing down their lives. She is able to again embody the voice she remembers in the physical shape of her mother, joining memory with substance through her story. The final section emphasizes this bonding, or collaboration, across generations as Andrea herself becomes the teacher, describing her mother to her own daughter.[6]

Andrea's knowledge of herself and her ability to write have their grounding in her mother's instruction and in the context of the Mennonite tobacco farm. Within a community governed by the Word — of God, of the bishop, of the husband and father — women's deepest

---

5. A number of reviewers identify this separation as the primary theme. In her review, "Daughters Eye View," in *The New Republic* (April 21, 1986), 34-35, Anne Tyler notes this separation as "something inevitable . . . and therefore all the more moving" (35). Ursula Hegi, in *The New York Times Book Review* (April 20, 1986), 17, describes the merging and separating process in almost Freudian terms, with the daughter shifting focus from the mother to the father. Mark Harris, Kauffman's biographer in *Dictionary of Literary Biography Yearbook* (Detroit: Gale Research, 1986), 306-311, describes the novel as a "lyric meditation on intergenerational conflict," in which the daughter "becomes the prototype of all daughters, anxiously scrutinizing their mothers for clues about how to be women" (311).

6. Because Kauffman never names her, Andrea's mother can be read as a kind of "everywoman," or perhaps a model for every woman.

desire, represented by Andrea Doria's mother, is not sexual, as one might infer from the mother's descriptions of her own satisfying love of other men, but oral, in her desire to gain power over language so that she can wield words on her own behalf, to tell her own story of her own experiences, regardless of the rules. Though she is not writing for a public forum, she uses language creatively in the one forum to which she does have access—the home. Al Reimer has noted in his work with Mennonite literature that:

> the real storytellers in Mennonite families were often the mothers, secret readers who nurtured the creative spirit in their children [by reading aloud] and were frequently the custodians of the oral tradition within the family no matter how voiceless they were outside of it.[7]

In Kauffman's novel, Andrea's mother and Ruth are the readers, writers and sayers who will teach Andrea how to read, write and speak the words that will create possibilities for her future. The male presence—of her father and brother—is almost absent in the first half of the novel.

Andrea's collaborations with her mother begin early in her life, before Andrea can think of herself as an independent being with a will of her own. She calls herself "simply a toy, with no power of my own." Andrea initially is as frightened by the power of her mother's words as she is entranced by the power of her mother's body as it slides through the ocean waves. The intimacy here almost overwhelms Andrea, but her mother soon begins to teach her the ways in which Andrea can claim power over herself—through learning to control her body in swimming lessons and controlling her mind and imagination through language. As with swimming, Andrea notes, "We'll practice when nobody's looking" (11). Before Andrea can learn the power of speech, however, she must learn the power of silence. Her mother assures Andrea that she does not have to speak; she does not have to answer the altar call during a revival. Even this act, which seems to be passive, demands incredible strength. Andrea describes her mother modeling this act of silence: "She brings her teeth together and closes her lips in a line, she is that powerful." Before Andrea can learn the power of speech, she must also learn that "you don't have to say a thing" to be powerful (13). It is the control of language—the choice to speak or not to speak—which enables self-determination.

Andrea is her mother's initiate at home, and as Andrea enters school she becomes her mother's "apprentice" and "accomplice" (41). Through a number of lessons, Andrea learns the power of language. She must

---

7. Al Reimer, *Mennonite Literary Voices: Past and Present* (Newton, KS: Bethel College, 1993), 39.

avoid the trap of yielding her responsibility for herself — of laying aside her own will and accepting the will of men or God or even her mother. After telling Andrea the story of her own near-rape, her mother tells her: "Dovie, you're a woman now, it's the truth. That boy has nothing to do with it. God has nothing to do with it" (33). Andrea must rely on herself, on her own understanding of self, and avoid accepting the role of victim. Language has everything to do with this self-reliance. She learns her next lessons in speaking and writing in the tobacco shed. In the tobacco dust, her mother writes words for Andrea to memorize, then erase. Though these words become a part of her vocabulary, Andrea continues to ask herself, "Which words can I claim?" (36). She begins to recognize the necessity of her own appropriation of language, beyond her mother's teaching. Beneath the sizing table are boxes storing more words — the letters her mother saves from her friend Ruth, who cut her hair and left the Mennonite community after she graduated from high school. Here is the physical, material communication between women, to be cherished and saved for future reference. Spoken words are equally important. Andrea's mother speaks in imperatives, emphasizing the significance of language as power — the power of remembering, of writing, of acting, of remaining silent. Language in its many forms is power, though Andrea is not yet able to wield it.

Because language is a powerful medium, "transport[ing] a human weaponry," words must be used with care (13). Andrea learns that those who control language do not always use it truthfully. Her mother insists on the truth, painful though it may be. Words can also be misused and can convey falsehoods, as Andrea finds out from her mother's description of Lars Skyrzinski, a sociologist who visits the farm for three weeks, then writes authoritatively if incorrectly about farming tobacco. With scorn, her mother reads the romanticized description of their lives, far from the truth of their experience (23-24). Later, after her mother's stroke, Andrea learns again of the equivocating nature of language, for she reports, "The word was, [Mother] is recovered," when Andrea knows full well that the woman inhabiting her mother's skin is smaller, less spectacular than the mother she remembers (91).

Slowly Andrea learns to challenge, to participate, to collaborate with her mother and with the widening community around her. Her mother claims that although bats get into the house even when "there's never a way to get in," she promises that no bats will get into Andrea's bedroom. Andrea is triumphant in her challenge of this paradox: "You said there's never a way in . . . but they get in," she points out (25-26). Her triumph of language play draws her closer to, rather than pushing her away from, her mother. Andrea's developing linguistic power is also noted by Ruth. During a visit to Ruth's home, Ruth welcomes Andrea into an adult female relationship, telling Andrea that there are to be no secrets between the three women, that Andrea should hear her mother's letters to Ruth, and Ruth's responses (50). This communication among women provides a model for both independence and dependence for Andrea — independence of thought and action, dependence on the support and encouragement of other women.[8]

This developing friendship with Ruth soon serves a more crucial role for Andrea. Just as Andrea is poised to enter womanhood, her mother's stroke forces Andrea immediately into the premature role of mother and teacher, taking on the responsibility to keep the words alive and flowing even as her mother lies unconscious, mumbling (65). Now Andrea must care for her as if she were a baby, wheeling her around the house, encouraging her attempts at speech. As her mother slowly recovers, Andrea realizes that the damage to her mother's outward personality is permanent. Her mother has lost her brilliant skills with words. The titan of language suddenly attaches very little significance to words. She avoids the word-play, the secret game she previously shared with Andrea. She throws away the carefully saved and cherished letters from Ruth, living solely in the present instead of savoring the past, the written record of her own and others' lives. Yet Andrea refuses to see this alteration as permanent. Somewhere inside, her mother's real self is buried. Andrea envisions her mother's mind, hoarding the words "in the rooms behind her eyes"(76). That woman must still exist for Andrea's own growth to continue.

With the loss of this verbal connection to her mother, Andrea Doria does appear to be sinking, like the ship after which she is named. She quarrels with Marlene, a family friend who encourages Andrea to "face facts" and accept that her mother is changed and the cord between them broken (73). She develops a sour disposition, according to her mother. Only through the letters Andrea types from her mother to Ruth, and reads aloud from Ruth to her mother, is Andrea able to reestablish a connection to Ruth and through Ruth to her mother.

Through a series of postscripts to these letters Ruth introduces Andrea to the medieval writer Marie de France, yet another model from whom Andrea can learn how to refute the oppositional structures that traditionally have constricted and demarcated women's words and lives. Not only does Marie de France represent a situation similar to Andrea's mother before her stroke, and to Andrea herself — a woman claiming authority through her words in a predominantly patriarchal society — but

8. Ruth's name reminds us of the biblical Ruth as well, with her petition to remain with Naomi and form a family based on female relationships (Ruth 1:16-18). Though Kauffman's Ruth remains physically at a distance, she offers a similar kind of love and support for Andrea.

the *lais*, or songs, Marie de France transcribes offer Andrea further models for resistance to expected behavior or, alternately, for claiming authority through language or other sign systems. Ruth describes the prologue to the *lais*, in particular, as a legal argument necessitating women's appropriation of language and as a justification for women's speech and writing. She tells Andrea to read the prologue to her mother as well, even if she isn't listening, as if Ruth also believes that somewhere behind the eyes a different woman lurks and listens and might be provoked into a response. For that woman, Andrea reads from Marie de France's prologue:

> Those whom God has given knowledge and full eloquence of speech, they must not be silent and secretive, but instead they must willingly reveal themselves. When something of goodness is heard by several, then it blossoms; and when it is praised, even by a few, then it opens its flowers (113).

In this written record from the past, the voice of the storyteller defends the right to write. This voice is embodied in the passive image of the flower, yet demands an active vocality as well, refusing the inanimate silence of the object. Marie de France justifies her own writing even as she offers all writers — female and male — a vindication for their appropriation of language. Marie de France, like Cixous, ultimately insists on an expansive wholeness of experience rather than a divisive hierarchy, and refuses the limitations of categories or binary oppositions. She appropriates authority for herself in a field dominated by men and argues for participation by a broader variety of writers, basing this authority on the need to tell a story rather than on gender. Thus she offers a model for Andrea that enables her to both challenge the societal restrictions on her own future and develop a new, more inclusive approach to language and life.

The references to the *lais* in *Collaborators* emphasize the way in which writing offers women in particular a method of combining immanence (words and meaning) with the bodily (concrete and material).[9] Marie de France uses instances of creative expression again and again in her stories to illustrate how necessary it is for women to refuse the passive role of "profound presences" by recording their personal experiences, by articulating their own stories, and through these, in certain extreme cases, to save their own lives or the lives of those dear to them. In her reading of the *lais*, literary historian Diana Faust emphasizes that the female characters often are involved in some kind of artistic creation —

---

9. Amy Holland, in her essay, "On the Materiality of Air: Janet Kauffman's Bodyfictions," in *New Literary History* 27 (1996), 503-25, suggests that Kauffman's later novel *The Body in Four Parts* continues this exploration of how language is material yet "enables limited transcendence of the constraints of bodily existence" (504).

writing, embroidery, painting a mural—which describes their experiences and enables them to communicate in a variety of sign systems.[10] Indeed, their work often communicates to other characters the truth of their lives, which has been silenced or usurped by the men around them. Though the truth does not always set these women free, it does provide solace during their captivity. The works themselves then represent a merging of the physical, material experience of the bodies of the women characters, imprisoned yet resistant through their artistic creations, with the more transcendental nature of language and meaning. These creative works are of special significance as acts of communication, despite the imprisonment of the physical body, through the collaboration that develops between the creator and her audience in order to share the story so that her audience—other characters and readers alike—understand and participate in the experiences which led to that creation. Only through these creative expressions can women begin to take control of their own "selves," telling the truth of their lives and deciding their own futures instead of passively allowing others to regulate their behavior. Through this model, Ruth realizes that for Andrea's mother—the mother Andrea remembers and cherishes—to be revived, Andrea herself must write her back into being. But Andrea must write both mothers—before and after the stroke—to embody the whole being, to tell the full story, and to incorporate her own self into that story since she also is a part of both mothers.

Marie de France's work models this embodying of the voice, which shows itself to be something more than the representation or justification of individual authorship, for it recognizes the collaboration that must exist among characters and between writer and reader. Faust suggests that Marie de France's work emphasizes the individual nature of the writer, who imbeds her name in the *lais* so that her own authority is clearly established.[11] Yet Marie's defense of her writing is also a recognition of the community for which she writes and the plurality of

---

10. In "Chaiteval" the heroine decides to write down the story of the four lovers who have fought for her and name it "The Four Loves," but the one lover left alive after the battle demands that she name the story after him. In "Milun" the heroine writes a letter and conceals it with her son in exile so that eventually he may discover the identity of his father. In "Guigemar" the heroine is imprisoned in a cave and paints a mural on the wall to entertain herself and record her story. —Diana M. Faust, "Women Narrators in the Lais of Marie de France," in *Women in French Literature*, ed. Michael Guggenheim (Saratoga, CA: Anma Libri, 1988), 17-27.

11. Faust notes that though Marie de France emphasizes the "I" in the prologue, she clearly recognizes the difficulties faced by women writers of her own time. Marie describes in the prologue that she writes at night, an act Faust reads as "furtive." Faust also suggests that Marie's own experience might be compared to that of the female protagonist in "Chaiteval," who had to submit her writing for male approval. —Diana Faust, "Women Narrators in the Lais of Marie de France," 18-21.

understandings which develops among writer and readers. The relationships developed through these collaborations — those she describes in her prologue and in the *lais* themselves — appear as significant as the artistic creations themselves. She does not write, then, to displace other voices but to challenge partial truths and fill in the gaps — or as Cixous will write centuries later, to "submerge, cut through, get beyond the ultimate reserve."[12] Here is a new model of authority, one which invites a plurality of participation. Thus the *lais* — and I suggest *Collaborators* as well — emphasize the need for women to "convert their experiences to a solid and durable form" and share that form with others in order to tell the whole story.[13] Only through these sign systems can they claim self-determination by clarifying for their intended audience the truth of their own experience and inviting others to participate in that experience. Here Marie de France's work seems most in line with the kind of writing pursued by Cixous and Kauffman; rather than posing a self which must be carved out completely independent of anyone else, all three writers suggest that the self is always, and productively, merging with others through language.

One final point must be understood in this reading of *Collaborators* in order to understand how Kauffman refuses to write a narrowly feminist novel in the *bildungsroman* tradition. In spite of Andrea's relationship to women in her emergence into language, her development as a woman is not predicated, as we might expect, and as is evident in the *lais*, on the explicit domination or oppression by male characters. Where, one might ask, are the juicy examples of repressive and dictatorial Mennonite males in this novel? There are none. Kauffman allows us as readers to fall into the trap of assuming the oppressiveness of the context — either in the conservative Mennonite community of Lancaster County in the 1960s or the male-dominated academic world which Ruth inhabits — without supplying us with proof of this assumption. Kauffman's novel, then, challenges this too-easy retreat back into a binary system of value by refusing to provide an oppositional masculine structure against which Andrea must find her voice. Kauffman moves beyond the theoretical possibilities offered by Cixous into creative application, forcing the reader to recognize her own traditional expectations and read beyond them. Rather than dominating or oppressing Andrea, Andrea's father is a quiet yet positive figure in her development. Indeed, for an assignment Andrea must complete for class, she chooses to write an essay about her father, so the novel actually includes Andrea's attempts to write both mother and father, feminine and masculine, rather than choosing one

---

12. Cixous, "The Laugh of the Medusa," 315
13. Faust, "Women Narrators in the Lais of Marie de France," 27.

over the other. Like Cixous, Kauffman refuses to simply reverse the hierarchies. Women must gain their voices but not simply to displace or replace men.[14]

Language ultimately becomes the "durable form" for collaboration in Kauffman's novel, between mother and daughter, and father and daughter, joining together what history has fragmented. Though Andrea's introduction to language suggests that it can be wielded as a weapon in order to gain power, Andrea recognizes that words, like machetes, can be used more productively as tools to build rather than as weapons to destroy.[15] Andrea's final words as narrator identify this use of language, of story, as the key component in a new kind of writing that builds on and interacts with the past rather than dominating it. She asks: "Who are the ones I could approach and ask, Did you ever know? Have you forgotten?" — questions to which there can be no answer unless she can provide the story, the words to record her father and revive her mother in the text (133). In telling this story, Andrea opens herself to the past and what has been forgotten or ignored. Andrea will refuse to be entrapped in the prisonhouse of binary value. Instead she will set free the woman imprisoned in the dying body of her mother by telling her story — her mother's, her own. By honoring this mother with words of truth and by telling Andrea Doria's story, Janet Kauffman proves that a Mennonite woman, as well as a Mennonite man, can be both a "profound presence" and a thinking, articulate being.

---

14. Janet Kauffman is currently working on a novel that continues Andrea Doria's story, exploring her relationship with her father after her mother's death.

15. It is telling that after Andrea's mother has the stroke and loses her power over language, she develops an almost obsessive interest in shooting the groundhogs that burrow on the farm. Andrea's last view of her mother follows her, gun in hand, as she wanders across the field. This image requires more thought on my part but certainly raises questions about the relationship of words and weapons. — Kauffman, *Collaborators*, 127-29.

COMMUNITY, THEOLOGY AND MENNONITE POETICS IN THE WORK OF JEFF GUNDY

DAVID WRIGHT*

Abstract: To pay closer attention to Jeff Gundy's poems in *Inquiries* and *Flatlands* as they speak in dialogue with his recent nonfiction work, *A Community of Memory*, is to encounter a distinctively Mennonite poetics of community and a compelling response to the literary and cultural landscapes of postmodernity. Gundy's prose work provides a necessary filter through which to view his poetry and its rich and challenging rendering of community and history, his implicit and explicit theological questioning, his sense of place, and his resulting poetics. Gundy's work offers a necessary refraction of Mennonite identity through the particularly important lens of storytelling and poetry, a provocative and humble vision facing an unpredictable response from both the church and the broader culture.

"Every telling of that story is a covenant with the past. . . . All remembering is equally a forgetting. Which is a reminder that we Christians can take the risk of remembering, and forgetting, that task we currently call history, because we know that God rightly remembers all those who constitute the communion of the saints."

> —Stanley Hauerwas from "Whose Church? Which Future? Whither the Anabaptist Vision?"

At the end of his comprehensive discussion of Mennonite poets in the United States, Jeff Gundy exhorts Mennonites to pay closer attention to their poetry-writing sisters and brothers. "I believe we will benefit from listening to our poets," Gundy writes. "I doubt that they will save us, but I believe they can make us a little less lost."[1] Such listening is precisely what this essay attempts to do with Gundy's own work: to consider Gundy's poems in *Inquiries* and *Flatlands* as they speak in dialogue with his recent nonfiction work, *A Community of Memory: My Days with George and Clara*. This dialogue between Gundy's prose and poetry produces a

---

*David Wright is Assistant Professor of English at Richland Community College in Decatur, Illinois. Since he completed this essay, he and his wife have joined First Mennonite Church in Urbana, Illinois.

1. Jeff Gundy, "U. S. Mennonite Poetry and Poets: Beyond Johnson's Dog," *MQR* 71 (Jan. 1997), 39.

distinctively Mennonite poetics of community and a compelling response to the literary and cultural landscapes of postmodernity.

However, let me quickly apologize, in the philosophical sense, for my position as listener. I am an eavesdropper. I stand just inside the fringes of Mennonite life and traditions, listening surreptitiously and sometimes wistfully to Mennonite talk of community, to the ongoing Anabaptist theological tradition and, in this particular case, to a particularly important Mennonite poet. From my position as overhearer, I will likely get wrong some or much of Gundy's writing and its import for Mennonites. I invite correction. I do not want to be like the tourists I heard about in Central Illinois Amish country who were convinced, from a safe distance, that those folks in black hats and coats and simple dresses were really Orthodox Jews. "We didn't know you had 'em like that out here," they said.

An eavesdropper's stance should invite a large measure of humility, one of the literary and critical virtues Gundy embodies and extols in so much of his writing. At the very end of *A Community of Memory* he writes about his own tenuous grasp on the truth, on the failures and risks of interpreting the world's text:

> And yet what do I know. Every fall in the pollen season my wife's bodily defenses go to red-alert and flood her system with histamines and misery while I blunder mildly onward, breathing easily. I am reminded each time of how little my senses really deliver of what goes on. I am reminded to beware of claiming too much certainty of whatever kind; there's more going on than I can explain or understand. We may be surprised, overtaken, drowned, raptured — tomorrow or today.[2]

Barring such apocalyptic interruptions and yet hoping for surprises, I will read through three key concerns that emerge in Gundy's work: his rendering of community and history, his implicit and explicit theological questioning and his resulting poetics.

COMMUNITY—"THE RISK OF REMEMBERING"

To those Christians (and non-Christians) who listen and watch from outside Mennonite circles, no ongoing reality appears more attractive (and, for some, more frightening) than Mennonites' understanding and practice of community. And as theoretical and political paradigms shift toward a broader cultural embrace of the idea of community, those traditions consciously struggling with such practices become sources of

---

2. Jeff Gundy, *A Community of Memory: My Days With George and Clara* (Urbana: U. of Illinois Press, 1995), 154.

envy and curiosity to other traditions attempting to correct and redirect the individualistic excesses of our churches and culture. Neo-Anabaptist theologies, analyses of discourse and interpretive communities, and communitarian movements abound. One well known Methodist theologian and ethicist actually calls himself "high-church Mennonite" as a way of describing his attempt to suggest "an image of the sort of church I thought not only should exist, but must exist for faithful witness to the Gospel."[3]

Similarly, literary and political theories gravitate more and more toward theories of activism and interpretation grounded in something(s) called communities. For some twenty years literary scholar Stanley Fish has been arguing that to interpret texts, and lives, we must conceive of persons "not as free agents, but as extensions of interpretive communities, communities whose warranting assumptions delimit what can be seen and therefore what can be described."[4] A range of communitarian political and environmental coalitions also ground themselves in a similar recognition of the necessity of social ties and limits. The most prominent of these groups, The Communitarian Network, articulates its vision and mission in terms of shoring up the nation's:

> moral, social, and political environment. We are a nonsectarian, nonpartisan, international association. We believe that individual liberties depend upon the bolstering of the foundations of civil society: our families, schools, and neighborhoods. It is through these institutions that we acquire a sense of our personal and civic responsibilities, an appreciation of our rights and the rights of others, and a commitment to the welfare of the community and its members[5]

For all their insight and noble intentions, Hauerwas, Fish and The Communitarian Network run the risk of forgetting that when speaking of communities we are not talking of abstractions or institutions or stances alone. We cannot simply invent a "high-church Mennonite" or an interpretive community. We inherit such worlds—sectarian, partisan

---

3. Stanley Hauerwas, "Whose Church? Which Future? Whither the Anabaptist Vision?" in *In Good Company: The Church as Polis* (Notre Dame: U. of Notre Dame Press, 1995), 66.

4. Stanley Fish, *Doing What Comes Naturally* (Durham: Duke U. Press, 1989), 152.

5. "The Communitarian Network," The Communitarian Network Homepage <http//www.gwu.edu/~ccps/> 22 October 1997.

and local — and we necessarily experience them in particular collections of people (others and ourselves) situated in particular places with distinct histories, stories, rituals, languages and geographies that shape us and involve us in their shaping. For such remembering, we need more than theorists or theologians. We need storytellers and poets as well.[6]

Paul Ricoeur describes the importance of creativity and poetics for understanding the myriad ways in which traditions and communities work, particularly theological and religious traditions. Such traditions are vibrant not as the "inert transmission of some already dead deposit of material but as the living transmission of an innovation always capable of being reactivated by a return to the most creative moments of poetic activity."[7] While theology, theory and sociology certainly map the terrain of this transmission and innovation, in the creative acts of storytelling and in the making and reading of poems we discover an additional and perhaps more uncomfortable (and therefore all the more necessary) aspect of community. We experience the risk and reward of speaking and hearing the truths of our own and our community's certainties and uncertainties in a context where those truths can be taken more seriously than anywhere else.

In other words, the complex and humble construction and reading of a story or poem occasions not only intellectual debate or reverential worship, but also invites us into perpetual self and communal examination through the imaginative identification with another person or community through language. The charged nature of poetic language pulls willing readers out of either unreflexive communal conformity or self-centered preoccupation and directs them into the fluid and necessary practice of interpretation. Unlike other forms of discourse, poetry, according to Gundy, is an intensified "artefact in language" designed to "sneak up on us." A poem contains within it layers of ambiguity that confront our intuitive understandings of a community's language or of our own boundaries by demanding interpretation. In Gundy's case, this confrontation results as much from a poem's stance as from its explicit message. As Gundy puts it, in a poem "it's critical not to

---

6. For a variety of perspectives on this claim see *Refocusing a Vision*, ed. John D. Roth (Goshen, IN: Mennonite Historical Society, 1995) where Stephen Dintaman, reflecting on Harold Bender's "Anabaptist Vision," claims that "perishing communities (and ideas) produce historians and sociologists and academic conferences. Flourishing communities produce preachers, missionaries, and prayer meetings. Right now the Anabaptist Vision is producing lots of the former, few of the latter" (50). One might ask, then, what sorts of communities, outside of these two extremes, produce poets, novelists and playwrights?

7. Paul Ricouer, *Time and Narrative*, Vol. 1 (Chicago: U. of Chicago Press, 1984), 68.

act superior to whatever I'm attempting to criticize, because I'm implicated in all the evil in the world I'd like to change. Where and how you position yourself makes an enormous difference. You need to go about the task with a certain restraint."[8]

In *A Community of Memory* Gundy recognizes in his accessible and restrained way many of the disuniting and disconcerting forces that have encouraged Americans to "find themselves," often at the expense of a strong and complex sense of community. The problem is not that we do not have any kind of community. We have all inevitably become, as Gundy writes, "connected over the years to an increasingly complex set of people we rely on, trust, and consider at least worthy of being saved. They may be family, lovers, children, friends, colleagues, fellow poets, plumbers, auto mechanics; we may feel we have too few, or too many, or the wrong ones, but no one I know lacks such a personal community."[9]

These communities of chance and choice, however, are too often displaced and fluid, too limited in a sense of their own history to counteract the homogenizing and atomizing forces of our culture and our nature. What Gundy recognizes in his nonfiction and in his poetry is that a specific, almost primary, community with its particularities and weaknesses as it interacts with the other contexts and practices of our lives, is what sustains and limits most of us, for good and ill. Thus he sets off to re-enter, through the voices of his ancestors and his conscious engagement with them, the intricate web of ethnicity, geography, faith and history that reveals the power and ambiguity of a genuine community, in all of its fallen necessity. He takes what Hauerwas calls "the risk of remembering and forgetting"[10] in order to remake what he believes most of us have lost: "a community of memory, one that extends backwards in time, reminding them of where they came from, who their people have been, how they have struggled and blundered, suffered and persevered."[11]

---

8. Gundy, "'Some Laughter, Some Work to Do': A Conversation about Poetry with Jeff Gundy," in *Trading Places: Images of Work and Home*, ed. Robert Grindy (Decatur, IL: Richland Community College, 1998), 27-33. For an extended discussion of the Mennonite writer's unique role as member of the community and creator of humble textual practices see Gundy's "Humility in Mennonite Literature," *MQR* 63 (Jan. 1989), 5-29.

9. Gundy, *Community of Memory*, 152-53.

10. Hauerwas, "Whose Church? Which Future?" 77.

11. Gundy, *Community of Memory*, 153.

The richness of the voices presented in *A Community of Memory* is overwhelming in its detail— John Strubahr's loss of homeland and discovery of Illinois as Eden; the endless trip on board a dirty, stinking ship to a muddy, swampy Ohio and Illinois that causes Marie Strubahr to say at her most positive, "For a little while it almost felt like a place where a person could live"; the loss of both mother and baby brother bringing Barbara Gundy to wish to die herself because "at least we could lie down and rest then and forget the bugs and the fevers and the smoke, and the work, work, work";[12] the theological ruminations of Joseph Joder, heretic and poet; the utter transformation of the prairie in Peter Nafziger's forty-nine years in Illinois; the farming of Jacob Gundy and the incongruity of a saint named Valentine Strubahr ("For me," writes Gundy, "it calls up only cheap cards bought by the pack"). Gundy bodies forth, with great claims to imperfection, the lives of women and men "silent and vanished now, but each of them [with] ten or seventy or ninety years of days and months and seasons, meals and work and loving and grieving and trips to the outhouse or the bathroom—myriad lifetimes of inner monologues whose contents remain only in the mind of God."[13]

The most resonant of these voices are, of course, George and Clara, Gundy's great-grandparents. They live and struggle within the demands of their particular community and make clear that, while not ideal or perfect, such community is invaluable and inescapable. As George and Clara struggle with the stubbornness and pride of their own congregation, it is their sense of community as a given ground of reality that they must continually re-embrace as gift, that provides them with reason to stay put, to talk themselves out of "just getting on the train with a suitcase and whatever money we could scrape together, heading off to see the world. For a moment I really thought we'd do it, get out from under everything and never have to worry again."[14]

George remained and completed his work, grudgingly and purposefully, because he saw himself as "part of a community, however minor and marginal and fallen it was, and knew that what he did mattered to others, if only a few. And finally he found his confidence, or something like it and went on with the work." This struggle to complete

12. Ibid., 22, 33-34.
13. Ibid., xvi.
14. Ibid., 136.

the work because of its mattering to others seems almost anachronistic to some of us, yet George's and Clara's "deep sense of themselves as part of a historical process, part of a group with both a past and a future, gives their work weight and substance."[15] Their identities, while strong and defined, are inextricably intermingled with others' lives and made from the concrete particulars of their daily history. "I never thought much about history," says Clara, "not the way you keep brooding over it certainly. But if you want to know, I think now that it's what is in the diary, the work we did and the people we knew, the illnesses and deaths and births."[16]

The dailyness of history as memory, conveyed in the context of a given yet chosen community, echoes strangely for those of us in a postmodern age. We each exist in multiple communities at one time; it is difficult for us even — and perhaps especially in the church — to sustain a sense of ongoing identity. As a result we affiliate ourselves with any number of groups and causes. Theologian John Cobb describes the situation: "The breakdown of traditional communities has made self-identification in non-geographical ways increasingly important. Multiple types of self-identification play major roles in different aspects of an individual's life."[17]

We are made, at least in part, of complex layers that feel, in Cobb's words, "non-geographical" and that multiply daily. One temptation is to choose a less fluid and seemingly more solid definition of the past than Gundy layers into his prose account of his own family. Yet as more and more Mennonites use the tools of theology and sociology to attempt to find a definitive group identity, one sociologist notes that "efforts to override Mennonite diversity in search of a singular, unifying definition have generated a plethora of competing interpretations of Mennonite peoplehood."[18]

---

15. Ibid., 138.

16. Ibid., 104.

17. John B. Cobb, "Defining Normative Community," in *Rooted in the Land: Essays on Community and Place,* ed. William Vitek and Wes Jackson (New Haven: Yale U. Press, 1996), 188.

18. Daphne Naomi Winland, "The Quest for Mennonite Peoplehood: Ethno-Religious Identity and the Dilemma of Definitions," *Canadian Review of Sociology and Anthropology* 30 (Feb. 1993), 110.

As we sort through this plethora of identities in light of history's competing interpretations, *A Community of Memory* reminds us that such interpretations take place in the slant light of daily work and wear. For Gundy, humans are constructed not of an abstracted, objective, unifying sociological theory, but of an accumulated set of peculiar histories, of thought and speech and memory:

> those things that flit through us while we are at rest or trying to sleep or about some ordinary business. The true substance of the world is in those images, feelings, words that come back to us, memories that simply arise and linger. . . . As real as any other piece of this terrible, humdrum, miraculous world.[19]

This imaginative, concrete patchwork of community forms a necessary filter for reading Gundy's poetry and discerning from him a distinctive Mennonite poetics.

QUESTIONING THEOLOGY: FINDING GOD IN PLACE

Gundy claims that except for one poem, "How to Write the New Mennonite Poem," "everything I have written on explicitly Mennonite subjects has been in prose."[20] He may indeed be right, but that leaves an enormous range of implicit theological, and very Mennonite, questioning lurking in his poetry. Like the psalms, Gundy's first volume *Inquiries* engages in the honorable theological work of questioning God, God's world and the place of human beings in "the landscapes of plenty and need, / the vehicles of good intentions, / the hurt to be done just moving / through our delicate terrains."[21]

Gundy's work poses both implicit and explicit theological inquiries on subjects ranging from the possible loves and dreams of chainsaws to the technology of hell: "barely medieval, / let alone postmodern."[22] The poems reverberate, like the rented jackhammer in one of the inquiries, with the same sorts of recollections and uncertainties that populate *A Community of Memory*. The questioning of God is the believer's and unbeliever's most powerful and legitimate tool, digging into and tearing up cracked foundations and inconsistencies. As Gundy puts it:

---

19. Gundy, *Community of Memory*, 155-56.
20. Gundy, "U.S. Mennonite Poetry and Poets," 29.
21. Gundy, *Inquiries* (Huron, OH.: Bottom Dog Press, 1992), 19.
22. Ibid., 15.

152

> And here in the basement
> with the rented electric jackhammer between
> my legs things are definitely happening,
> I have as big and nasty a weapon
> as any irritable pacifist could want.[23]

The "irritable pacifist" does not want to overlook any of the elements that make up a midwestern Mennonite poet's world; he looks closely at all of the details and finds them wanting. And as he pokes through such details, it helps to be reminded of Gundy's conversation with a poet friend who says, "I don't believe in God. I believe in details." Both this notion and its inverse strike Gundy as "equally pernicious" and "radically poverty-stricken" ways of being in the world.[24] Mapping the ambiguous terrain between these two views is the work of his poems.

In one particularly theological poem, "Inquiry on the Proposition that All Things Work Together for the Glory of the Father," Gundy tells the tragic story of a former teacher's work and his many losses. Eventually, the poem's speaker listens to a tape of an old class session. He hears the teacher sing from the tape, "his voice rising over all the rest / like honey, / like the wine / of flowers gathered and pressed / out of pain and time and beauty / that we all might drink somehow, / that we all might live some way / in the grace of things unseen / in the peace we cannot understand."[25] In this reel-to-reel memory, the poem reminds us of the ways in which the details, the particulars of faith and history are pressed and transformed by moments of transcendence which emerge seemingly from nowhere. All things work together, sometimes.

But at other times all things, all the details, resist the comforts of grace, as happens when Gundy brings the larger world's questions to bear on the comforts and easy platitudes of a midwesterner's domestic realm. In one poem a preacher encourages the flock to consciously "refuse notions not conducive / to the mental health and Christian / prosperity of the suburbs" by choosing two worries, daily, to ignore. Instead, Gundy writes ironically and bitingly of the speaker's perverse and inverse need to be:

> profligate I am choosing
> only two things a day to worry.

---

23. Ibid., 53.
24. Gundy, *Community of Memory*, 153.
25. Gundy, *Inquiries*, 52.

Today I forgot the drought,
acid rain, forest decline, the ozone hole,
nuclear proliferation and the escalating
deadliness of all our means of inflicting pain
at short, middle or long range,
and worried the psychosocial difficulties
of children whose T-ball teams
are insufficiently oriented toward success. . . .[26]

Juxtaposing these details demonstrates the futility of being only local, of believing mostly in a God who cares about comforts and graces within us, and not without. In other words, Gundy orients the speaker and the reader outward, toward the rest of the damned world.

Finally, though, in his theological questions, Gundy forces readers toward the ground of his later prose work, asking if it is possible to say no to the demands of our community, our family, our closest others. His "Inquiry into Simply Responding in the Negative" suggests the simultaneous impossibility and attraction of doing so. Saying "no" he says:

will make you better.
It will improve your digestion and lower
your triglycerides. Are you an American
or what? Remember the great
and enduring values on which
your fathers stood like the black muck
of Illinois, the generations
of dead flora and fauna who made it rich,
who might have been you.
The rotted, dark bluestem brooks nothing
it does not give the time of day.
If it could it would tell
how long the time for saying yes will be.[27]

These poems, swaying, as Scott Sanders says, "between anger and joy,"[28] are grounded in the intransigent and inescapable soil, in the truth that humans, and perhaps Mennonites in particular, are folded into and grow out of the "generations" and the "rotted bluestem" of a past that points them uncomfortably toward an uncertain and unavoidable set of tasks.

---

26. Ibid., 36.
27. Ibid., 22.
28. See Sanders' blurb on the cover of *Inquiries*.

Community, Theology and Poetics in Jeff Gundy's Work

GUNDY'S MENNONITE POETICS OR "HOW IT DID NOT QUITE KILL US YOUNG"

For Gundy, then, these tasks have been the making of poems and the ongoing construction of a poetics that engages in a restless relationship with his community's history, theology and geographic and cultural place. Gundy's poetics stand out in the postmodern landscape precisely because of his poetic reverence for and groundedness in details, tempered by his unwillingness to elevate the concrete to the status of the divine. His poems refract his own and his community's particularity through their unresolved relationship with the Mennonite past, their profound theological questioning, and their rootedness in, as Keith Ratzlaff puts it, "the Midwest with all the ambivalence that landscape holds."[29] In his latest collection *Flatlands* the poet works his way, at times carefully and often recklessly, around and within these concerns. A brief look at three of this collection's poems gives a small sense of Gundy's poetics as it has developed most recently.

As a poem dealing with the conflict of a Mennonite childhood, "The Universe Is A Safe Place for Souls" describes in prose lines an ongoing battle with junior high nemesis Gary Eden: "He was the best athlete in our class, but being / a north-of-town Lutheran he got into hot cars and beer and never / went out for anything after eighth grade."[30] The poem details how for years "I went around in fear of his picking at me" until finally, after a myriad of petty tortures, the "blond, lean-good looking . . . and dumber than I was" Lutheran inexplicably stops:

He held his hand out. Sorry, he
said. Sure you are I said. No, I mean it, he said. Sure, I said, and
looked at his hand. Sure you are. We got dressed. After that we
quit fighting. We never talked. We were not friends. I don't know
now if he meant it or not.[31]

And because we don't know for sure if our enemies mean it or not, we cannot be sure if the universe really is "a safe place for souls." The poem itself cannot give the poet, the community or the eavesdropper the answer. As Gundy writes in "Worms": "What are these stories, anyhow? they leave us slack and defenseless, crippled and brain shocked, dreaming the bones."[32]

---

29. Keith Ratzlaff, "Poetry from Mennonites," *The Mennonite*, Feb. 13, 1996, 22.
30. Gundy, *Flatlands* (Cleveland: Cleveland State U., 1995), 30.
31. Ibid., 30.
32. Ibid., 17.

Standing uneasily rooted in the light of such troubling stories gives way, of course, to what Kevin Walzer describes as Gundy's "larger questions of rootedness in spirituality or human connections to God."[33] In one section of "Big Dog and Little Dog, or Where Is God" the poet suggests that such connection "is a question of looking, / of forgetting the little wounds / and petty complaints."[34] Or, in another stanza, it might be enough to observe the simple act of touching a key to a lock and seeing that "a delicate / tiny blue-white spark often flashes, / and each time I am reassured. / No. Reminded."[35]

So if we cannot be reassured, it must be sufficient to be reminded of both our connectedness to God and to our past. The most compelling reminders in Gundy's work grow from the landscape itself. In the same way his prose work recognizes the socio-historical nature of family and religious identity, so Gundy's poetry demonstrates the conviction that identity is also shaped by places. The connection to a particular geography, recognized in the title of the collection, exemplifies Gundy's belief that "no artist is truly an isolated individual. Whatever the particular relation to the community, both artists and their works are inevitably and complexly linked to their social and physical environment."[36]

He displays this sense of the place-bound nature of the artist in the biting "For the New York City Poet Who Informed Me That Few People Live This Way." After enduring a condescending critique of his poems, not unlike the young junior high boy taking his classmate's stinging towel in his bare backside, Gundy affirms his own place in the universe, or at least on the map. Addressing the city poet, he writes: "We're out here, working and eating, playing games that / mean nothing, but make us stronger. An old machine / cleans the streets, wakes us to the dawn. We listen. / I remember your name. Nobody else here knows you from Adam." This invocation of the poet's Adamic role and the outsider's inability to see that people do indeed live, and "get stronger this way," demonstrates the centrality of Gundy's own place, his town and history,

---

33. Kevin Walzer, "Space and Time," *Cincinnati Poetry Review* 27 (1996), 57-59.
34. Ibid., 57.
35. Ibid., 58.
36. Gundy, "Humility in Mennonite Literature," 11.

and echoes the words of Wendell Berry, who insists that every "writer is a regional writer, even those who write about a fashionable region such as New York City."[37]

Such a relationship with place, however, cannot be merely defensive or nostalgic. "Where I Grew Up" includes such a defensive stance: "Where I grew up we hate people telling us / how bad we've got it, how deprived"; but the poem moves on to its own ambivalence about the community, history and landscape of growing up in the rural Midwest. The stories and songs by which this mixed past are communicated mingle pride at having survived with worry for the future:

> We teach our children all the stories
> of the blizzards and tornadoes,
> the droughts and the black deep soil,
> its grand slow rolls only idiots
> and easterners could call flat—
> how we love it, how we hate it,
> how it did not quite kill us young.[38]

That the land breeds both love and hatred, and that it has "not quite kill[ed] us young" begins to summarize the distinctive poetics that I see emerging from Gundy's work and humbly label as Mennonite.

As in his prose work *A Community of Memory*, what makes Gundy's poetics uniquely Mennonite are the distinctives of humility and history, grounded in place and in the honorable tradition of theological questioning. Yet Gundy also instantiates in his poetics the tension between the power of his Mennonite heritage and what Gerald Biesecker-Mast calls the plurality of "truths discerned in the various communities" to which we inevitably must grant competing authority.[39] Gundy's intensification of this dilemma through poetry and storytelling makes powerful use of narrative and irony to map an angry, good-humored, uncertain and vital place in both Mennonite life and the broader life of contemporary American literary culture.

The response of these two groups of readers is wildly unpredictable. As for the church, Gundy himself describes the risk for Mennonite poets when he discusses the frustrations of engaging the church by telling it truths about its own "past, present and future communal life, [truths]

---

37. Wendell Berry, *What Are People For?* (San Francisco: North Point, 1990), 79.

38. Gundy, *Flatlands*, 37-38.

39. Gerald J. Biesecker-Mast, "Anabaptist Radicalism and Postmodern Publics: A Discussion Paper," Anabaptists and Postmodernity <http//www.bluffton.edu/~mastg/publics.htm> 24 May 1998.

that we need to hear."[40] He questions whether poets will participate in the transformation of the church or become fodder for either liberal or conservative agendas. I will watch to see how the larger Mennonite church responds to him and the other poets and writers represented in this volume of essays.

As for the rest of Gundy's readers, I find hope in Denise Levertov's comment that "We often hear it said that there is much spiritual hunger in our society—but I have been surprised by how much quiet, unadvertised religious *commitment* there is among people one can loosely characterize as intellectuals—the people who constitute the audience for contemporary poetry in twentieth-century America."[41] If such readers are indeed eavesdropping, they should tune their antennae toward Jeff Gundy's poetry and prose, listening with care. But it may be harder to hear than I have suggested. Like the trickster Menno Simons, Mennonite poets are surely craftier than we know and may turn out to be like the geese in one of Gundy's inquiries who "have learned / to talk as loud as they want / and give nothing at all away."[42]

40. Gundy, "U. S. Mennonite Poetry and Poets," 8.

41. Denise Levertov, "Work that Enfaiths," in *New and Selected Essays* (New York: New Directions, 1992), 255-56.

42. Gundy, *Inquiries*, 23.

LABORING THROUGH *THE WEATHER BOOK*:
THE VALUE OF WORK IN
THE POETRY OF JANET KAUFFMAN

TODD DAVIS*

Abstract: Although Janet Kauffman is connected to the Mennonite community by ancestry, much of her work to date does not dwell conspicuously on Mennonite matters. Outside of her novel *Collaborators,* set in the tobacco-growing country of Pennsylvania on a Mennonite farm, and her poem "Mennonite Farm Wife," collected in *The Weather Book,* little in her writing would lead to an instant recognition of Kauffman as "Mennonite." This is not to say, however, that her work does not suggest some connection to Mennonite themes and ideas. In fact, as Julia Lisella explains in *The Village Voice,* Kauffman's "Mennonite background figures into her writing, autobiographically in the early work, and later as a thematic hush." This "thematic hush" may be most evident in Kauffman's use of work as a subject in both her poetry and fiction. Such ideas align her with Mennonite attitudes and ideals concerning work and its importance for drawing one into community and communion.

> You know what work is — if you're
> old enough to read this you know what
> work is. . . .
> —Philip Levine, " What Work Is"[1]

> Through my history's despite
> and ruin, I have come
> to its remainder, and here
> have made the beginning
> of a farm intended to become
> my art of being here.
> —Wendell Berry, "History"[2]

Critic and poet Lionel Basney speaks compellingly and convincingly of the late nineteenth and early twentieth-century shift in focus and attention toward work as a subject in literature. Basney explains that until this time much English fiction and poetry ignored the very real

---

* Todd Davis is Associate Professor of English at Goshen College.

1. Philip Levine, *What Work Is* (New York: Knopf, 1991), 18.
2. Wendell Berry, *Traveling at Home* (San Francisco: North Point Press, 1989), 29.

culture of work because the "novel-reading bourgeois in nineteenth-century England was not expected or allowed to work."[3] While clearly exceptions to this statement may be found — in American literature, Whitman's extended odes to the laborers of the fields and factories come immediately to mind — many of these exceptions have only recently been given critical attention, perhaps for the very reason that these writers concentrated, at least in their literary efforts, on work that the critical establishment deemed ill-suited for "art."

In speaking about the poetry of Gary Snyder and Wendell Berry, Basney proposes one reason for the importance of a poetry of work in the contemporary world: "It would place the body in a social context and in this way make it an instrument for articulating relationships with the world and with other people. Of course, the poet must ask, What sort of work will best serve this purpose? For society's vision of work is as defective as its consciousness of the body."[4] Basney chooses to deal with Berry and Snyder for just this reason. Berry's efforts at farming are inextricably linked with his career as a poet, essayist and novelist, as are Snyder's concerns with Zen Buddhism and the environment in his own poetic career. Both Berry and Snyder suggest, often in polemical fashion, that our connection to the earth and the human community must be understood in terms of our spiritual practice, and of course neither writer is pleased with the state of such matters at present.

The post-industrial, technologically driven, urban world that America has become presents little in the way of craft and consciousness as it is linked to the body; few see their work as something related to their physical and spiritual beings. Rather, the late twentieth-century landscape often appears to be little more than a world caught in cyberspace: humans attached to machines, driving back and forth from the suburbs into the sprawling din of decaying cities, never fully free because of the electrical umbilical cords wrapped around their waists that frequently take on the forms of beepers and cell phones and lap-tops. Because America has, in less than a century, moved from an agrarian economy to an industrial economy and most recently to a service-oriented, post-industrial economy, it is not surprising that feelings of dislocation and disassociation are widespread. Many professions demand that laborers be transient. Compared to life during the first two decades of this century, few people today are allowed to live in the same communities where they were born and reared.

---

3. Lionel Basney, "Having Your Meaning at Hand: Work in Snyder and Berry," in *World, Self, Poem: Essays on Contemporary Poetry from the "Jubilation of Poets,"* ed. Leonard M. Trawick (Kent, OH: Kent State U. Press, 1990), 130.

4. Ibid., 133.

Connections between children, parents and grandparents are lost because of transfers to towns that many times did not even exist fifty years ago, places that often look bizarrely the same from region to region because of strip malls populated by national chains and restaurants where all food tastes the same. Such conditions do not encourage a sense of responsibility to place and to the work that one does in that place. Sadly, the life of the earth and its inhabitants suffers.

While Janet Kauffman's writing does not take on the overtly polemical dimensions of Berry's or Snyder's texts, she does chronicle in striking images and a rather spare, lyrical style what remains of rural America, more specifically that of Pennsylvania, where she was reared on a tobacco farm, and Michigan, where for many years she farmed before recently placing her land in a trust that prevents its development in the future. Most know Kauffman as a writer of fiction, but, like another Michigan novelist, Jim Harrison, she began her career as a poet, writing her first poems around the time she moved to Michigan after completing a dissertation on the Michigan poet Theodore Roethke and graduating from the University of Chicago with a Ph.D. Several critics suggest that Kauffman's apprenticeship in poetry has served her well, and I would go so far as to say that much of her prose borders on poetry, especially a short story like "Women Over Bay City,"[5] a text comparable to the prose poems of Jim Heynen.

Although Kauffman is connected to the Mennonite community by ancestry, much of her work to date does not dwell conspicuously on Mennonite matters. Outside of her novel *Collaborators*,[6] set in the tobacco-growing country of Pennsylvania on a Mennonite farm, and her poem "Mennonite Farm Wife," collected in *The Weather Book*,[7] little in her writing would lead to an instant recognition of Kauffman as "Mennonite." This is not to say, however, that her work does not suggest some connection to Mennonite themes and ideas. In fact Julia Lisella claims in *The Village Voice* that Kauffman "is an ethnic writer" whose "Mennonite background figures into her writing, autobiographically in the early work, and later as a thematic hush."[8] This "thematic hush" may be most evident in Kauffman's use of work as a subject in both her poetry and fiction. Such ideas certainly align her with Mennonite attitudes and ideals concerning work and its importance for drawing one into community and communion.

---

5. Janet Kauffman, *Obscene Gestures for Women* (New York: Vintage, 1989), 3-4.

6. Janet Kauffman, *Collaborators* (New York: Knopf, 1986).

7. Janet Kauffman, *The Weather Book* (Lubbock: Texas Tech Press, 1981), 6.

8. Julia Lisella, "Young Americans: Janet Kauffman Faces the Nation," *The Village Voice*, Jan. 9, 1990, 57.

In "'Work and Hope': Tradition and Translation of an Anabaptist Adam,"[9] the Mennonite poet Julia Kasdorf proffers an engrossing and rather comprehensive study of the image of a laborer digging in a field accompanied by the phrase, "Work and Hope," which until 1990 was prominently placed on the title page of most editions of *Martyrs' Mirror*. The importance of the phrase, "Work and Hope," cannot be underestimated in the Mennonite community. In "Gelassenheit: The Rites and Redemptive Processes in Old Order Amish and Old Order Mennonite Communities,"[10] Sandra Cronk suggests that "the rite of work" actually leads toward the creation of community and the strengthening of the bond of love through its expression in work. In fact, this idea that love must be expressed through action is an important part of Mennonite theology. Based in part on Christ's example of active discipleship and particularly the Sermon on the Mount found in the gospel of Matthew, as well as on the admonition found in the second chapter of James which suggests that faith without works is dead, Mennonites have long expressed their faithfulness to God and to one another through their work, thereby demonstrating how discipleship and devotion to God may be reflected in daily labor.

In Mennonite circles the kind of work one does takes on significantly different dimensions from American society at large. Mennonites tend to recognize that, to a great extent, work represents what and who one is. Such a conclusion is not startling when one stops to consider that the greatest percentage of one's waking hours spent on earth is consumed by work. What is startling is that so few people in American culture are willing to accept that what they spend their time doing professionally represents and shapes who they are as people. In his typically pithy, aphoristic style, Kurt Vonnegut speaks to such people in the preface to *Mother Night*, warning them about the deception of such a dichotomy: "We are what we pretend to be, so we must be careful about what we pretend to be."[11] Vonnegut's admonition leaves no room for a separation between what one does at work and who one is at home—an idea especially suited to those who live on farms because on the farm there is no separation between where one lives and works. A family that farms actually lives in the very place where they work, a reality which may potentially lead to a deeper understanding of stewardship for the land, animals and family members. Such a setting allows for a much clearer view of the interdependence of all life in producing, using and

---

9. Julia Kasdorf, "'Work and Hope': Tradition and Translation of an Anabaptist Adam," *MQR* 69 (April 1994), 178-204.

10. Sandra Cronk, "Gelassenheit: The Rites and Redemptive Processes in Old Order Amish and Old Order Mennonite Communities," *MQR* 60 (Jan. 1981), 5-44.

11. Kurt Vonnegut, *Mother Night* (New York: Delacorte Press, 1966), v.

replenishing sources of our physical and spiritual need. Of course, the same may be said for the writer, because the life of one's mind — where words and ideas and images coalesce — is a home of sorts, one that can be left behind only with great difficulty and loss and one that must be cared for with the same diligence as the farmer cares for the land if it is to remain fertile. This is not to say that all farmers or all writers recognize and treat their "homes" with care. Certainly some Mennonite farmers use environmentally unsound practices, just as some writers abuse alcohol or other damaging substances. But as we turn to Kauffman's work, we should note that she does indeed value both human and earthly resources — which is why she put her farm into an environmental trust.

Fittingly, Kauffman's *The Weather Book* begins with the making of a new home. As a farmer and a writer, Kauffman offers insight into the possibilities of work as a means of discovery and bonding. In the prefatory poem "Beginning of the Book," the speaker tells of her first winter on what we assume is a newly purchased farm:

That was a time for scraping the womb
clean, for combing hair, bathing,
and walking the toppled fields in cold
lively winds, snow thrashing among weeds.[12]

The speaker in the poem addresses an imaginary friend, "a neighbor, farther than Nebraska, / who lived quietly, with a certain pallor / and a mind made up,"[13] and, through the creation of this friend and the writing she addresses to her, the speaker comes to understand that she is "alive," that her life has meaning. By writing — an act of creation, a kind of work that demands commitment and craft — she discovers that she has been working with words "out of love" for this other: "At first it was not out of love / I wrote, I thought; but at last / I'm sending the book of weathers."[14] By writing "the book of weathers" from her life and from the place where she lives that life, the speaker begins to gather strength from the new perspective she gains in her relationship with the "neighbor," and, from this communion that is begun in the sharing of her work, she moves from that "first winter here without wood" when she chewed her cheek, "shaping hollows" and starving herself, to the most recent card she sends to her neighbor "showing white mules and hay," an image of fertility. By sharing her work — both her writing and her farming — the speaker in the poem establishes a communal

---

12. Kauffman, *The Weather Book*, 3.
13. Ibid.
14. Ibid.

relationship that appears to lead toward growth, a beginning of a new life.

Writing about *The Weather Book* in *The American Poetry Review*, poet and critic Dave Smith suggests that Kauffman's poetry is "a harvest wrought by work," not about people "who go out to the farms but those who are inextricably of the farms."[15] Indeed, in Kauffman's poetry one never feels deceived. In her descriptions, there is a closeness to the real work that takes place on a farm that belies any romantic reinterpretation. Despite a lyrical voice that allows her to describe the beautiful green world of topping tobacco plants as "blessing and breaking, blessing, breaking,"[16] she never loses sight of the danger hidden by the green leaves — which many pastoral poets conceal with a blanket of words.

Perhaps this refusal to romanticize rural life is most evident in the poem "Mennonite Farm Wife." Over the last several decades, as the population in rural areas has dipped dramatically and fewer and fewer people participate directly in farm life, there has been a nostalgic look back toward the country, one that tends to focus on pastoral scenes and to forget the demands and trials that inevitably accompany a life lived on the land. Such an idealization of rural life is especially evident in the commercial depiction of Amish and Old Order Mennonite families. Artists like N. A. Nöel and P. Buckley Moss have provided images of Amish farmers and their children for a national audience, while television and movies continue to provide rather simplistic and highly unrealistic glimpses of farm life. Although the beauty of life lived in connection with the earth is not to be denied, Kauffman does not allow the reader to forget that all life harbors loss, that growth and fertility must lead toward mortality. Remarkable for the depth of insight achieved in such a short poem, "Mennonite Farm Wife" describes in direct, understated language the washing of laundry by the farm wife:

> She hung her laundry in the morning
> before light and often in winter
> by sunrise the sheets were ice.
> They swung all day on the line,
> creaking, never a flutter.[17]

After this straightforward description, however, the poem turns toward the beauty the speaker sees when the woman takes the sheets from the line as the sun sets:

---

15. Dave Smith, "Some Recent American Poetry: Come All Ye Fair and Tender Ladies," *The American Poetry Review* 11 (Jan./Feb. 1982), 39.

16. Kauffman, *The Weather Book*, 12.

17. Ibid., 6.

At dusk I'd watch her lift each one
like a field, the stretches of white
she carried easily as dream
to the house where she bent and folded
and stacked the flat squares.[18]

Rather than deny the scene's loveliness, Kauffman demonstrates how the work of this woman achieves its own beauty, almost dreamlike except for the fact that the sheets, like the fields, are mapped out in squares. Strikingly, Kauffman uses this pointed image to bring the poem to its culmination: the square corners of the sheets, dried in freezing weather, are "like thorn." Like the rose whose beauty is guarded by thorns, so too is the work of this Mennonite farm wife. The hands of the woman who handles these sheets will become rough and chapped from her work. Like the farmer who works in the fields that these sheets resemble, this woman's physical body is touched by her work, which offers a deeper connection to it. The poem staunchly refuses to make this woman's work any more or any less than it is.

The barrier of nostalgia is not the only boundary Kauffman attacks as she writes about work. As a woman who farms, Kauffman consistently breaks down gender distinctions erected by our culture. In *The Feminization of American Culture* Ann Douglas contends that women lost much of their economic and social power during the nineteenth century as America became increasingly industrialized.[19] In an agricultural nation of small, subsistence farms, women by necessity were intimately involved in production; however, with the shift toward industrialization women were relieved of their duties and stripped of their power. Products that once were made by their hands now were mass produced in factories or grown and shipped from larger and larger farms to be purchased in stores. In spite of this, during the farm crisis of the 1980s an interesting shift occurred on family farms. While women never truly disappeared from the family farm altogether—Kauffman's own life as a farmer attests to this fact—during the farm crisis more and more women began to take on increasing responsibilities because many men were forced to find other work outside of the farm to help make ends meet.

Kauffman's short story "Patriotic," collected in *Places in the World a Woman Could Walk*,[20] looks directly at this issue and suggests other possibilities for understanding some of the speakers in the poems found in *The Weather Book*. The story's narrator is a woman whose husband finds seasonal work in construction and leaves her to take care of the

18. Ibid.
19. Ann Douglas, *The Feminization of American Culture* (New York: Anchor Press, 1988).
20. Janet Kauffman, *Places in the World a Women Could Walk* (New York: Knopf, 1983).

farm and hire her own help. The story chronicles a day spent putting in hay with Floyd Dey, a local farm kid who will be a senior in high school, and Mrs. Bagnoli, a neighboring farm wife who drives a John Deere diesel because her husband works at the Ford plant. Mrs. Bagnoli, we are told, has a "magical accord with machinery." The story includes an epiphany in which the narrator takes off her shirt, like Floyd, baring her chest to the work of the hay wagon and Mrs. Bagnoli's blouse burns on the tractor's muffler, leaving the buxom driver in nothing more than a black bra. What the story reveals, beyond the cultural boundaries of who may or may not take off a shirt to work, is the bond created by good work: Mrs. Bagnoli drives the tractor so smoothly that neither rider has to shift for balance; all three workers witness the harvest of fine hay; and the blue sky above seems boundless, hinting at the wonderful possibilities such a world may hold for their community of three. Although the story culminates with the narrator and Mrs. Bagnoli sharing a drink together as they speak about Floyd in the kitchen — "Wouldn't you say," Mrs. Bagnoli says carefully, "that he is encouraged by what he has seen of womanhood?"[21] — it is the absence of gender roles that marks the story. In "Patriotic" women and men seem to have found equal footing; there is work to be done on the farm, and the able-bodied must do that work. Of course, as the narrator has explained throughout the story, Floyd Dey is an exceptional young man. He means it when he tells the narrator that it is nothing to him if she takes off her shirt, and he easily commends Mrs. Bagnoli's driving without feeling threatened by her doing "men's" work. That is why the narrator feels "patriotic": the story intimates what the world might be like if we could begin to see people for the kinds of work they do, rather than what they appear to be physically, as constrained by gender and class expectations.

In her poetry Kauffman's speakers also break down such gender and class expectations. Like Mrs. Bagnoli, who has a "magical accord with machinery," the speaker in the poem "The Womb in the World" also finds herself connected through her work to the earth — not as an Earth Mother whose body becomes a metaphor for the land but as one who is so intimate with machinery that she may address a roto-tiller in an invitation of union:

Meet me, machine —
tiller, attuner, that we might engender
anomaly: the steel leek,
mechanized berries (wired
to cluster), aromatic pipewrenches,
the interchangeable root.[22]

21. Ibid., 63.
22. Kauffman, *The Weather Book*, 8.

This is the machine in the garden, indeed, but here it is woman, not man, embracing the possibilities of mechanization.

Kauffman's poetry, however, does not offer simple role reversal. Her vision of men and women joined in work goes far beyond merely transposing cultural norms. Rather, she bridges the two worlds, demonstrating that individuals are not essentially masculine or feminine but a combination. In "Fall Plowing," a poem similar in its setting to "The Womb in the World" — earth worked into furrows — Kauffman cultivates a more organic image. The work has been done; the speaker is no longer an active participant but an observer of a field lying in wait. Here we find no machinery, only a woman lovingly drawn to an earth described as "luxuriant, yeasty, / feisty, glutinous, / umbrous, precious / amber loaf."[23] Baking, a task often deemed the work of the farm wife, supplies the images in "Fall Plowing," but what is remarkable is that such work rests easily beside the images described in "The Womb in the World." There is no contradiction for the speaker in these poems. She loves both machinery and the earth. One love does not cancel the other but, rather, the two loves feed one another: farmer riding machine, machine touching earth, earth springing forth with life, life harvested by machine and transformed into the bread which will in turn feed the lives of those who care for the earth.

With the work of the harvest complete, Kauffman is brought full circle in *The Weather Book*. The value of work ultimately holds no merit beyond the connections it affords with the earth and with one's community as an expression of faithfulness. Fittingly, Kauffman uses "December: Drying Corn" as the volume's final piece. In the last month of the year, as the days grow short, harvested corn is dried and stored:

> Two-story bins whirl through the night;
> inside, yellow grains collide in their shriveling,
> plummet through fanned winds
> like rolls of a universe;
> propane thrums, and the sweet roasted
> yum yum galaxies crackle.[24]

The tension in the poem emanates from the speaker's concern for her neighbor, who lights and cares for the propane fire. She explains that the work of drying the corn "unwinds a scented wilderness / unimagined by sure-fire grandfathers, / unknown to the first women threshing seeds."[25] Both genders have done this work, which brings them closer in understanding and respect because of its necessity, its burden. But now

---

23. Ibid., 48.
24. Ibid., 70.
25. Ibid.

the burden falls to the farmer who lives down the road, and we are told that the speaker has not revealed her fear to him:

> I have not told my neighbor I fear for his life,
> lighting the fire at dusk. Its roar
> drives over fields, vibrates through houses,
> behind the TV flickering. Past midnight
> when he checks the moisture and cuts the gas,
> in the silence, the silence fallen in curtains,
> I can tell that he takes a handful of corn,
> rattles it like dice, then brushes his dry cheek
> for comfort, with the back of his hand.[26]

Although the farmer comes to his work in the hours past midnight, described as a "specter,/ another traveler through the dry winds of space," he is not alone. Because the speaker in the poem is acquainted with her fellow farmer's work, she cares for him. The farmer who walks the night, insuring that the harvest will be fruitful, is brought back into community by the empathy of the poet, her work with words. Through an understanding of the value of work, a type of communion is achieved: it is more than the comfort of his own hand that "brushes his dry cheek"; it is the bond created by the one who watches him and writes with words of love and fearful hope.

At least in part, Kauffman's desire to write such words of love and fearful hope may be linked to the "thematic hush" of her Mennonite heritage, her early years growing up on a tobacco farm in Pennsylvania. Clearly the presence of Kauffman's devotion to work as an act of faithfulness that leads toward compassion and ultimately community — while an anomaly in much of the contemporary world — suggests the power of her religious heritage as it works in combination with her concerns as a feminist and farmer whose voice continues to ripple outward across the fields of literature in the United States.

---

26. Ibid., 71.

SPEED THE PLOW: JULIA KASDORF'S
SLEEPING PREACHER

JOHN J. FISHER*

Abstract: A key metaphor operates throughout *Sleeping Preacher*, i.e., to write verses on paper is to plow furrows in a field. Through this traditional metaphor of plow and pen Julia Kasdorf synthesizes her heritage from the rural Amish/Mennonite community in the Big Valley of central Pennsylvania with her commitment to being a student poet in New York City. The volume draws upon three interrelated archetypes: (1) The Garden, (2) Coming of Age and (3) The Dedicated Poet. These archetypes energize the genre structure—pastoral elegy—whose elements infuse many of the book's poems and which climaxes in "Morning Glories," itself an explicit pastoral elegy. The poet's empathy with Western literary culture is both technically conservative and spiritually celebrative. The redemptive tone in "Morning Glories" does not come as a surprise.

In *Sleeping Preacher* Julia Kasdorf has struck a chord among both Mennonite and other readers.[1] The book's success springs, I think, from the poet's sensitivity to certain interrelated archetypes imbedded in the Western literary culture that she has studied with profit and out of which she speaks. Those archetypes are a familiar part of our Judeo-Christian cultural heritage: (1) The Garden. Kasdorf refers to it as "that story" about the Garden of Eden, exile, labor and redemption; (2) Coming of Age, here in the form of an urban Vision Quest with roots in the tribal home community; and (3) The Dedicated Poet, one who has chosen to undergo the linguistic discipline requisite to an informed mastery of the art.

The archetypes in *Sleeping Preacher* are embodied in a particular genre, the pastoral elegy, employed masterfully in Christian tradition by such poets as Milton, Gray, Yeats, Auden and Seamus Heaney. While the more generalized pastoral mode is readily apparent in *Sleeping Preacher*, the traditional elements of pastoral elegy in particular shape Kasdorf's book.[2] Originally, pastoral imagery had to do with shepherding. In later

---

*John J. Fisher is Emeritus Professor of English, Goshen College, Goshen, Indiana.

1. Julia Kasdorf, *Sleeping Preacher* (Pittsburgh, PA: U. of Pittsburgh Press, 1992). Witness the book's reviews, its many author's readings, the publication of selected poems in *The New Yorker* and the church press, readings by Garrison Keillor on National Public Radio, and the publisher's repeat contract for the next book. However, no sustained critical analysis of the book has yet appeared in print.

2. See respectively, "Lycidas," "Elegy Written in a Country Churchyard," "Easter 1916," "In Memory of W. B. Yeats" and "The Strand at Lough Beg." Insightful studies of the genre are included in Sukhanta Chaudhuri, *Renaissance Pastoral and Its English Developments*

agricultural economy it came to reflect fertility and seasonal rebirth. Thus, cultivating the soil in the spring acquired ritual significance. Since a key agricultural image, the plow, helps unify *Sleeping Preacher,* we shall be examining how, in a present-day pastoral setting, Kasdorf uses the plow as a metaphoric bridge between her religious/cultural heritage and her urban poetic vocation.

I will then attempt to place *Sleeping Preacher's* archetypes, particular genre and dominant metaphor in both its Mennonite and general cultural contexts. It is a measure of Kasdorf's artistic maturity that these two settings are realized as more complementary than conflictive. All of the above elements coalesce in a coherently structured and richly textured volume.

Even before opening *Sleeping Preacher* we are struck by its singular front cover. An author's attractive photograph at the back of her book is not unusual, but her stylized portrait on the front invites our notice. In her bed, a young woman lies sleeping beneath a picture of a modest Amishman with his horse and buggy and beside an opened book turned down on a chair. In its dreamlike quality we might find the scene analogous to that presented in Henri Rousseau's "Sleeping Gypsy." Given the courteous Amishman, there may also be a folkloric echo of Sleeping Beauty or Snow White, each waiting to be revived by a qualified suitor. More threatening literary analogues would include the aroused poet in Coleridge's "Kubla Khan" or Yeats's awakened rough beast in "The Second Coming." One would like to know what book is on the chair. In any case, historically speaking, sleeping preachers in Amish/Mennonite circles — and often poets — have tended to be viewed as exempt from the control of local authority.[3] Given these suggestive parallels, and with considerations of gender aside, are we to assume then that Kasdorf when awakened — flashing eyes and floating hair — is herself a sleeping preacher?

In light of Jeff Gundy's recent ironical interpretation of Kasdorf's poem "Mennonites," we may note some incongruities that cast doubt here on such a tempting assumption.[4] For one thing, the title *Sleeping Preacher* that accompanies the portrait differs from that of the book's title poem "The Sleeping Preacher." Second, in that poem the preacher's

(Oxford: Clarendon Press, 1998) and Sidney Burris, *The Poetry of Resistance: Seamus Heaney and the Pastoral Tradition* (Athens, OH: Ohio U. Press, 1990).

3. Don Yoder, "Trance Preaching in the United States" (12-18) and Harry H. Miller, "The Sleeping Preachers: An Historical Study of the Role of Charisma in Amish Society" (19-31), both in *Pennsylvania Folklife* 18 (Winter 1968-1969).

4. Jeff Gundy, "U. S. Mennonite Poetry and Poets: Beyond Dr. Johnson's Dog," *MQR* 71 (Jan. 1997), 7. He examines "the understated but radical irony of the poem." I would say, "modest ambivalence."

attack upon the things of this world ("jewelry, fancy dresses for women, and photographs") seems a rather superficial model for a serious lyricist. Finally, in the poem the only bequest that survives from Kasdorf's great-grandma's exposure to the preacher's ministry leaves "nothing / for us to touch or see / except this stubborn will to believe."

Belief is a recurrent theme in *Preacher*, e.g., "The Amish believe," "It is easy to believe," "we cannot leave the beliefs" (see "Freindschaft," "That Story" and "Mennonites"). Throughout the book Kasdorf inclines toward the gracious example of doubting Thomas, who demanded to touch and see before confessing, "Lord, I believe, help thou my unbelief!"[5] In addition, John L. Ruth in his *Mennonite Identity and Literary Art* reminds us of W. B. Yeats's pejorative phrase about the "will trying to do the work of the imagination."[6] Readers are not inclined to value a poet's imposed belief nor her imagination when it is "stubborn." The aims pursued by Kasdorf and by her great-grandma's sleeping preacher differ.

Whatever incongruities we find in the title poem, and with the book's cover illustration in mind, we are made aware that on the poet's part there is considerable ironic posturing or, in other words, self-conscious performance. Indeed, she seems to be a bit of a tease, daring the reader to speculate about what kind of "preacher," if any, she really is. At the same time, we are openly invited to identify the voice in the *Sleeping Preacher* volume as that of the poet herself. She presents specific persons in geographically accurate settings from her own personal point of view, recounting in a poem like "The Interesting Thing," for instance, concrete childhood details about a moment of sibling cruelty or an episode of sexual jeopardy. Exiled from the Garden, a Dedicated Poet on a Vision Quest, Julia Kasdorf consistently speaks not as a hypothetical persona but as Julia Kasdorf herself.

I shall assume little, if any, separation between Kasdorf the person and the "I" of the poems. She may stage other people in dramatic postures of stylized characterization, but for her there is no mask. Without relinquishing aesthetic distance and ironic self-awareness, as a lyric poet Kasdorf speaks about her own self in her own voice. For example, in "The Sleeping Preacher" Kasdorf's employment of interior

---

5. Kasdorf's allusion to Thomas' bodily proof is illuminated by her article "Bakhtin, Boundaries and Bodies," *MQR* 71 (April 1997), 169-88: "The resurrection—mirroring the miracle of embodiment first enacted in the incarnation—made it possible for Jesus to be seen by grieving followers. He recognized the necessity of a bodily presence, the need for the physical gaze or consummation which would serve as a proof of his identity and basis for belief" (177-78).

6. John L. Ruth, *Mennonite Identity and Literary Art*, Focal Pamphlet 29 (Scottdale, PA: Herald Press, 1978), 50.

rhyme coincides with her distribution of metrical accents in the line "swóon across the front péw" — reinforcing the melodramatic effect of the preacher's behavior — heightens our awareness of Kasdorf's own subtly skeptical attitude, which is in turn consistent some lines later with her sincere "touch and see" allusion to doubting Thomas.[7]

Forthright self-disclosure has already occurred in the opening poem, "Green Market, New York." There Kasdorf recounts how, in an early springtime escape from her desk, "buoyant, my coat open," she comes upon an Amish woman from upstate New York selling pies in Union Square. They discover their native ground to be the Big Valley of central Pennsylvania, "around Mifflinburg, around Belleville." Herself a Peachey (Kasdorf's mother's family name), the Amish woman sighs, "What a place your folks had, down Locust Grove."[8] Both women are displaced persons: Emma Peachey peddles pies; Julia Kasdorf, poems. Asked whether she likes the city, Kasdorf answers:

> I don't like New York, but sometimes these streets
> hold me as hard as we're held by rich earth.

She continues:

> I have not forgotten that Bible verse:
> Whoever puts his hand to the plow and looks back
> is not fit for the kingdom of God.

To explain her strong attachment to the city, Kasdorf employs an image from the Valley. Looking forward, she offers encouragement to her fellow refugee and to herself. Hand on plow, no looking back — both country and city belong to the kingdom of God. Their work can be redemptive.

Besides the disciplined plowing of furrows, what Kasdorf is talking about and demonstrating here is her dedication to the poetic calling. In literary culture the farmer's plow has been a conventional symbol for the poet's pen. Etymology reveals that to plow a field is to compose a poem, to write lines of verse, since the English word "verse" derives from Latin

---

7. Kasdorf is not an unmetrical poet. A careful prosodist, she employs a relatively conservative verse form, which in turn enhances — rather than deconstructs — meaning. See John R. Cooper, "Intonation and Iambic Pentameter," *Papers on Language and Literature* (Fall 1997), 392-421.

8. Gundy (29-30) has rightly noted that both persons have left the Valley, one now in New York City, the other from upstate. They are, then, self-consciously aware of their journey thence. But the Locust Grove congregation, according to John A. Hostetler, is "high church" in the Valley scale "of cognitive orientation," that is, relatively worldly by strict, Amish standards. *Amish Society*, 4th ed. (Baltimore, MD: Johns Hopkins U. Press, 1993), 290-97. The two women's separation from the home community, while marked, seems not overly sharp. Emma Peachy is fondly reminiscent. In Kasdorf's case, there were her juvenile residence in Irwin, Pennsylvania, college (including a term in China) and university, graduate school and married life in New York, before *Preacher* was completed.

versus, meaning "turn." Hence, the turns at the ends of plowed furrows and of lines of verse are metaphorically the same. A commonplace among classically educated poets, the plow-pen metaphor would at least be known to Kasdorf in its modern practice. W. H. Auden, for example, in his elegy for W. B. Yeats, writes, "In the farming of a verse, make a vineyard of the curse." Auden alludes here to the poem "Adam's Curse," where Yeats sighs, "A line will take us hours," to which his female companion murmurs, "We must labor to be beautiful." Both poets note that plowman and poet alike must pay the post-lapsarian penalty.

More recently, Seamus Heaney has wrought a two-sonnet sequence out of the same extended metaphor. At the end of the second sonnet the metaphor is explicit:

> Vowels ploughed into other, opened ground.
> Each verse returning like the plough turned round.[9]

All three poets incisively point up the association between Adam's sweat-of-the-brow labor, "the farming of a verse," and its aesthetic reward, a poem, "a vineyard."

Kasdorf has also employed the plow-pen metaphor in a highly specialized recent poem. When she came to write an elegy for Warren Rohrer, the noted abstract painter out of Lancaster County who died in 1995, she named it "Boustrophedon." In ancient Greek "bous" means ox and "strophe" refers to the turn of a line of dancers in the theater, and hence of lines in a poem. A boustrophedon is, then, literally a sequence of ox-plowed furrows. For her memorial poem in English, Kasdorf composed a sestina about the abstractly rendered field furrows in Roher's paintings.

No

> one back home sees or knows what he makes:
> the way light shifts on those scarred rows
> of pigment, though he paints as they plow.[10]

---

9. Seamus Heaney, "Glanmore Sonnets," i and ii, *Selected Poems 1966-1987* (New York: Farrar, Straus and Giroux, 1990), 124-25. He wrote the pair of sonnets at the time he had taken the occupational risk of a life devoted wholly to poetry. A similar occasion is presented in the first poem published by Heaney, "Digging." Heaney has remarked upon the words a workman spoke to him on the way to school: "The pen's easily handled. It's a lot lighter than a spade." In respect to the pen in his hand, Heaney at the end of "Digging" says, "I'll dig with it." In these poems, using farm vernacular, Heaney the poet is encouraging himself to "speed the spade," i.e., the plow. The latter familiar saying occurs sporadically in English literature and folk culture. It represents "a wish for success and prosperity in some undertaking. It is a very old phrase." *Brewer's Dictionary of Phrase and Fable*, rev. Ivor H. Evans (New York: Harper and Row, 1981). An interesting tangential usage occurs in Milton's "Lycidas," in the sardonic line at the expense of the corrupt clergy: "What recks it them? What need they? They are sped."

10. Julia Kasdorf, "Boustrophedon," *College English* 59 (Sept. 1997), 577.

The complete poem celebrates the sheer power of art—Rohrer's and the poet's—in which function may even follow form. Of particular interest is the presence of the plow-pen (or, in this case, -brush) metaphor in both "Boustrophedon" and in the last poem in *Sleeping Preacher*, "Morning Glories," both of which are pastoral elegies.

The plow-pen metaphor operates throughout *Sleeping Preacher*.[11] The plow-implement may be a single steel share, a garden cultivator, a spade or even a hand trowel. While in all these instances it is literally still a plow, at the same time it participates in the metaphor. In the opening poem of the book "Green Market, New York," the plow figure enables the poet to compose a poem about her poem and about her dedication to her calling. Each of the plow poems to be discussed below, "That Story," "Freindschaft" and "Morning Glories," is also self-consciously reflexive about one's dedication to poetry. The practice of lyric self-consciousness is an extended one, including, for instance, Milton, Gray, the Romantics, Whitman, Dickinson, Yeats, Plath, Eavan Boland and Heaney. Kasdorf participates in the tradition.

Moreover, as Jesus knew and every plowman knows, to turn proper furrows is to keep looking straight ahead. When in "Green Market" Kasdorf quotes the Gospel of Luke about right plowing, she puts her reader on notice that, while not forgetting her rich Valley heritage (which she will explore in the immediately succeeding series of poems), she is determined to move forward into the city in good style. Indeed, the fact that the words "Whoever puts his hand to the plow and looks back" constitute so long a line reveals the poet's technical choice not to break that line after "plow," but, for rhetorical emphasis, to extend it with "and looks back." She declares that in order to become an accomplished poet she will keep looking forward toward New York.

Along with establishing the pertinence of the plow-pen metaphor, I have been attempting to characterize a quality of artistic self-disclosure usually referred to as "confessional." Julia Kasdorf—like those acknowledged masters of this mode, Robert Lowell or Plath or Heaney or her teacher Sharon Olds—while particularly honest and unflinching about herself is at the same time resonantly universal. At her poetic best, the metaphoric medium is the message. When Kasdorf draws her

---

11. Kasdorf's practice seems unique. The plow image, of course, occurs widely among rurally based Mennonite writers, especially wheat-farming Russian Mennonites, but not as plow-pen metaphor. Sometimes sexual connotations having to do with fertility are present, as in the opening, plowing chapter of Rudy Wiebe's *Peace Shall Destroy Many*. A more fundamental myth not irrelevant to *Preacher* is worth noting: "Brighid was a Celtic goddess of poetry and learning. St. Brigid was her Christian namesake. Her feast day coincided with the pagan festival Imbolg, the first day of spring, and the advent of spring plowing." — Peter Somerville-Large, *Ireland: the Living Landscape* (Boulder, CO: Roberts, Rinehart, 1994). See also the related folk custom of "plough Monday" cited in *Brewer's*.

readers into singular situations that are peculiar to her, with technical virtuosity she simultaneously renders them familiar to the readers' imaginations. "The Body Remembers," for instance, a New York poem placed later in the volume, recapitulates two wedded Mennonites' respective Swiss and Dutch ancestries. I agree with Rudy Wiebe that this poem does fuse style and content, "snarl the music with the thought," as Gerald Stern says in his back-cover blurb.[12] Though her readers may not be inter-ethnic marriage partners, Mennonite or otherwise, they sense in the meter's heavily "knocking" intercourse rhythm the cross-cultural tensions and attractions that exist in their own heritage, and then through a metrical shift toward a lighter rhythm discover that they too are "nothing special, just a woman and a man on a floor in Brooklyn." It is the poet's stylistic control that involves her audience in so intimately private an epiphany.

The major confessional poem in the book, "Freindschaft," is by far the longest. Its epigraph from II Corinthians refers to the "unequal yoke" between light and darkness. At an inbred family's annual Valley reunion, after painfully listening to the gossipy catalog of her clan's genetic misfirings, the poet cries out:

> With parents who are distant cousins and their
> parents before, my greatest fears
> get told in the stories I already know.
> What can I do to change my fate
> but take a strange lover and cleave
> to my work?

Like the family narratives that expose Kasdorf's fears, these poetic lines ominously evoke also those greatest fears that, in whatever domain, are our own. Genetic deformity is posited first in "Freindschaft." And biological anomalies, of course, may also stand for the spiritual dislocations that threaten any creative artist dependent solely upon a tightly closed community. As Kasdorf has stated elsewhere, in reference to the body of Christ: "Mennonites in traditional ethnic communities could claim their community as a body in actuality. To be enmeshed like this can be pleasurable, comfortable and secure, although it sometimes breeds freaks of flesh and soul."[13] But more universally, such anomalies also threaten us with chaos, or at least the intrusion of unpredictable, random chance upon us and our descendants. Nevertheless, for an

---

12. Rudy Wiebe, "The Body Knows As Much As the Soul: On the Human Reality of Being a Writer," *MQR* 71 (April 1997), 197. Evidently in context with "The Body Remembers," Wiebe goes on immediately (198) to make passing reference to the exclusion of Eve and Adam from Eden and their consequent "sorrow" in childbearing and in agricultural toil. See also the discussion of the poem "Freindschaft" below.

13. "Bakhtin, Boundaries and Bodies,"171.

ethnic community defined physically by bloodlines these fears are personal and palpable. The equal yoke provided by a closed community is purchased with a price.

The "strange lover," David Kasdorf, we have already met. A son of Mennonite Brethren refugees from Russia, now of Fresno, California, he is the gifted painter of what presumably is his wife's cover portrait.[14] When married, the young Kasdorfs chose to settle in New York City.

At the moment, however, we are interested in what "to cleave" means in another, related sense. In Eden, Adam cleaves, is bonded, to Eve. In New York Kasdorf takes her strange lover, but, like Eve tending the Garden, places fundamental value also upon her work—her poetry. Kasdorf's "cleave to my work" expresses again the same plowman's resolve that she voices at the end of "Greenmarket, NewYork," and, as we shall see, both commitments draw upon the metaphoric equation between plowing furrows and writing lines of verse.

After genealogy, "Freindschaft" moves on through theology, then agriculture and finally poetry. When we read the poem's closing lines, immediately subsequent to those just quoted above, we find that, as in the conclusion to "Green Market," we eventually cross what Seamus Heaney has called "the frontier of writing."[15] The two lines, "but take a strange lover and cleave to my work. / The Amish believe," serve as a nexus in this progress. The poem is not about a conversion to poetry but rather a rededication to the continuing task. Moreover, in a collection of unrhymed poems the rhyme "cleave believe" stands out; it helps strengthen the link between biological and theological fears.

By means of the stresses marked in the lines that follow, I attempt to indicate the poet's use of structure for meaning:

> The Amish believe
> it is sinful to be súre
> their souls are saved.
> The only defense against théir worst fears
> is work and hope, *arbeite und hoffe*.[16]

---

14. In her Bakhtin article (178-79) Julia Kasdorf has stated that "I modeled for many artists, unconsciously seeking the images that would help me to know and appreciate myself differently."

15. "From the Frontier of Writing," *Selected Poems 1966-1987* (New York: Farrar, Straus and Giroux), 236-37.

16. "Assurance of salvation" in Amish faith and practice is hardly a clear-cut doctrine. See Julia Kasdorf, "Work and Hope: Tradition and Translation of an Anabaptist Adam," *MQR* 69 (April 1995), 199-200; John S. Oyer, "Is There an Amish Theology?" (288-89) and John A. Hostetler, "The Amish as a Redemptive Community" (346-55), both in *Les Amish: origine et particularismes 1693-1993*, ed. Lydie Hege and Christoph Wiebe (Ingersheim, France: Association Francaise d'Histoire Anabaptiste-Mennonite, 1996). Assurance comes only after a lifetime of faithful labor and obedience. Easy assurance, cheap grace, is sinful because it undermines faith. "Their worst fears" revolve around manifestations of this sin.

"The Amish believe": their humble faith has at this point not yet been appropriated by their descendant, the poet, who is concerned about her assurance of salvation, at least about her odds in the gene-pool. But the poem concludes:

> The work that they mean
> darkens your skin with sun
> and roughens your hands; you must strain
> as a horse against a harness, as light
> against the darkness.

By now the parallel between the Amish plowman's devoutly earnest work and the poet's has converged. The pale poet works indoors with soft hands, it is true, but in her own way, line by line, she too strains at the plow.[17]

The key to this compactly structured passage is Kasdorf's unforced appropriation of her Amish heritage and its belief. Her anxiety, originally genetic, then spiritualized, is alleviated by the ancestral faith she shares with Amish farmers. As if in harness, she too strains to shed light on darkness.[18] "The work they mean," tilling the soil, yields crops. Kasdorf's work, turning verses, produces poems. She has come to see that her work, if patiently and faithfully pursued, can also be salvific. The Amish motto *arbete und hoffe* is also hers.

Kasdorf has explicitly acknowledged this faith elsewhere. In an *MQR* article, "Work and Hope: Tradition and Translation of an Anabaptist Adam," she begins by reproducing the very passages from "Freindschaft" that we have just been discussing.[19] She then traces the evolution of the emblem portraying a farmer who digs with a spade, which, bearing the caption *Arbeite und Hoffe*, appears on the title page of early editions of the *Martyrs' Mirror*. "What does the little man hope for?" she asks. "Might his effort be connected with a desire for eternal life as my poem suggests?" (199) I agree: the digger is a post-lapsarian

---

17. An obscure seventeenth-century anti-pastoral poem by Francis Quarles begins this way: "I hear the whistling Plough-man all day long,/ Sweetning his labour with a chearefull song:/ His Bed's a Pad of Straw; His dyet course;/ In both, he fares not better than his Horse." —Cited by Burris, 5.

18. The light-dark imagery derives from the poem's epigraph: ". . . what communion hath light with darkness?" i.e., the unequal yoke. I count as many as sixteen instances of light-dark imagery in *Sleeping Preacher*, none of which makes the sharp distinction drawn in II Corinthians. Those usages tend to be transformational rather than nonconformist, softening this part of Kasdorf's Amish heritage, quite possibly through her mother's family's association with the Locust Grove congregation. In Biblically based communities, and in *Sleeping Preacher*, the unequal and equal yolk are in constant tension.

19. Julia Kasdorf, "Work and Hope: Tradition and Translation of an Anabaptist Adam," *MQR* 69 (April 1995), 178-204.

farmer who, in the spirit of Paul's charge to the Philippians, is working out his salvation.[20]

It may properly be said that the humble digger's labors, both their merits and their frailties, "in trembling hope repose," in the words of Thomas Gray. This diction appears near the end of the epitaph that climaxes his pastoral "Elegy Written in a Country Churchyard," published a century after *Martyrs' Mirror*. The grave marker is erected in memory of the humble countryman who on his humble neighbors' grave stones carved the crude lines that record "the short and simple annals of the poor." Whether the motto of the *Martyrs' Mirror* icon registers with all Kasdorf's readers or not, its valorization of humility is not limited to Mennonite faith. It is part of our general literary heritage. As it appears in pastoral elegy this Christian virtue is a significant strand in Western cultural tradition.[21]

In conventional literary form the "Elegy" celebrates Christian humility in attitude and behavior when facing death. Gray's country churchyard also is paradigmatic for Amish cemeteries in the Big Valley, where short and simple annals also mark the graves. Kasdorf, in fact, specifically mentions the ancestral burial sites of her maternal grandmother ("Vesta's Father"), her paternal grandfather ("Grossdaadi's Funeral"), as well as his wife and daughter ("Dying with Amish Uncles"). She also cites the deaths of her paternal and maternal grandmothers and of her step-grandmother Bertha Peachey Spicher Sharp ("August"). Not only does she echo Gray's elegiac mood, but she employs a similar kind of "poetic diction" as well. Like Kasdorf's Amish laborer, Gray's plowman, whose "furrow oft the stubborn glebe has broke," also "homeward plods his weary way," leaving the world "to darkness." Working within a widely shared genre convention, both elegists bring forth poems out of the meditative darkness.

Toward the end of her Anabaptist Adam article Kasdorf makes another statement related to "Freindschaft": "I am drawn to the one who toils alone outside the walls of the village as I—a woman who wonders if she writes like a Mennonite—try to make my way in a city university" (203). Under the aspect of the digger emblem, associated for Kasdorf

---

20. In relation to work, Hostetler's qualifying statement is pertinent here: "The Amish are not obsessed with . . . excessive anxiety about their souls. A way of life that includes hard manual labor is important to them, but it does not assure salvation. Assurance is hoped for by living in a redemptive community." —*Amish Society*, 352-53. An interesting question outside the scope of this study would be the nature of the redemptive community that sustains Kasdorf's artistic-spiritual quest.

21. In respect to humility, "Clearly, we would be guilty of hubris if we thought Mennonites the only writers, or the best ones, to wrestle with this theme." —Shirley Hershey Showalter, "Bringing the Muse into Our Country: A Response to Jeff Gundy's 'Humility in Mennonite Literature,'" *MQR* 63 (Jan. 1989), 27.

with her writing, to work in hope can save both poet and plowman. Although they can not literally repossess it, digger and poet may in spirit regain the Garden that is lost.

In the next key plow poem, "That Story," the Valley is explicitly designated the Garden of Eden, and New York City is Babylon. In the present-day version of the story, Kasdorf's father, years after leaving his Amish home in the Valley, resides in town. Now resting from the toil of plowing his garden, where "his children stooped over the furrows behind him," he looks back: "Doomed to office work," he plows in despair over what he has lost. But his daughter, a Cain "who slays with words" (strongly put by Kasdorf yet not out of keeping with the post-Edenic context), has moved to the city, where she tends her little hardscrabble garden in Brooklyn and no doubt writes her share of hardscrabble poems. Remembering how at home she watched her weary father, she now finds it "easy to believe that story" about the lost Garden. Like her father was, she is now weary, but unlike her father she works in hope. By looking forward, when she keeps her hand to the plow her patient labor, her poetry, can be redeemed. From her vantage point in New York, though weary like Israel's children in Psalm 137 (another exilic situation), her belief in "that story" from Genesis can enable her like them not only to endure but prevail. "Next year in Jerusalem" articulates the faith that will carry them through. In John Ruth's words (a striking anticipation of Kasdorf's allusion to the Psalm):

> The artists who are sons and daughters of Zion will not strum the harp or indite a song for aesthetic effect only. By not forgetting Jerusalem they will remember who they are, and they will write of what they remember (71).

The poems in the later portion of the book, those set in New York, are not so much confessional as reportorial of surface phenomena. They report violence, noise and claustrophobia. Friendships suffer under stress. The urban Vision Quest undergoes its necessary trials.[22] These poems explore themes and situations that reflect the relative rootlessness of city life, in contrast to a few interspersed "leftover" Valley poems: "What I learned from My Mother" is a resumé of Valley domestic healing culture. Likewise, Kasdorf writes her friend Weatherly, still in New York, that inland "the fireflies rise / off the cornfields, and apricot clouds butt against the mountain's spine." In another transplanted poem, "Sunday Night Supper for a Mennonite," she carefully explains the Valley's ethnic ritual about bean soup. Such an interpenetration of past and present suggests that in critical literary practice Kasdorf, in *Sleeping*

---

22. See, for instance, "Mother," "For Weatherly, Still in New York," "Piano, New York" and "Morning Glories."

Preacher at least, remains a modernist with a relatively conservative stance akin to T. S. Eliot's notion of the relationship between tradition and individual talent. She interprets splintered metropolitan culture through its continuing debt to a meaningful provincial pastoral past: the temptations and dangers of postmodernist indifferentiation are thus placed in an enabling perspective.

Yet in the opening section of the book New York has already impinged on some of the earlier Valley poems: "Green Market," "Along Ocean Parkway in Brooklyn," "First TV in a Mennonite Family" and "That Story." Exceptions to the rule of simple binary opposition tend in proper pastoral to soften what might otherwise be a forced, artificial stand-off between city and country.[23] In *Sleeping Preacher* neither place is perfect. In both, for example, fatal accidents occur, too much liquor is imbibed and—a sharp detail—cats are cruelly abused. The complex world of *Sleeping Preacher* is both ideal and real.

These later city poems remind us that the Valley is actually not a Garden of Eden, though in "That Story" the weary poet, stuck with her second-hand garden in Brooklyn, has so named it. In fact, the Valley is a Garden of Hope for Heaven, where *Arbeite* is sacral ethic. For instance, as recorded in "Freindschaft," the poet's Spicher grandfather, with a bit of unredeemed pride "ran from house to barn to get the milking done before his neighbors." R. W. B. Lewis, in the prologue to his history of nineteenth-century New World ideas, *The American Adam*, has pointed out that the optimistic Emersonian view of America as a free enterprise Eden inevitably provoked a reactive conviction that America was as depraved as Europe. Disillusioned, the American Adam became a tragic figure. Dialectically, says Lewis, the two views produced a third, which he calls tragic irony, where Adam in mature self-knowledge on his westward journey carries both optimistic and pessimistic spiritual genes. This, I venture to suggest, is the significance of the Valley-New York overlap poems. They provide a livable paradox by which exclusive loyalty to either place is matter-of-factly, pragmatically transcended.

Moreover, since an exclusive concentration upon Adam and Eve's expulsion runs the risk of turning sour—life in a large city can be grim— we might also note a citation by Lewis from Hawthorne's *The Marble Faun*: "Adam saw it in a brighter sunshine, but never knew the shade of pensive beauty which Eden won from his expulsion" (110, 126). "The shade of pensive beauty," if it means thoughtful aesthetic perception from afar, characterizes the tone of Kasdorf's poems about the Valley,

---

23. "The distance between 'court' and 'country' constantly fluctuates in pastoral: their relationship assumes all possible proportions from direct to inverse. Hence each can be assessed in terms of the other to any desired degree of interpenetration." — Burris, *Poetry of Resistance*, 2.

poems which in practically all cases were written from a New York resident's point of view. Although condemned like her Amish emigré father to a life of toil in a "second" garden, Kasdorf, a daughter of Adam and Eve, a Christian poet necessarily aware of her own human fallen condition, in hope brings pensive beauty to light.

By maintaining intellectual perspective and aesthetic control within a generic structure Kasdorf avoids a merely sentimental attachment to the lost Valley paradise. Indeed, *Sleeping Preacher* gains overall coherence if it is viewed as a sustained book-length pastoral elegy. Psalm 137 itself falls within those generic boundaries. "By the waters," it not only mourns a loss but also nourishes memory with hope and resists oppressors. The oppressors in the Psalm (through their little ones) will suffer in due course, as will Milton's corrupt clergy ("they are sped") and Gray's revelers in "the pomp of power." Kasdorf in her turn resists, for instance, both Mennonite/Amish patriarchy and the meretricious elements in metropolitan culture.

At the same time, the poet's residence in the city should not be viewed as an unrelieved Babylonian captivity. While this exile poet works in hope she sings songs of Zion. Even in a poem with disagreeable subject matter like "At the Acme Bar and Grill," her lyric grasp is firm and clear. In Kasdorf's hands, from a dirty, noisy Valley chickenhouse vantage point the Acme Bar and Grill becomes a vehicle of wry urban satire. In "Riding Bike with No Hands," an easier instance, the poet breaks into singing "Christ the Lord Is Risen, Today."

The New York poems help set the stage for the book's last poem, "Morning Glories," which assimilates work and breathes hope.[24] In "Morning Glories," as with earlier poems, the Valley and the City play against each other in conventional literary pastoral fashion. In this case, however, between them exists a vital link, a remarkable woman named Bertha, the step-grandmother on her father's side—whom Kasdorf in her growing years had a chance to know and love. Fondly attached to Bertha ever since her childhood visits to her Spicher parents' Valley homeland, Julia was nurtured by her grandmother's gentleness, piety and compassion, qualities richly enhanced by Bertha's enterprising, self-reliant behavior:

> Who could begrudge all those children a mother
> besides it was she who taught that proud Amishman
> to drive in her own new, black Plymouth.

---

24. The four preceding poems are already lightened in tone. They take pleasure in the music of an African-American taxi driver, in laughter at men's leers, in regaining the skill of riding bike with no hands and in Holy Week sunshine in Prospect Park.

Bertha's portrait is derived from this poem "Leftover Blessings," and also from "August," "Where We Are," and "Sunday Night Supper for a Mennonite." In "Where We Are" we learn that it was Bertha who after Grandpa's death accompanied his body home by air.

In her later years Bertha's unaffected piety was expressed, for instance, by "breathing desirous prayers" ("Where We Are") and by off-key singing of "Tis So Sweet to Trust in Jesus" ("Sunday Night Supper for a Mennonite"). Unlike the great-grandma of "The Sleeping Preacher," she was a various yet complete woman, one whose identity requires a wide imaginative compass to describe.

After Bertha's death in 1990 Kasdorf composed "Morning Glories" in her memory. It is an urban pastoral elegy, evoking Milton's loss of Lycidas, whom he mourns in the most influential pastoral elegy in English. It also serves as a closing epitaph for the whole volume, much as the formal epitaph at the end of "Elegy in a Country Churchyard" does for that poem. To the poet in the city, the loss of Bertha, who died unexpectedly while canning peaches at home the previous August, has been grievous. While mourning Bertha, she mourns also the loss of the Valley. She regains it, however, while cultivating her garden in Brooklyn.

Once more, in "Morning Glories" the human activity is work. In *Preacher*, sequentially from Amish farmer's field through father's town plot to mini-garden in the city, the focus narrows down. The appropriate implements have been a plow, a cultivator and now, no doubt, a trowel (in all cases metaphorically a pen). Here Kasdorf is clearing away dead morning glory vines from her neglected city garden, which was described in "That Story" as "only as wide as a sidewalk [where] stray cats pee on her ragged tomato stalks." It is hard work, "scattering seeds and straw on my head / up my sleeves." It is work that must get done "under a grey sky / in a cold wind, the first week of the year."

Like the young Milton composing "Lycidas," Kasdorf the poet is obliged to "shatter . . . leaves before the mellowing year." She too does not feel qualified to address the "sad occasion." Her first words are, "Would you approve . . .?" Bound like Milton by "bitter constraint," she faces the task of pastoral elegy. Quite independently, it seems, Kasdorf's reading of Bakhtin has prepared her to fulfill this mission: "Only near or after the death of someone you love can you see his or her entire life and understand its meaning. . . . Thus, grieving a loss is not only the process of letting go, but also the process of keeping through creative acts like writing, with which you continue to consummate the other.[25]

---

25. Kasdorf, "Bakhtin, Boundaries and Bodies," 180.

To Kasdorf, the onerous labor of tending the garden—and, we can now understand, of composing this poem—represents "whatever is left of my life [in the city] that you [Bertha] would accept." Living in New York, away from the domestic haven of the Valley, Kasdorf confesses that her relationship with Bertha had become somewhat tenuous. According to this poem (and also "Where We Are") Bertha would "never visit until I moved from this city." Reinforcing the somber mood (and evoking Milton's "heavy change now thou art gone . . . and never must return") are the harsh cement wall, chain link fence and barbed wire that, no matter how adorned by morning glories, in a violent neighborhood protect not only the poet's garden but also her personal safety.

Confession implies penance, out of which grows forgiveness. The genre of pastoral elegy is itself informed by that rooted pattern of human experience. Milton, for instance, acknowledges the vested interest of an elegist:

> So may some gentle Muse
> With lucky words favor my destined urn,
> and as he passes turn,
> And bid fair peace be to my sable shroud.

Here the morning glories in their simplicity bring blessing—more so it seems to me, than does the flood of flowers in "Lycidas" that merely "interpose a little ease." At the time of Bertha's death:

> this wall was lush
> with leaf-hearts and fluttering maroon
> and heavenly blue bells that unfurled
> new each day, then withered
> into used tissues by dusk.

The flowers that unfurl each morning signify hope. These lines—pleasuring the ear with repeated *f*'s, *oo*'s, *l*'s and *r*'s, enriched at the end of the first line by the iambic accent on the word "lush," its hovering sound echoed with a solidly iambic "by dusk" at the end of the sentence—are a gift of ineffable abundance and beauty.[26] In the ambience of Kasdorf's memory of those blossoms, Bertha has come, under a cold sky in January, to feel "as close as the flesh." The Vision Quest is complete.

Here at the end of *Sleeping Preacher* the binary opposition between Valley and City, farmer and poet, Bertha and Julia, the Old and the New Garden, and Adam is not so much compromised or resolved as

---

26. A recent poem by Juanita Brunk, "This World," presents morning glories in botanical detail much like Kasdorf's. Brunk's morning glories, while at first etherealized, are finally "of this world," while in Kasdorf's poem they point from earth to heaven. — *Brief Landing on the Earth's Surface* (Madison, WI: U. of Wisconsin Press, 1986), 3.

transcended. The critical, though caring, attitude toward the Valley evident in such poems as "The Sleeping Preacher," "Vesta's Father," "The Mean Words of Jesus" or "Mennonites" has become through Bertha—who personifies the Valley community at its ideal best—transformed. On her outward journey the poet has been sustained by "the shade of pensive beauty" that comes only with expulsion. In her rough work with the morning glory vines the poet is visited by Bertha through the memory-imprint of those "heavenly blue bells that unfurled each day" in the Valley during the summer month of her step-grandmother's death. Kasdorf's earlier spirit of determination, expressed in her move out of the Valley, persists; here she is intent on "keeping enough space clear for tomatoes next spring." The elevated status of work, whether plowing or writing, remains. But the scattered morning glory seeds promise a harvest more lasting even than canned tomatoes, more beautiful than all the mundane glory of Solomon. The gifts symbolized by the morning glories is the gift of grace, theologically anticipated in the title poem "The Sleeping Preacher," implied in "Freindschaft" and now lyrically transformed through inspired linguistic and imaginative discipline that can even snatch a grace beyond the reach of art. Because each flower unfurls only once before it is "withered into used tissues by dusk," what it symbolizes is not immortality but resurrection, the basis for Christian faith and hope, a gracious expression of the ingrained Amish humility sometimes known as *Gelassenheit*.

John Ruth's call in *Mennonite Identity and Literary Art* for writers to articulate the "holy meaning of our identity" appears to be answered in *Sleeping Preacher*. He looks for the Mennonite literary artist, grown to be "a whole person," who speaks "from the core of a tradition which gave . . . the priceless gift of identification with the Kingdom of God." Kasdorf demonstrates that while post-lapsarian language may be broken, in the hands of artists it is capable of being meaningfully redeemed. We may continue to be puzzled by thorny patches like that about the poet as Cain who slays with words—passages of unplumbed confessional power—but Kasdorf in her own way has come remarkably close to fulfilling Ruth's wish for the kind of Mennonite artist who will "*penetrate* and *articulate* the unique values of our ethos" (63).

In "Morning Glories" we might perhaps feel also a sense of supernatural forces stirring in that little garden: Christian, but not exclusively or necessarily so. There may be a touch here of ethnic superstition, not unlike that associated with the aura of sleeping preachers, or with blood lineage, or pow-wow practitioners. The dead Bertha is now "as close as the flesh." A little Puerto Rican neighbor girl runs from Kasdorf's hand waved in dead Bertha's glove. Seeds that in ancient folk medicine are considered hallucinative burrow into the winter earth. In "Lycidas" Milton took pains to acknowledge pagan elements in the pastoral tradition that fell outside the boundaries of orthodox Puritan faith:

> For so to interpose a little ease,
> Let our frail thoughts dally with false surmise.

Not that Kasdorf need be consciously emulating Milton's elegy. She is vulnerable to her own surmise. It is simply that the pastoral elegy dialectic of despair and hope resonates throughout literary history. It is in the air; it is at hand. Acknowledging the presence of doubt and humility in the face of death, it offers a modern Christian poet struggling with grief and its catharsis some freedom of movement, some therapeutic breathing space.

As pastoral elegies, the poem and the book end in apotheosis. After mourning deeply, Christian pastoral looks in hope to the future, shedding light on darkness. The poet's labor, like Bertha's, will be rewarded ultimately in heaven. "Lycidas," written upon the death of Edward King, is essentially not about King (nor "Morning Glories" about Bertha) but about John Milton, a self-conscious young poet who, fearful about the future, where "the blind Fury . . . slits the thin-spun life," must work in hope. Like the weary Kasdorf wondering what part of her present life as urban poet Bertha would accept, Milton finds that vocational assurance must come from a tested hope of heaven:

> Fame is the spur that the clear spirit doth raise
> (That last infirmity of noble mind)
> To scorn delights, and live laborious days.

But Fame is no plant that grows on mortal soil. It:

> . . . lives and spreads aloft by those pure eyes
> And perfect witness of all-judging Jove
> As he pronounces lastly on each deed.

According to Milton and Kasdorf, God's judgment on a faithful poet's self-transcending work is at last redemptive.

Milton the Dedicated Poet sets out "Tomorrow to fresh woods, and pastures new," much as Kasdorf, missing the Valley, in "Green Market, New York" looks forward nevertheless to her beckoning vocation. And with the tools at hand that have come to her—archetypes, genres, metaphors, techniques—Kasdorf will scratch in her new garden, plant tomatoes and, at the same time, inadvertently stir the soil for dormant morning glories.

For Valley natives it would seem that tomatoes are a staff of life (all that canning!). Tomatoes are their discipline, their daily prose. Kasdorf works hard to make hers grow. At the same time she is doing the work necessary to create poetry, a gift of morning glories inspired by the memory of Bertha, rooted in the Valley and nourished by hope. The Vision Quest is rooted in the home community. Risen out of fresh fields and pastures new, these poems give beauty to the dark mountain walls of the Valley as they do to the City's chain link fence.

Julia Kasdorf's final, forward-looking words in *Sleeping Preacher* articulate a fusion of discipline and grace:

> It will take all I've got to keep enough space
> clear for tomatoes next spring, when this plot
> comes up all morning glories.

There are more morning glories, more poems to come from her new garden. Like the darkened, roughened hands of dedicated poets gone before, her hand is on the plow.

THE POETRY OF JEAN JANZEN:
A THEOLOGICAL APPROACH

Laura Schmidt Roberts*

Abstract: This essay explores theological themes and imagery in the recent work of Jean Janzen by considering poems from an as yet unpublished manuscript *Tasting the Dust*, the first section of which is a collection of poems about the San Joaquin Valley of California. I will focus on three poems from the first section of *Tasting the Dust*: "Claiming the Dust," "In Tule Fog" and "The Mountain." In these poems Janzen's identity as a San Joaquin Valley poet and as a Mennonite/Anabaptist poet is most visibly intertwined. The experience and geography of the valley become powerful imagery for expressing theological themes from her ethno-religious tradition.

". . . THIS HARD EARTH NOT OUR FINAL HOLDING PLACE AFTER ALL . . ."

At a poetry reading in the Fresno Art Museum a student asked Jean Janzen whether she intentionally included verbs in so many of her poem titles.[1] Indeed, the sense of movement that emerges in the titles of many of Janzen's poems is a defining characteristic in the theology of the poems as well.[2] "Claiming the Dust" demonstrates this theme strikingly, dominated as it is by images of motion and change, especially in relationship to the earth and people.

---

* Laura Schmidt Roberts is a faculty member of the Division of Biblical and Religious Studies at Fresno Pacific University, Fresno, California.

1. "I Keep Forgetting," "Holding Back," "Burning Apricot Wood," "Curbing the Appetite." — Jean Janzen et al, *Three Mennonite Poets* (Intercourse, PA: Good Books, 1986). "Potato Planting," "Questioning the Cold," "Reclaiming the Land," "Eating Stones," "Flying With the Light," "Singing Yourself to Death," "Driving in Fog." — Jean Janzen, *The Upside-Down Tree* (Winnipeg: Henderson Books, 1992). "Identifying the Fire," "Dividing the Night," "Going West," "Finding the Pearl," "Looking for the Soul." — Jean Janzen, *Snake in the Parsonage* (Intercourse, PA: Good Books, 1995). Her unpublished manuscript "Tasting the Dust" continues in this tradition: "Claiming the Dust," "Listening for the News," "Looking at Nilsson's *Being Born*," "Beginning Again," "Getting it Right," "Reading the Fields," "Raising the Dust in Siena," "Tasting the Dust."

2. See, for example, "Sometimes," "Postcards To My Sister" (*Three Mennonite Poets*), "Double Rail," "Reclaiming the Land," "River," "One for the Road" (*The Upside-Down Tree*), "Women of the Cloth," "Home," "Looking for the Soul," "Photographs of the Wild" (*Snake in the Parsonage*).

CLAIMING THE DUST

Like nomads we come
to this subtropical valley,
our borrowed space
under the sun. Once
an ancient lakebed,
the July ground powders
under our feet, lifts
in puffs to welcome us.
The children rise, then
run out to pound acorns
under the oaks, calling
to each other from
their rings of stones.
Pale bird-of-paradise leans
out of its gravely bed.
It takes dynamite to plant
an orange tree, our neighbor sighs.

This is our new home,
this valley's layered clay
which offers its sunbaked surface
to the scuffing of our feet,
as if our fragile lives
are enough to rouse the ages.
The slightest breeze, and the dust
becomes skittish, whirls
to settle in the next yard.
But mostly, stillness,
so that the beige siftings
are almost imperceptible.
Fig leaves in a talcum haze.

It is the night we finally learn
to claim. At dusk the children
float their sheets like flattened tents
and sprawl face-up into the warm
‚darkness, and we join them
in this rehearsal—a summer
night travel, the sky's black
curtains pinned back with stars.
That open stage.
This hard earth not our final holding
place after all, but the air
into which we sail,

breath by dusty breath,
toward a different shore.
— *Poetry*, 166 (July 1995), 201-202.

Janzen introduces the earth initially as space borrowed by nomads who come to the valley. This space is not static, whether in regard to its history or its present state. Rather, the substance of this space, the dust of the earth, is dynamic. It has layers of history that mark its journey, from ancient lakebed to dry dust. The dust itself is figured as nomadic, puffing and whirling at the slightest breeze. It will leave the yard of one new home for the next, not seeming to notice, particularly, to whose borrowed space it supposedly belongs. The "beige siftings" may be almost imperceptible, but they occur nonetheless. Granted, not all of the earth is so easily moved ("it takes dynamite to plant an orange tree"), but the abundance of orange trees in the valley bears testimony to the fact that even the hardpan can be changed. This world of borrowed space is a place of change where the earth is moved, whether by wind, feet or dynamite.

Movement is characteristic of the people in the poem as well. Figured as nomads, whose lives consist of moving from place to place, their latest move is to the new home of "this valley's layered clay." However, Janzen makes clear that this borrowed space does not mark the end of the journey. The people are nomads in a more elemental sense. At night, with their faces directed not toward the hot, dusty earth but the warm, dark sky, the journey's end becomes clear. The face-upward sprawl is figured as rehearsal for the final move from the holding place of this earth to the "distant shore."

At least two theological convictions inform the images in "Claiming the Dust." First, the portrayal of both the earth and the people as nomadic implies a view of creation as mutable rather than constant.[3] In Christian scripture and theology the mutability and finiteness of creation is sometimes presented as a contrast to the constancy and infiniteness of God and the eternal.[4] God, however, does not appear as a point of

---

3. This view is present elsewhere in Janzen's work. See, for example, "Temperature of Cruelty," "To My Aunt Dying in Autumn" (*Three Mennonite Poets*); "Osprey," "How It Looks at You" (*The Upside-Down Tree*); "Looking for the Soul," "Movement of Vaulted Chambers," "In November" (*Snake in the Parsonage*); and "Saskatchewan Harvest" —Jean Janzen, *Words for the Silence* (Fresno, CA: Center for Mennonite Brethren Studies, 1984). On occasion Janzen contrasts the relative age or permanence of aspects of non-human creation (mountain, granite, river) with the transience of human life. However, in such poems the movement or change of non-human creation is at least implied. See, for example, "Czar" (*Words for the Silence*), "Note To Conrad Grebel From Mt. Pilatus" (*Three Mennonite Poets*).

4. See, for example, Thomas Finger, *Christian Theology: An Eschatological Approach* (Scottdale, PA: Herald Press, 1989), 2:407-30 and Jurgen Moltmann, *God in Creation* (San

comparison in "Claiming the Dust." What develops in the poem is not the difference between creation and God, but the contrast within the created order between humanity and the rest of creation. For Janzen, humanity shares the mutability of the created order, but with a different end result.

This difference stems from the second theological conviction present in the imagery, that this world is not, in the end, home for humanity ("This hard earth not our final holding place after all"). In "Claiming the Dust" humanity moves and changes, as does the earth itself, but humanity journeys ultimately to leave this world for the next, "breath by dusty breath," in a way that the rest of creation apparently does not.[5]

This notion of life as journey from this world to the next is prevalent in Mennonite/Anabaptist theology.[6] Anabaptists have always felt a strong sense that this world is not home for the believer. Yet coupled with that belief has been the equally firm conviction that the life lived in this world is of the utmost importance; the kingdom of the world to come has broken into this world, and the faithful must live as citizens of that kingdom here and now.[7] The result is a profound tension between yearning for that final home and yearning for the land that is home for now.[8] Both of these longings are present in "Claiming the Dust," as the nomads inhabit their "new home" and in so doing are also reminded of the final journey that awaits them.[9]

Francisco: Harper and Row, 1985), 72-103. This contrast relates to the distinctions in essential nature between Creator and creation. Delineation of these differences has long been a topic of discussion and debate in systematic theology.

5. Janzen is largely silent, here and elsewhere, on the fate of the rest of creation.

6. See, for example, Paul Erb, *The Alpha and the Omega* (Scottdale, PA: Herald Press, 1955), especially Part III; Finger, *Christian Theology: An Eschatological Approach*, 1:135-76; Harry Loewen, "The Anabaptist View of the World: The Beginning of a Mennonite Continuum?" in *Mennonite Images: Historical, Cultural and Literary Essays Dealing with Mennonite Issues*, ed. Harry Loewen (Winnipeg: Hyperion Press, 1981), 85-95; "Eschatology," *ME* 5:247-48. Since this conviction is a central aspect of eschatology, the prevalence of articles on eschatology in North American Mennonite confessions also bears this out. See Howard Loewen, *One Lord, One Church, One Hope and One God: Mennonite Confessions of Faith in North America* (Elkhart, IN: Institute of Mennonite Studies, 1985), 36, 43-45.

7. See, for example, Finger, *Christian Theology: An Eschatological Approach*, 99-115; Robert Friedmann, "The Doctrine of the Two Worlds" in *The Recovery of the Anabaptist Vision*, ed. Guy F. Hershberger (Scottdale, PA: Herald Press, 1957), 105-18; Gordon D. Kaufman, "The Mennonite Roots of My Theological Perspective" in *Mennonite Theology in the Face of Modernity: Essays in Honor of Gordon D. Kaufman*, ed. Alain Epp Weaver (North Newton, KS: Bethel College, 1996), 1-19.

8. See, for example, *Visions and Realities: Essays Poems, and Fiction Dealing With Mennonite Issues*, eds. Harry Loewen and Al Reimer (Winnipeg: Hyperion Press, 1985), 9-10; Calvin Redekop, "The Mennonite Romance with the Land," in ibid., 83-93; Waldemar Janzen "The Great Trek: Episode or Paradigm?" *MQR* 51 (April 1977), 127-39.

9. See also Janzen's "Wild Grapes" (*Snake in the Parsonage*).

". . . WALKING OUT WE JOIN IT, OUR HAIR AND BREATH BECOMING ONE WITH THE PAST. . . ."

The idea that the coming kingdom has broken into this present reality implies that the other, eternal world may be experienced in the here and now. This conviction informs the imagery of "In Tule Fog."

IN TULE FOG

It rises from the fields
like an ancient seabed
come back from the dead,
and hovers. Walking out
we join it, our hair and breath
becoming one with the past.
We're fish again, finning
through a millennium risen
for us, to cushion us,
to slow us for new sounds.

And she being born into this
diffusion, heaves from one float
into another — her mother's arms.
Her pulse flutters
in quick rhythm against
the slower, steady one.
And surrounding them both
is this rising of the ages,
as though she is not really new, but
fresh to us — given, so we can press
against our cheeks the wonder
of that time, or no-time,
from which she came, to which we go.

The fog itself (typical of the valley in winter) seems to function as a figure of timelessness or the eternal. In walking one encounters not merely fog, but the past resurrected from the dead. In the fog, time has collapsed. The hovering of the fog is perhaps the first great hovering over the waters; there is devolution and we are back at creation ("we're fish again"). Or perhaps the "finning" image is that of the womb, of floating cushion and muffled sound. Either way, present merges with past, producing images of death, resurrection, creation, new life. We join the fog of the resurrected past, if only with our hair and breath. Likewise, the birth of the child in this poem is an encounter with the eternal, and she too is somewhat ethereal. She floats, she flutters. In pressing our cheeks to her we experience not mere flesh but "the wonder of that time, or no-time, from which she came, to which we go." It is as if she comes with eternity still on her, her body not yet having had the chance to get in the way.

These two images of encounter with the eternal reveal a tension between the tangible and the ethereal. Fog and child are tangible, physical realities, tied to this world. Yet for Janzen these become two occasions when we experience the other, eternal world.

The journey imagery is present again, but here Janzen has cast it in the arena of time rather than space. The child has come from "that time or no-time" and we go to "that time or no-time." It is as if she, and we, appear in this world for a window of time but are connected to eternity before that appearance and after it. We journey from this time toward "that time or no-time," as we journeyed from this hard earth toward a distant shore in "Claiming the Dust."

". . . WHERE IS HOME? . . ."

In "The Mountain," Janzen moves back and forth between valley and mountain, using a mixture of images that communicates ambivalence: both places are home, yet neither is home.

THE MOUNTAIN

From their cool, shaded rooms
we carried our children into the sun's glare,
past the burned hills,
and into the immense canyon.

We lifted them, pointing.
The river roared, battering
and shining in its swiftness,
and the walls it had made through

millennia stood taller than the world.
This is home, we said,
but they couldn't hear us.
Not until we carried them

back into their safe beds
did our voices enter them again.
Sleep, we whispered,
and stepped back into

192

our own solitudes, spaces
that couldn't hold us now,
but vibrated outward without end.

In spring the first slopes
are lacy with snowdrops, lupine, and fiddleneck
in a wild band of curve and curl —
the whole field bending
to lure us up and into the mountain's
huge embrace, up to the silence
of a high meadow's chilled nightfall,
the sudden precipice, and its white peak
like the *Sanctus*, overhead.
Over its granite lap, the mountain
has made a bed for us all,
pine-fragrant with dew gathering
for our lips, a place we had only
imagined until we entered like a child.
For the mountain calls the child,
the one who awakens early, who hear
the small sounds of seekers beside the streams.
In the silence of dawn, the rustled of leaves
where the chickaroo leaps, the cracking
of seeds, the jay's blue streak.
No one sees him turn his back to the campground;
he doesn't hesitate, but follows
the source, pumping his arms in a run
before he pauses to turn back,
and discovers he has lost his way.

Where is home?
Is it this magma cooled and lifted,
the rocky ledge where poppies cling,

the roaring river cutting in,
and the peak with its icy distance
and sustenance?

Or is it our ancient valley seabed
which the mountain feeds,
where cotton bolls thicken and vines

swell with grapes?
Grace and necessity, the endless paradox.
Hungry, we open our mouths and arms,

and there, over the other's shoulder
we see the mountain, its craggy peak crowned
and waiting, even when it is hidden among clouds.

The "cool, shaded rooms" and "safe beds" of the valley become too confining a space after the experience of "the immense canyon" ("spaces that couldn't hold us now, but vibrated outward without end"). The mountain offers its "granite lap" and even "has made a bed for us all." These may be comforting domestic images, but the mountain is also a place of danger where the child loses his way. The third section of "The Mountain" finally asks the question outright: "Where is home?" The mountain, with its grandeur and life-giving water and danger? Or the valley with its ample sustenance for human life and its flat confines? "The Mountain" ends with a hungry embrace of the valley's abundance, but with the mountain ever present. Janzen somehow must have both in sight, for her home must include both: the grace of the mountain's water, and the necessity of the valley's abundance. The endless paradox.

Perhaps it is the sense of paradox that keeps Janzen moving. For "Where is home?" is a profoundly theological question for her as well. Where is home for the nomads in "Claiming the Dust" — the new home in the valley dust or the final destination, that "different shore"? Where is home for mother and child in "In Tule Fog" — this world in time, into which one is birthed and one lives, or "that time, or no time, from which she came, to which we go"? The prominence of journey imagery and the theological conviction that this world is not our home means that Janzen is often working between the two poles of this world and the next, and in some ways never quite settles in either.

These three poems then embody several pairings in theological tension: permanence and transience, mutability and constancy, this world and the next, the tangible and the eternal. The interrelation of things and the tension between polarities are themes often present in Janzen's work.[10] This vision of life lived out between polarities or within

---

10. Several of Janzen's manuscript titles bear out this notion: *Words for the Silence, The*

paradoxes keeps Janzen on the journey, between valley and mountain, day and night, earth and sky, this time and no time, this world and the next. She thereby reflects a fundamental conviction of the Christian faith, that truth comes in paradox: divinity and humanity, transcendence and immanence, sovereignty and free will, righteousness and forgiveness, the now and the not yet.

Upside-Down Tree, Snake in the Parsonage. Specific poems include "The Chalk Mountains" (*Words for the Silence*); "The Temperature of Cruelty," "Red," "Solo," (*Three Mennonite Poets*); "Double Rail," "Vermeer Had It Right," "River" (*The Upside-Down Tree*); "Going West," "Flash Flood" (*Snake in the Parsonage*).

WHEN FLESH BECOMES WORD: CREATING SPACE FOR THE FEMALE BODY IN MENNONITE WOMEN'S POETRY

BETH MARTIN BIRKY*

Abstract: This essay explores the representation of the female body in poetry by Juanita Brunk, Jean Janzen, and Julia Kasdorf. Like many women, these three Mennonite poets write from a history of patriarchal condemnation of and restrictions on the female body and attitudes that have alienated women from their own bodies. Such a dualism between body and self not only undermines a woman's self-esteem, but also her spirituality because she is denied the unity of body, spirit and self that is represented most powerfully by Christ as the incarnation of Word in flesh. In their intimate, lyrical exploration of the female body in their poetry, these poems offer a unique incarnation of flesh in word, a fusion of image and thought that captures the way mind and spirit are bound to physical reality.

And the Word was made flesh, and dwelt among us . . . full of grace and truth.

—John 1:14.

In "The Laugh of the Medusa" Hélène Cixous declares: "Woman must write her self: must write about women and bring women to writing, from which they have been driven away as violently as from their bodies."[1] As a French feminist critic exploring female body and language, Cixous calls female writers to awareness, acceptance, and more intimate exploration of the relationship of body and self than society has historically permitted or encouraged. Cixous claims that "by writing her self, woman will return to the body which has been more than confiscated from her, which has been turned into the uncanny stranger on display. . . . Write your self. . . . Your body must be heard."[2] And indeed, since Cixous' famous 1975 essay, numerous women have written about self and body and explored voice and identity in unprecedented ways.

Cixous identifies and responds to patriarchal oppression and repression that has controlled women's bodies in language and in

---

*Beth Martin Birky is associate professor of English at Goshen College.

1. Hélène Cixous, "The Laugh of the Medusa," in *Feminisms: An Anthology of Literary Theory and Criticism*, eds. Robyn R. Warhol and Diane Price Herndl (New Brunswick, NJ: Rutgers U. Press, 1991), 334.

2. Ibid., 337-38.

experience throughout a long history that does not require summary here. This same history has been shared by Mennonite women, with issues of female body and identity further shaped by theological and cultural definitions of and restrictions on physical appearance as well as on women's roles in the community and church. From the question of women wearing head coverings to restrictions on ordaining female pastors, the female body and voice have been integral to issues facing Mennonite women. I remember, for example, my mother's story about not being able to teach Bible school in the early 1950s because the bishop found out she used curlers in her hair. (The bishop never bothered to discover that she only curled her thin, straight hair so it would better conform to the shape of the modest roll at the base of her neck.) Her perceived transgressions of the accepted female body became a reason to silence her. Although I experience more freedom in the church and in society than my mother did, I still live with the legacy of what Di Brandt has referred to as a "tradition which has designated [women] as subordinate, silent, and sexually *other*," a history that has placed many restrictions on the voicing of life in a woman's body.[3]

My awareness of this alienation of body and self has been heightened by my reading of Mennonite women's poetry, where I find other Mennonite women heeding Cixous' call to women's identity and body through writing. In the poetry of Juanita Brunk, Julia Kasdorf, and Jean Janzen, in particular, I have found an honest exploration of life *as* a female body, whether negative or positive, whether rejecting patriarchal limitations or asserting personal discoveries. And I intentionally say *as* a female body, not *in* or *with* a female body, because these poets write their lives as women who experience, explore, and give voice to a self that is both mind and body. I examine the way I have experienced their poems as acts of incarnation, of flesh becoming word in a way that has allowed me to grow into fuller understanding of my self as a spiritual and physical being. As a Mennonite woman and feminist critic, I do not claim to be what Susan Suleiman would call the "ideal reader" of Mennonite women's poetry, nor do I claim that my reading is shared by what Stanley Fish would call my "interpretive community." I can only attempt to describe the discoveries I have made in the private conversations between poet and reader, discoveries that center on the intimate realities of life as a female body.

In Mennonite women's poetry I have encountered a complex exploration of body and self that I refer to above as incarnation. By this I mean an incarnation in language of each woman's physical and

---

3. Di Brandt, *Dancing Naked: Narrative Strategies for Writing Across Centuries* (Stratford, ON: Mercury Press, 1996), 38.

emotional experience, of flesh becoming word in a powerful parallel to
the Word becoming flesh offered by God's incarnation of spirit in flesh.
Janzen captures the relationship between the incarnation of spirit in flesh
and spirit in language in her poem "Overflow":

> Our stories are too big
> for our bodies. Our first heartbeat
> is spill-over, and we are born
> in a rush of water and cries.
> With our whole body we lift
> our first vowels to the air —
> a stream, pressing
> from a place we do not know.[4]

Incarnation: the Word becomes flesh, but also the flesh becomes word in
voice and in poetry. And in the textual bodies of Mennonite women's
poetry, I have felt the truth and grace of incarnation, of the powerful
spirit in body that makes up the self. As intimate, lyric expressions of
feeling in the first person, these poems offer the distilled intensity of
experience, the fusion of image and thought that captures the way mind
and spirit are bound to physical reality. The two cannot be separated.

Unfortunately, the pervasive dichotomy between body and soul in
Western thought, as Nancy Mairs observes, often results in attitudes and
language that separate identity from body. In a collection of essays,
Carnal Acts, Mairs notes that we even speak of our body as something
separate, saying for example, "I have a body" rather than "I am a body."[5]
But the relationship between body and self is complex. We understand
our experiences and express ourselves through language, language that
is not possible without body, as Janzen's poem "Overflow" reveals.
Instead of exploring that connection, Mairs says, we tend to "widen the
rift between the self and the body" and "treat our bodies as
subordinates, inferior in moral status."[6] We resort to a dualism that
denies the embodiment of spirit in flesh and the integral relationship
between the body, language, and self-understanding.

As these Mennonite women poets write the female body, their poems
resist this dualism and create a space for the female body in which I can
consider my own experience. In her 1992 essay "Bringing Home the
Work," Julia Kasdorf claims that the "work of poetry requires that the
writer gain deep access to her emotional life and write to make sense of

---

4. Jean Janzen, "Overflow" *Gospel Herald* (Oct. 14, 1997), 6.
5. Nancy Mairs, *Carnal Acts* (New York: Harper, 1990), 84.
6. Ibid.

it."[7] When a writer finds that emotional life inextricably linked to body, the two coalesce for the reader as well. With a similar goal to write from her emotional and physical experience, Mairs urges the woman writer to "tell the truth about her body. . . and its passions" and "giv[e] tongue to her own delight and desire."[8] Such writing, Mairs says, is a gift to other women.[9] In telling the truth about their bodies and exploring the intimate connection of body and self, these three Mennonite women poets offer me the poetic truth of their experience and expand my own sense of body and self. By forging this experience of body in language in her poems, each woman has given me language for my own self-understanding.

A poem that captures well my experience with the way Mennonite women poets create space for the female body is Juanita Brunk's poem "On this Earth," from her 1996 collection, *Brief Landing on the Earth's Surface*:

> To love my own, my body,
> to know without saying, *legs, you are good legs,*
> and feet and stomach and arms, good, and the spaces
> under my arms, and the brown pigments
> splashed across my back like tea leaves.
> To love my body the way
> I sometimes love a stranger's: a woman
> on the subway, tired, holding her two bags,
> a child slumped against her like another sack
> as the train stops and starts and the child says something
> so quietly no one else can hear it,
> but she leans down, and whispers back,
> and the child curls closer. I would love my body
> the way a mother can love her child, or the way
> a child will love anyone
> who gives it a home on this earth, a place
> without which it would be nothing, a dry branch
> at the window of a lit room.[10]

Here I find several important themes that resonate with poems by Kasdorf and Janzen. The first is an intimate and private, yet very ordinary, account of a woman's body, one that rejects or replaces the tendency to eroticize the woman's body for male pleasure. The second theme concerns nurturing and enlightening relationships to other

---

7. Julia Kasdorf, "Bringing Home the Work," *Festival Quarterly* (Spring 1992), 10.

8. Mairs, *Carnal Acts*, 60.

9. Ibid.

10. Juanita Brunk, "On This Earth," in *Brief Landing on the Earth's Surface* (Madison: U. of Wisconsin Press, 1996), 25.

women's bodies, relationships so unlike the competition between women, the measuring self and other women against a standard size 8, standards so prevalent in popular media and pervasive in many young women's minds. Finally, in these poems I find an affirmation of and hope for the unity of body and identity that is so often destroyed by society's classification of the female body as "other," as an object to be worshipped or reviled. Although these poems ultimately assert the centrality of body to identity, they also acknowledge the struggle and pain involved in reclaiming and creating space for the woman's body, whether in language or in experience.

The first feature I observe in Brunk's "On this Earth" is the startling normalcy of the description of a woman's body – unlike that found in so much other poetry. Gone are the flowing hair, longing eyes, sensuously round mouths. Instead we have feet, stomach, arms, and even underarms, and "the brown pigments/ splashed across my back like tea leaves" (5-6).[11] In a similar way, Kasdorf's poem "Knees" recalls her childlike intimacy with her body that is later altered because of society's expectations for her mature woman's body:

> Every spring I split a knee.
> Mom said, you'll never be a majorette
> with knees like that. Sit still.
> I squirmed, picked scabs,
> everyday at least, peeled the crust
> to see if it was clean and pink
> underneath. Or watched it bleed —
> slowly, like a bloom opening
> then the thick red petal
> sliding down my shin until
> it was stopped by a finger or tongue.
>
> Now knees seldom bleed.
> They just work
> under hose or jeans,
> and I laugh at men who look.
> Knees, just gristle on bone,
> and there are scars on these.[12]

Knees as objects for men to ogle cause the speaker to laugh. Her knees are really just "gristle on bone" (16), and they still carry scars of an

---

11. Ibid.

12. Julia Kasdorf, "Knees," in *Sleeping Preacher* (Pittsburgh: U. of Pittsburgh Press, 1992), 56.

earlier intimacy, of "peel[ing] the crust" to explore the relationship of the physical surface to the interior reality.[13] The speaker remembers a sense of pleasing curiosity about her body ("to see if it was clean and pink/ underneath. Or watched it bleed—/slowly, like a bloom opening") and expresses her current sense of loss ("Now knees seldom bleed").[14] The bleeding, scarred knees give way to the menstrual blood that marks womanhood, that also marks a shift from the normalcy of body to the absurd roles a woman's body must sometimes play in society.

The second element I find is a sense of connection to other women's bodies, a connection of solidarity and sympathy. In Brunk's poem, the speaker actually loves another woman's body. In her snapshot of a child slumping against mother, accepting unquestioned comfort provided by her body, we are given a glimpse of the way body can connect to self-love. The speaker offers metaphors for a relationship between body and self in a mother's unconscious giving of love or a child's blind acceptance of love, a curling closer of the self to the body.

In Kasdorf's "Ladies Night at the Turkish and Russian Baths" we also get a sense of woman's body in community, with a tension between isolation and communion. As the speaker descends into the steam room, she says,

> . . . an old woman looks up;
> slender gourds hang off the cage of her ribs,
> and when she wrings the pink cloth on her crotch,
> I see a bun, bald as a girl's, and think *crone*,
> ashamed. She runs weary eyes down my form,
> then closes them (8-13).

But one woman's assessment of another dissolves in the steam bath,

> . . . in the hot cave where women drape
> between streaming spigots. Some murmur,
> most are silent, except when one
> grabs a bucket and dumps it onto her chest
> with a groan. Our eyes meet and we grin,
> grateful to show and view the real shapes
> of ourselves: so many different breasts
> and hips that get smoothed over by clothes,
> none of us looking like we're supposed to! (26-34).[15]

Later she lies on a cot, stretched out by a "stunning young woman" who "cries silently,/ tears sliding like sweat into her turban./ Whatever her

---

13. Ibid.

14. Ibid.

15. Julia Kasdorf, "Ladies' Night at the Turkish and Russian Baths," in *Eve's Striptease* (Pittsburgh: U. of Pittsburgh Press, 1998), 53.

reason, I feel bound to that/ sadness" (40-43).[16] To love other women's bodies is to share their pain and to discover their power and the power within our own bodies. Unfortunately, women's bodies are so often linked to weakness, and women's identity and spirit develop in relationship to this perceived isolation and weakness.

A third theme concerns the way identity can be connected to body rather than alienated from it, although quite often that connection only follows a conscious act of defiance or rejection of assumed alienation from and powerlessness of a woman's body. Within the assumed dualism between body and self described above, we often feel the need to extend control of the self over the body, a move that can result in self-loathing. "In fact," Mairs says, "we treat our bodies with very much the same distance and ambivalence women have traditionally received from men in our culture. Sometimes this treatment is benevolent, even respectful, but all too often it is tainted by outright sadism."[17] Mairs describes the current obsession with body-building regimens designed to beat bodies into shape, an attitude toward exercise that surpasses the concern for healthy living. Mairs says, "Bodies get treated like wayward women who have to be shown who's boss, even if it means slapping them around a little."[18] In women's writing, and in some Mennonite women's poetry, undercurrents of female masochism and resistance to body exist in conjunction with or prior to assertions of body love or acceptance of self as body.

In the opening line of "On this Earth" the speaker directly confronts this pattern of female self-loathing, which is so often linked to body loathing, by asserting her conscious effort "To love my own, my body." In fact, the verb "love" is repeated in each of the three sentences that constitute this poem. Even as Brunk's poem reinforces my own desire to love my body, the speaker emphasizes the conditional quality of this love, the focus on the future, not the present, a recognition that this type of body love does not yet exist. Beneath her confident assertion of body love lies a longing for a relationship of self to body that cannot be known "without saying, *legs, you are good legs*" (2). As the poem progresses, her repetition of "[t]o love" becomes not so much an affirmation of her confidence but a confession of her knowledge that the love is only occasional, only felt "sometimes": "To love my body the way/ I sometimes love a stranger's" (7-8). And when she begins the final sentence in the poem, the speaker states only, "I would love my body"

---

16. Ibid.

17. Mairs, *Carnal Acts*, 84.

18. Ibid., 85.

(14), with the word *would* indicating an unrealized condition repeated later by the conditional words *can* and *will*. In this poem the speaker explores what it would be like to love her body, but at the same time she admits that it takes deliberate effort to make space for the female body in society, in language, and in her own sense of identity. By concluding that the body is "a home on this earth, a place/ without which it would be nothing" (17-18), the speaker maintains that the self in body is not negotiable; it is reality.[19] Yet she also demonstrates that the relationship between body and self can be very strained and often unrealized.

In a similar way, Kasdorf exhibits the need to address the alienation of the body and self and the constantly evolving relationship between the two before finding acceptance of body *and* self. In "Ghost" the tension between body and self is so strong that the speaker feels like a disembodied spirit:

> In stories brought back from brief deaths,
> patients hover above frantic doctors,
> hoping they will not find a way to pull
> the ghosts back into wracked bodies.
> One of those ghosts slipped out
> when I was a child and a man caressed
> the cleft in my panties. In all memories
> I see the scene from three feet away.
>
> Later, the ghost sat in a back seat
> admiring my boyfriend's face
> as it shifted in a kiss,
> his hand drifting across a shoulder
> to a breast. Even in marriage, the ghost
> taunts from above the bed: *Is it good?*
>
> Walking home late from the train,
> I clutch keys between my knuckles.
> (Why don't I think it would help me to scream?)
> Instead the ghost foresees it all from above,
> and I rage against the vulnerable socket
> I cannot gouge out of this body.
>
> To keep the ghost in place, I lift weights,
> strain against that good force
> binding me to earth. Mine, I instruct
> my brain, my strong arms, my fists,

---

19. Brunk, "On This Earth," 25.

my sweat, the ache of myself in my calves.
And I straddle my love like a bench,
pressing hard so my thighs bulge up
into all their beautiful shapes.

I take the sun like a lover, lie naked
under its radiant gaze, finally safe,
like when a young man faces me on the train
and begins to sketch my crossed legs.
Can I take the touch of his eyes
tracing an ankle, moving up my black tights
from five feet away? *All flesh is grass.*
The priest gently lifts my bangs
and strokes a cross of ash on my forehead,
Remember, from dust you were made.
By morning, it's soot in my pores.[20]

"Ghost" explores the way sexual violation in childhood results in the forced detachment of self from body. Even in the speaker's lovemaking, she does not even claim her own body, referring only to "a shoulder," "a breast." As an adult, her "rage against the vulnerable socket" (19), the physical core of her female body, is evidence of her self-hatred.[21] Her straining "against that good force binding me to earth" resonates with Brunk's title "On This Earth." The determined declaration of "Mine, I instruct/ my brain" (23-25)[22] mirrors the plea of Brunk's speaker, "To love my own, my body/ to know without saying" (1-2).[23] Even with a physically strong body, "thighs" that "bulge up/ into all their beautiful shapes," the speaker does not feel secure. Although she confidently "take[s] the sun like a lover," safe under the sun's "radiant gaze," her self-confidence dissolves into a question when facing a strange man's look: "Can I take the touch of his eyes" (33).[24] By creating her disembodied self, her ghost, the speaker resists the fear of violation and the fear of her own physical vulnerability, but that disembodiment comes at the cost of constant control over and condemnation of her body. The emotional pain that results from this process haunts the self that is created.

---

20. Julia Kasdorf, "Ghost," in *Eve's Striptease*, 12-13.
21. Ibid., 12.
22. Ibid., 13.
23. Brunk, "On This Earth," 25.
24. Kasdorf, "Ghost," 13.

A woman's alienation from her body can result from many messages in our society and in the Mennonite community, as well as from actual physical abuse, but some alienation emerges from the ongoing changes experienced in women's bodies. Sometimes our bodies do feel like strangers, and the changes that take place are frightening. In "The Gardens of the Body," Janzen writes:

> I fear my body
> crushed or stopped, this fabric scrim
> which falls, the way a garden falls,
> the way one fleshy pear falls, holding
> within it an entire tree, the sucking
> roots, the bridal bloom, and the light,
> which in Vesalius glowed in a place
> he never found. (19-26)[25]

The body holds possibilities as a pear holds within it an entire tree. But with that power comes fear: fear of the potential, fear of the unknown, the surprise of regular or irregular menstrual cycles, the sexual stirring, the desire to give life, the fear of infertility, the strangeness of giving birth, the changes imposed by time. All are a part of a woman's life as a female body. Denial of and control over the body can be responses to the inexplicable changes that have historically marked a woman's body as other; celebration and exploration of body can be another response.

In exploring the relationship of this unpredictable body to self, Janzen's poems reveal the need to perceive of and experience the uncontrollable qualities of a woman's body as strength not weakness. In some of the poems, this strength comes from the ability of our bodies to transcend expected boundaries. In sex and in pregnancy, birth, and motherhood, women take others into their bodies and give out from their bodies. In Janzen's poem "Once In The Rain" she remembers:

> how once in a warm autumn rain
> you took me naked to the deck,
>
> how as I lay curved in your arms, your dampness
> entering all of me,
> we dissolved together as if
> God had never separated
> land and sea,

---

25. Jean Janzen, "The Gardens of the Body," in *Snake in the Parsonage* (Intercourse, PA: Good Books, 1995), 56.

how we drifted up over the cedar tips
and the slant of the roof
and hovered there (12-23).[26]

Unlike the hovering ghost of Kasdorf's poem, Janzen's speaker experiences a spiritual transformation that results from the extension of oneself to another, a joining of the physical and spiritual that enlarges her. Giving of body or giving of self can be a powerful merging, where boundaries dissolve into a sense of wholeness that surpasses the experience of an isolated body, a separate self.

Janzen's "Curbing the Appetite" also offers an interesting exploration of the boundaries between mother and child, with the unexpected feelings of separateness and union, estrangement and longing, that accompany giving birth:

They brought them to me
bound in blankets
like cooked sausages,
the fat cheeks bulging
for kisses, their mouths
rooting for my own skin.
I thought of our mother cat
devouring placentas
and umbilical cords,
licking and licking,
barely able to keep
her sharp teeth out
of the soft, flabby necks —
that dark intertwining
of love and possession.[27]

The interesting tension between detachment and possession: babies referred to as "them" and compared to "sausages," cat's sharp teeth devouring, forcing detachment that is needed for growth. Yet detachment is balanced by connection: "cheeks bulging for kisses," "mouths/ rooting for my own skin."[28] The permeation of boundaries between self and other that these poems create conveys a sense of welcoming the other into one's sense of self, not giving or taking, adding or losing.

---

26. Jean Janzen, "Once in the Rain," in *Three Mennonite Poets* (Intercourse, PA: Good Books, 1986), 18.

27. Jean Janzen, "Curbing the Appetite," in *Three Mennonite Poets* (Intercourse, PA: Good Books, 1986), 22.

28. Ibid.

The truth of the incarnation is that a special power exists in the union of spirit *and* body and in the living of self as spirit *and* body. The incarnation of the Word in flesh enlarged human understanding of God; the incarnation of flesh in word in these poems enlarges my understanding of myself. The normalcy of body, the connection to other women, the combating of body loathing, and the hope for unity of body and self: these qualities of life as a female body represent only a fragment of the wide range of women's experiences to be embodied in language. But each woman speaks so that, as Cixous says, the female body is heard. By putting the experiences of life as a body into word, these Mennonite poets have created a space for the female body that offers me a home on this earth.

TRIBUTES TO THREE PIONEER MENNONITE WRITERS

Editor's Note: During the closing session of the conference on Mennonite/s Writing in the U.S. at Goshen College, October 23-26, 1997, speakers paid tribute to three pioneers in the field: John Ruth, Elmer Suderman and Warren Kliewer. Edited versions of these tributes follow.

JOHN RUTH

JULIA KASDORF*

Picture a bookish boy, growing up between English and Pennsylvania Dutch: listening to sermons, listening to bawdy jokes you can tell only in Dutch, listening to Branch Creek in the pasture or, on Sundays, to the singing of poultry processors and market farmers who distrust smooth talkers.

See him leave home for Lancaster Mennonite High School one morning in the '40s, driving down the road before dawn, when light glowing in milkhouses and stables makes him realize: there are other families like ours. One afternoon after classes he turns a corner and hears the men's chorus practicing, and that harmony grabs him with such force that he stalls in the hallway, weeping. Strange boy.

After one year at Eastern Mennonite College his name falls into the lot back home, and once again he cries, mystically made a minister of God and Franconia Conference, for life. It is 1950; he is 20; this call—to the new mission at Conshohocken—he cannot refuse. So, he finishes at Eastern Baptist College, then continues to study literature at Harvard, wearing his preacher's plain suit like a shield at Cambridge cocktail parties. And Roma digs in the bottom of her purse for change to get her winter coat back from the dry cleaners. There are children now. He gets the Ph.D. in 1968, already an English professor at Eastern but, in 1976, leaves academia altogether—to make films and write the unwritten stories of Mennonites in the New World, still working as associate pastor at Salford.

Each time they ask, he writes a book—more than ten, by my count—for these people who sometimes would rather not read, who are both too eager to grant authority and also suspicious of authority. His four

---

* Julia Kasdorf is Assistant Professor of Writing and Director of the Writing Workshop at Messiah College, Grantham, Pennsylvania.

lectures at Bethel College are published as *Mennonite Identity and Literary Art*, a manifesto that will inspire and vex Old Mennonite writers for a couple of decades.

His is a singular, strong voice, yet the last three videos he has made are about congregational singing. And now, having shown us how to make a literature from our past, having admonished a generation to sing the songs of a strange land in their mother tongue, he is finally working on the one book no one asked him to write. It is supposed to be *his* book, but it comes from yards and yards of 4 x 6 cards filled with notes and gossip. He writes with his ear to the ground, there by the Branch, with his ear to the lips of the old folks. This is the work.

It is about language and all that got lost when we started talking English. It is about all that John Ruth has gathered from listening all these years.

ELMER SUDERMAN

DALLAS WIEBE*

Elmer Suderman was the first person I met who took the idea of a Mennonite literature seriously, at a time in the late 1940s when no one else seemed to consider it a possibility. Certainly his subsequent career proves that very early on he imagined something like a Mennonite literary world and he set out to make it.

He has published extensively, not only in Mennonite periodicals but also in other journals of national standing. Many of his over 200 published poems appeared in *Mennonite Life, Journal of Mennonite Studies* and *Mennonite Mirror*. When his poems appeared in other journals such as *Kansas Quarterly, Cimarron Review, Midwest Quarterly* and others, the subject matter of the poems was often something pertaining to his Mennonite associations.

His efforts to establish an awareness of a Mennonite literature and an audience for it extend to his many articles and even some short stories. In 1949 he published the article "The Mennonite Pioneer in American Literature." In 1992 in *Mennonite Life* he published "Mennonites, the Mennonite Community and the Mennonite Writer," which remains one

---

* Dallas Wiebe is Emeritus Professor of English at the University of Cincinnati.

of the most important and most thoughtful statements in regard to a Mennonite literature.

Probably the most important aspect of his career is the way in which he has kept in touch with Mennonite writers. He has provided a focus for writers and encouraged them in their efforts. He has been a teacher, an advisor and a critic. He has served as a kind of clearing house for information about current literary activity in the Mennonite world. He has always been a repository of information about the historical and current bibliography of Mennonite writing.

Elmer Suderman seems always to have known that someday there would be a "Mennonite/s Writing in Canada" conference and a "Mennonite/s Writing in the United States" conference. He seems to have known that someday there would be a group of writers who were Mennonites or of Mennonite origin and of national importance — writers with substantial publication, writers of national merit quite apart from their Mennonite heritage.

He, as much as anyone else, made that situation possible.

WARREN KLIEWER († JULY 29, 1998)

Lauren Friesen*

The artistic contribution that Warren Kliewer has made and continues to make cannot be summarized in one brief statement or even one essay. His accomplishments span the artistic spectrum — playwright, poet, director, literary scholar, producer, designer, editor, and he developed an enviable reputation as a professor of writing at Earlham and Bethany Colleges and Wichita State University. The serious reader will find his poetry in the *Beloit Poetry Journal, Antioch Review, The Christian Century, Kansas Quarterly, Dramatists Guild Quarterly, Descant* and other notable journals. The short list of his plays includes more than forty titles, and a significant number of these are listed in the Samuel French and Baker's plays catalogs.

There are three published collections of his work — *Red Rose and Gray Cowl; Moralities and Miracles; Liturgies, Games, and Farewells* — and, in addition, he is represented in a number of major anthologies, including

---

*Lauren Friesen is Director of Playwriting at the University of Michigan – Flint. We note with deep regret the death of Warren Kliewer on July 29, 1998, at the age of 66.

the University of Minnesota series, *Playwrights of Tomorrow*. For seven years he was the co-editor of the journal *Religion and Theatre*. He has also made a landmark contribution to literary scholarship. The editors of Arnold Dyck's four-volume collected work claim that Dyck was essentially an ignored figure, even in Mennonite literary circles, until Warren's analysis appeared in 1959. His incisive commentary was the first in what is now a succession of studies on Dyck's plays and novels.

Kliewer's Mennonite roots reach deeper than might be evident at first glance. His plays explore the weight of his heritage to a greater extent than many that focus simply on the decorative, quaint or peculiar expressions of being Mennonite. He has avoided wearing the soft veneer of ethnicity, even though it may have garnered greater headlines and profits. Instead, his journey has been marked by a quest to give dramatic and poetic shape to the human quest for meaning and significance. His dramatic journey began with a search for an integration between religion and theater and was followed by an investigation into the twentieth-century spirit of dislocation. This pilgrimage of an aesthetic soul across the treacherous terrain of the recent decades is diligently recorded in his plays and poems. Through all of this, he has maintained a strong interest in the connections between literary expression and Mennonite culture. Ask him about a Mennonite poet, playwright or novelist and he will usually provide extensive details on their work. That is what it means to belong to a tradition. That is what it means to be a literary Mennonite.

I will highlight only one of his plays. *A Lean and Hungry Priest* is a landmark work because it incorporates the most demanding and innovative of contemporary dramatic form, "epic" theater. This is a form rooted in the theories of Berthold Brecht, who advocated that theater needs to entertain as well as instruct. *A Lean and Hungry Priest* is replete with dramatic inversions, movements of dramatic "alienation," poetic escapades in scatological humor and, in a manner consistent with epic theater, the spine of the work is rooted in an ethical vision.

As a freshman at Bethel College, I had my life changed when I walked into the bookstore and saw a copy of *Moralities and Miracles* by Warren Kliewer. It had never dawned on me that Mennonites could create their own literature. That encounter resulted in my own experiment with pen and paper.

For all of these gifts to us, Warren, we thank you.

BOOK REVIEWS

A Year of Lesser. By David Bergen. Toronto: HarperCollins. 1996. Pp. 215. $12.

David Bergen's first novel hums with the conviction that the twin longings of spirit and flesh register most clearly when held in counterpoint, a continual tension that at its best recalls the dualism of Graham Greene, or more recently, of John Updike. The overcoming of this split metaphysical consciousness obsesses Bergen. But it's precisely the rendering of the split that makes Johnny Fehr, his central protagonist, so compelling.

For Johnny, the old pieties no longer satisfy. It could be that some of this has to do with his father, a Mennonite Brethren farmer who committed suicide by hanging himself from a branch of the tallest elm behind the house. Now Johnny lives on the place with his wife, a big Rempel girl grown too fond of hard liquor. Charlene offers little in the way of consolation, sex or consolatory sex. Johnny must find ways to bide his time.

He seeks ecstatic experience in the small prairie town of Lesser, and the first and foremost venue for this is Loraine Wallace, the widow of a local chicken farmer. Loraine—smart, pretty, tough as nails like the best pioneer women—ably runs an agribusiness operation of 20,000 birds. She also happens to be a sexual ball of fire, lit only for Johnny. It doesn't do justice to their relationship to call it one-dimensional lust, though some readers may begin to wonder when their single-minded vector toward the bedroom will start showing wear and tear. Nor is it an exaggeration to say that the quality of their passion occupies Lawrentian dimensions, something that embraces the sheer physicality of rutting mammalian love but transforms it nonetheless.

We cheer for Loraine and Johnny mostly because Loraine embodies a kind of endurance and grit that is impossible not to admire. Endlessly adaptive, she struggles to find her way in the murky moral landscape. When Johnny gets her pregnant—just one of the book's many fine plot turns—she must contend with, among many other things, her teenage son's conflicted response.

What should a mother do when her boy Chris gets his tongue pierced in solidarity with his p.k. girlfriend Melody who has done her nipple with the same dirty needle? Certainly, Bergen seems to be saying, we are not in Steinbach or Gnadenau anymore. Or we're in a Steinbach that the preachers aren't able to recognize. Loraine may hold more answers than the masters of divinity.

But the preachers obsess Johnny. Once an MB, always an MB, looking to be saved, worrying one's salvation like a dog gnawing a bone. Johnny's repeat baptisms by Phil Barkman, the local charismatic divine, have become something of a standing joke in Lesser. Yet Johnny persists in the spiritual quest. He believes each renewal will do the trick and demonstrates stoic equanimity while the neighbors hide their smiles. Granted lots of free time—in fact maybe too much (his father carried a large life insurance policy, allowing the bereft son financial if not psychological security), Fehr seeks to put his life to some good use through service to others. He establishes a drop-in youth center in Lesser where the borderline delinquent townies can get off the streets, play a little pool and listen to Johnny's drawling cautionary tales about the evils of hallucinogens. Of course, Johnny does not necessarily pass himself off as a moral beacon. That's much of his charm: forthright willingness to admit fallibility.

If the book has a weakness, it comes in the middle. Here Bergen introduces new characters, including rather amorphous New Age women friends of Loraine's, and a university physicist whose patent agnosticism seems too visibly constructed for the book's organic integrity. The physicist carries on sporadic dialogue with Johnny, letting drop a few bon mots about Jesus (he was quite possibly homosexual) and Christianity ("one is not converted" to it, rather "one has to be sick enough for it"). This chapter, portentously titled, "Theory of Everything," reveals to us an author looking for another angle of purchase on the practically manichean split infecting his central character's worldview.

Yet it is the staunchly dualist nature of Johnny Fehr that spells our fascination for him and makes this novel work. I, for one, am relieved when Johnny comes away from his last baptismal immersion most emphatically *not* with a memory of the ineffable raptures of spiritual transformation. Rather, he finds himself remembering with comic delight the glimpse he got of his minister's shockingly diminutive phallus while they changed into dry clothes afterwards.

It would be tempting to read this snapshot as some kind of allegorical comment about patriarchal religious authority in general. But the Rabelaisian humor of that moment is tribute, I believe, rather to a larger comical understanding of grace and honesty about the human experience. Bergen courageously records the shifting awareness of his battered and confused protagonist's vision of the world. In not flinching at the outrageousness or the disjunctions, Bergen gives us not a Theory of Everything, but a perspective that embraces with courage the totality of experience. Here the high and the low meet. Such moments could be called moments of grace, and I'm happy to say that David Bergen's novel is full of them. It is a splendid book.

Marietta College DANIEL BORN

Dancing Naked: Narrative Strategies for Writing Across Centuries. By Di Brandt. Stratford, ON: The Mercury Press. 1996. $16.50.

Dancing Naked, a compilation of short essays, is the latest offering from Canadian poet Di Brandt. These essays, many of them originally written as presentations for various conferences, roam freely over such topics as Brandt's past as a Mennonite woman, language and community, and, most often, poetics — the "how" of poetry, the creative process and the specific narrative strategies a writer employs.

The beauty and power of Brandt's narrative strategy is that it is rooted in the body. Critics often speak of the poet's "voice," but this can unfortunately elicit images of a sound that begins in the throat and travels a short distance to the mouth (or hand). What is implicit in Brandt's four books of poetry and explicit in these essays is that Brandt's voice emerges from a much deeper place in the body. In one essay she describes the experience of writing a poem as moving from the semiotic to the symbolic: "All this unspoken, unspeakable explosive energy being channeled, received into the words. It's magical — another conception, birth-giving, being born" (120). Writing from this deeper place gives both Brandt's poems and essays a raw emotional honesty. The reader senses that as her words emerge from within her, they pick up and carry to the surface all the pain and joy of being an embodied being in the world — and, specifically, of being an embodied former Mennonite woman.

To Brandt's surprise, many of these essays wrestle with being that Mennonite woman. In the introduction, Brandt writes that she had intended to put together a collection of essays on the topic of poetics. However, looking back over the essays, which were written over a roughly ten-year span, she discovered how often the "Mennonite question" came up — specifically, "how long it took me to recover from the trauma of breaking through the strict codes of separatism and public silence I grew up with in the Mennonite community of south-central Manitoba" (9).

The portrait Brandt paints of the Mennonite community is that of a thoroughly patriarchal institution built upon dynamics of domination, violence and the centuries-old suppression of women's voices, what she calls "the great silencing." Such a grim assessment is based on her own story, which we read often in these essays: of how, despite the voices in her head that warned her she would be killed for doing so, she wrote and published the poems that would form her first book, *questions i asked my mother* (1987); of how she survived the fallout for this "betrayal" of her community, in the process leaving almost all of her old identity and community ties behind; of how she healed from the physical, sexual and emotional abuse of her past through the help of other Canadian Mennonite writers and the feminist community in Winnipeg; and of how she eventually reconstituted a self through writing, in the process becoming an acclaimed writer on the Canadian literary scene.

Few poets from Mennonite background writing today have as dramatic a story to tell as Brandt, and her ability to powerfully articulate this story has put her on the cutting edge of the Mennonite literary movement in Canada. This is how she describes this movement (and explains the significance of the book's title): "The new Mennonite writing exists as a transgression, a violation of the authority of God and the Bible and the father. It begins to give voice to the children and women silenced by the tradition. And it does this by a kind of striptease, taking off the clothes of the official story, layer by layer, stripping away the codes we have lived by to get to the stories underneath of our real, aching bodies in the world" (36). The writers are part of this striptease. Through the raw emotional honesty of their writing, they are themselves publicly disrobing, turning the act into a kind of dance that exposes the lies of the Mennonite community's "authorized story" and strips it of its hegemonic power, according to Brandt.

Canadian literary critic Hildi Froese Tiessen, in a speech delivered at the recent "Mennonite/s Writing in the U.S." conference, takes rebel Mennonite writers and critics (including this reviewer) to task for the kind of binary thinking expressed in Brandt's analysis. Conceiving of personal/cultural existence in binary terms leads such thinkers to postulate monoliths such as "the Mennonite community" and "the Mennonite master narrative" (or authorized story) that must then be resisted. According to Froese Tiessen, such binary thinking negates the complex personal and cultural situations in which contemporary Mennonites live. I found myself thinking of, and agreeing with, Froese Tiessen's analysis when reading this book. The fact is, there is not one monolithic Mennonite community but numerous communities, all of which contain mixtures of life-giving and death-dealing dynamics. What I longed to read in Brandt's book was more recognition of these multiplicities.

I understand Brandt's anger and applaud her sense of moral clarity and outrage, born of hard experience, that sees violence and domination the rest of us might be too desensitized to see. I know why she had to run as far away as possible from the Mennonite community. And yet I found myself wanting her to turn her face toward home again and discover if she sees something there other than violence and repression. Perhaps that is already happening. In the last essay of the book, Brandt writes that becoming a writer for her meant breaking the "rules of language and sensibility and behavior" (159) that she learned from her grandfather, whom she characterized as an authoritarian, violent leader in her Mennonite community. And yet, she admits that she feels deeply connected to him and his vision of a spiritual community and goes on to list the gifts of "creativity and hope and desire" she acquired from her maternal ancestors. Is Di Brandt finally going to make the journey home again? We can only hope that such a perceptive and passionate writer will start taking tentative steps in that direction, and that she will write about what she finds when she gets there.

Oakland, California   SHERI HOSTETLER

Brief Landing on the Earth's Surface. By Juanita Brunk. Madison, WI: University of Wisconsin Press. 1996. Pp. 54. $17.95.

Brief Landing on the Earth's Surface begins with a poem about the self in "This World." The opening problem is to "wake up" the consciousness to the offerings of a lively, expanding world, after experiencing the deaths and separations of the past:

> I want to wake up again
> to this world, this time a throat, wide open,
> this time one of many, on a vine, shouting, for one day
> before they shrink to tiny fists,
> to wizened purple:
> oh, blue, blue world, a cup of light
> we have to drink, our potion,
> a morning holding out its glory.

The expansive perception of a "blue, blue world" is not sustainable, however. Section II in this collection explores the reasons why no one can really have an extended merger of sensation and imagination, feeling and thought, world and self, that is so strongly desired in recompense for the later, inevitable shrinkages caused by experience and grief.

As the poem "Anniversary" establishes, to enter the world is not always to enter a readable, meaning-offering structure like a flower: flowers are user-friendly instruments, offering beauty as symbolism; they have names that drop broad hints about their meanings. In contrast, "Anniversary" presents marriage history in terms of its most unreadable archive — the garbage, the daily excess, the bag splitting open as a necessary sort of archeological site. The poem explores how the world presses itself out of its bag onto the holder, almost demanding to be read, but is not fully legible anyway. Even one's own family life and marriage eludes interpretation: "that blankness" of the world becomes irreconcilable with the desire to see and understand "what you think you saw" (9).

Section II continues as a troubling catalogue of ways in which the modern mind does not experience a merger of mind and world, but romantically wants that full connection anyway in the context of relationships, spiritual searches and other post-Edenic conditions (as signaled most clearly by "After the Garden"). It ends with perhaps the best list poem I've seen in a long time. "Valentine" piles up a tirade of all the wrongs of relationships gone wrong and the terrible things people really do say to each other as a self-consciously predictable, escalating melodrama, and then turns that momentum into an epiphany of the holiday spirit which brings the pleasure of the body back: this is a smart and fun working up of the holiday that refers to a massacre and love at the same time. In the context of the poem, the cultural history and language structure that brings the pleasure of Valentine's Day is the same structure that understands romance as a series of imported power relations and ventriloquized clichés. The poem alludes to the broad range of poems by Sylvia Plath and others who use the historical, public histories of violence to provide the metaphors of the mutually degrading power relations possible in love gone awry. But the poem ends with all the romanticism of Romanticism, as sexuality asserts its quirky holiday spirit despite what the consciousness knows about public histories and relationship traumas:

> Right now the moon is as fine
> as a baby's fingernail up in the sky
> and a tiny thread hangs from the hem of a long black skirt,
> one tug and it all unravels,
> one tug and I'm naked, it's Christmas,
> it's Valentine's Day, it's March,
> it's April, it's Halloween.

Section III starts over with the wakening of potential. "Green Waters" begins the section by posing an old man recovering memory and a young girl experiencing a sexual awakening. One of Brunk's strengths as a poet is her ability to complicate metaphor and structure in a coherent, doubled structure. Although this section focuses on childhood, the doubled structure of an old man's memory with a young woman's changing body prevents a naive treatment of childhood as the era of unadulterated happiness. In "Green Waters," both aging memory and young expanding consciousness are developed through the metaphorics of algae: Brunk very precisely exploits the proliferating qualities of algae cells and the interiority of the operation, inside, under the "green weight" of skin.

Across this section, poems articulate linkages between language and the body in order to find moments of fullness called for in the opening poem of the collection. In "Letter to Myself as a Child," the resonances of the phrase "Amazing Grace" linger and transfer to a wide range of experience, some of it vaguely threatening, some of it about the plenitude of the body. The richness of childhood in "All Sweet Things, Like Forgiveness, Are A-Falling" compensates for the poem on the facing page, "My Father's Tongue," in which a father does not communicate love through words. Rather, expression is channeled into his obsessive rites of reclamation: the constant repair and collection of old cars, dolls and household items left out as trash.

The section is well shaped. The final poem in this section pulls away from the fullness found in these poems, and develops a turn into the final section of the book: I see it as the cusp poem in the work. Just past the cusp of youth myself, having turned 35, the poem "At Thirty-Four" moved me. Placed on page 35, positioned just after its own passage, the poem speaks of the longing to be past all the heroism of youth: "Suppose it were alright / to be small," it begins, already knowing it would not be alright, that family, friends, publishers and history itself expects some form of progression. The speaker thinks of being "not the letter / but the seal," knowing that the poem always already is "the letter," that is, meaning in language, and that language is turned loose. The ironic edge of the poem in its opening supposition is that language never seals itself or the thinking, perceiving consciousness off from the world.

Finally, Section IV offers a short series of poems with wilder metaphors: the book shifts away from precisely interpreting the revelatory quality of images of everyday life into questing for other, different realities: the final poem is the title poem, and the "brief landing" is the "lift and wave" of "corners of tablecloths" that might mean something when transformed into writing, or might not. Successful flashes of the Romantic merger of mind and world, subjectivity and the exterior object world, are realizable only as a series of singular events, or even as one event, a "brief landing" in the title metaphor.

The success of this book is the repeated tracing of desire for the entry into the changed world, and then, over and over, the parallel tracing of a resistant structure of knowledge, experience and the narrowing of expectation. Sometimes that structure takes on the religious structure of "After the Garden"; sometimes that structure offers a search with an open form.

Bethel College, North Newton, Kansas AMI M. REGIER

Eve's Striptease. By Julia Kasdorf,. Pittsburgh: University of Pittsburgh Press. 1998. Pp. 88. $25.

In one of the concluding poems of Julia Kasdorf's remarkable new book, *Eve's Striptease*, the poet's ledger lists three major personal investments with uncertain yield. In each case, the accounting notes the memory of a different Mennonite woman who helps to endow and firm up these investments just as the investor is about to say no out of fear or confusion. And then the bottom line: "When I wonder / how I should live this only one life, / I think of how they tell these stories: / honestly, without explanation." Such a telling is also the return on Kasdorf's undertaking in her book as a whole. But one should not overlook her three cold-sweat investments, for they dominate the reader's attention throughout: trying to separate "my own desire / from the wishes of others," setting "out once more alone" from the known, and tracing "one more sorrow back to its source." Here we have the three principal impulses of the book and the order of its distribution of emphasis.

To "separate my own desire" means, in this book, to write the complicated, inconsistent, irreducible, glorious, distressing history of the body — but here emphatically a woman's body. Such a writing, mentored by the recognition that "we all loved our bodies before learning / to feel ashamed," is underwritten by the memory that mother "let me learn for myself all the desires / a body can hold, how they grow stronger / and wilder with age, tugging in every direction/ until it feels my sternum might split / like Adam's when Eve stepped out, / sloughing off ribs." In her way Kasdorf, of Amish background, has followed Whitman's lead of singing the "body electric," which few women poets have done until recently. Writing the woman's body and its desires as memorably as she has done is still new and thrilling after two or three decades of notable precedents. Her body language and all the ineluctable, zany and often painful desires it holds are unforgettable, an assurance of things hoped for, the evidence of things too rarely seen, not only in Mennonite or Amish writing but also in American poetry.

A squeamish reader or two may respond to the first half of Kasdorf's book as Whittier did to his presentation copy of Whitman's 1855 *Leaves of Grass* or as my tenth- and eleventh-grade English teacher did to "Song of Myself." Not far into Whitman, Whittier added the book as an inflammable to logs glowing in his fireplace, and no farther into Whitman than the school curriculum mandated as minimum, my teacher harangued us on the apparently related and clearly disgusting subjects of Whitman: personal voice, physicality, sensuality, baseball and assertive women. Most important to him was right doctrine, which he found in Milton, commentaries by Jewish and non-western scholars notwithstanding.

But most readers will be grateful for the gift outright of Kasdorf's achingly beautiful language of desire and of a "full store" of unavoidable passings from discovery to dark discovery and from expectations and surprises of childhood to retrospections and surprises of adulthood. Startled body-spirit, we might say, for which, in Wordsworthian fashion, "That breath before words" is "so laden" that the words may "one day in memory, finally collapse / against the other's stunned form." Kasdorf's language registers both that laden breath and memory's stunned forms. Poems such as "The Knowledge of Good and Evil," "Eve's Striptease," "A Pass" and Bulbs" (the latter two recalling how a male insinuated his desire across the threshold of violation into the confused awareness of the child and adolescent respectively) are notable examples of these stunned forms. The ruminating anger and sympathy of "A Pass" and "Bulbs" present an adult speaker who refuses to be a victim, and who refuses the safety of denying her past, her body or the passions her mother "passed on to me" and passed on in poems "the way humming / is rolled into notes and strung on a staff." The adult's wonder and amazement over the history of her desires and how these desires still call on the body are affirmed despite the recognition that "The heart that cannot forget its desire / drags the body behind it like the driver / who, admiring a lily by the road, / ends up in the ditch." But safety, too, is important, as the conclusion of "Sixth Anniversary" and its lover's cravings make clear: "I see us,/ gripped by our slow heaving, / and wonder what form of animal / we finally are, / who crave / both safety and hunger."

Some scholars, no doubt, will place the Kasdorf I've just discussed between the covers of Foucault's *History of Sexuality*, or in the same room as, say, the arguments of a Jane Gallop, Hélène Cixous, Luce Iriguay, Judith Butler or Elaine Scarry. Others will revisit traditions of typological, allegorical, sacramental or incarnational interpretation so as to make profitable sense of her work. More often than not, precedents suggest, they will conceal precisely what her language is so insistent on revealing.

They may fare better with the second major burden of *Eve's Striptease*, the difficulties of our love as we set out for the unfamiliar. "Eve's Curse," both title of a poem and theme of a number of poems, refers to the love of place and a life integrated in it that follows us like baggage as we move to the unknown: "your curse/ will be to ache as you've never imagined." Nonetheless, "you will leave," and the new work "will make/ you strange in the end." This theme, anticipated in the opening poem, is strongly signaled at the end of the first half of the book. Small gifts of everydayness in the Brooklyn apartment tallied in "Before Dawn in October" are threatened by the sojourner's knowledge of passing. The physically, spiritually and imaginatively regenerative places of "Our Last Neighborhood in Brooklyn" are left behind but not abandoned — the simple rich excessiveness of Flatbush, for example, as poignantly registered in "Loud," or the diasporic remembering of Jerusalem/Brooklyn in "On Leaving Brooklyn," a poem that rewords the haunting repetitions in the middle of the 137th Psalm. The difficulties of our love are many. There is the love of "complex/lineage of attachment and loss" (a love that "collects in us like trace heavy metals"); there is a special love for "one/ layer of tissue out of seven that survived" and the pink "map of the known world" that healed over the burn; a love of Turkish and Russian baths "stained with a century's grit"; and a love of the "stiff oatmeal coat" the speaker's mother has passed on to her ("so much I stand to inherit"). A friend is clutched in the full knowledge that the metastasis of lymphatic cancer may soon take that friend away. Two thugs by the city pier test the security of her at-homeness. Through her love of nature she learns "this is how you use language/ to know what you will never possess." Her love of literary knowledge and of teaching it is upstaged by cherry leaves falling outside the window "too early and all out of season." Maxine Kumin survives the suicide of her confidant, Anne Sexton, and then survives "her own beauty to keep writing alone," defying "anyone who'd concoct a cautionary tale/ of her life." Despite recurrent loss and sorrow, Kasdorf's speaker refuses to deny her many loves: "*There are too many nos in the world/ to add one more.*"

But many of these sorrows are traced back to their source, and such tracing is the third major emphasis of the book and its pilgrim poet. Sorrow is located largely in love itself — love of place left behind, of family, friends, childhood or youth recalled like flammable skirts and not returned, of good labors that must give way to a new vocation, of an open-ended poetry writing that is always leaving what we know. And of the body and passion we have consented to: "Aging, /our bodies collect wrinkles and scars / for each place the world would not give / under our weight. Our thoughts get laced / with strange aches." This poem, which opens the book, ends with a girl who makes love for the first time: "She's too young to see that as we gather / losses, we may also grow in love; / as in passion, the body shudders / and clutches what it must release." Gathering losses; growing in love. And so like the painters suspended from Brooklyn Bridge, where they are going about their work, "we dare not let go of even sorrow" because "that hanging on, fearless and afraid as these men, is our only home."

With this her second book, Kasdorf takes her place among the major new poets in the United States.

Purdue University   LEONARD N. NEUFELDT

The Cock's Egg. By Rosemary Nixon. Edmonton: NeWest. 1994. Pp. 167. $12.95 Can.

Citoyen Mwanza in the title story of *The Cock's Egg* must educate his future wife when he brings her an egg, "the small brown oval warm within his hands." Mademoiselle Emma is delighted that her hen has started laying, but Citoyen Mwanza corrects her quickly. "The village rooster has shown your young hen how to lay an egg. Now you will certainly be blessed with many eggs to fill your stomach in the days to come" (93-94). The village rooster who wields power with his "con/cocted stories" has provided Mwanza with a black yolk to be buried in the ground, thus taking with it the spirit of bad luck.

Readers of Nixon's provocative short stories set in the western Congo at Kimpese, Kinshasa and Vanga around 1980 will find their interpretative keys in "The Cock's Egg," which shows how the hungry and lustful teacher Mwanza, with the help of his magic egg, succeeds in marrying Emma, the British Baptist biology teacher. The cock controls his harem and his counterfeit egg serves as a perfect symbol of illusion. The rooster, linked with lies and betrayal, makes it possible for the witch doctor to manipulate his followers, for Mwanza to marry his missionary and for neo-colonialism to cooperate with Mobutu. The themes of witchcraft, male chauvinism or misguided missionary idealism reappear in many of the other eighteen stories.

Exploding tampons, copulating rabbits, army ants, jiggers, fearless rats, cockroaches, thieves, a half-burned toad, a heat-infested breeze, sweat, worms — all paint a picture of exploitation and moral depravity that colors the experience of the main characters, young Canadians teaching in secondary schools who rub shoulders with the Congolese and other expatriates. Nixon is a skilled writer with an accurate eye for details that capture the essence of the two years that she taught history and English in the Congo.

The main characters struggle with alienation from each other and from cultures not their own. In "From the Inside Out" Frieda dreams of book club meetings in Calgary, of cheesecake, of airplane rides, "that drawing upward upward into blue" (7), but home alone by herself she must contend with lizards, snakes, cockroaches, trash and prolonged menstrual bleeding while her idealistic husband is off at some other mission station giving seminars or selling hoes.

In "Trappings" Annie traps rats and learns about the mysterious Makita, a young girl glimpsed as a spirit in the forest, who was ostracized, driven to death by her community, "just another black girl dreaming of America." Velma's hope for an idyllic escape to a Mombasa beach with Doug turns into a sweaty, boring trip with Alicia: a night train and then a hot, windowless, seatless matatu on bumpy roads, the hotel a "collection of thatch-roofed huts" (71), no towels, salt water showers, a broken bed . . .

At times one wishes for more continuity, some main characters who would tie the stories together, but then one realizes that Nixon has unified her collection through common settings, the reappearance of certain characters in minor roles and, most important, through references to the rooster and witchcraft. Her use of magic realism is designed to bridge the gap between traditional African religion and western secularism. Her central symbol, the cock's egg, works brilliantly in holding her complex series of stories together, each of which could stand on its own.

No matter how creative and accurate Nixon's portrayal of the expatriate experience in Congo may be (reminiscent as it is of the Teacher Abroad Program of Mennonite Central Committee), it remains, nevertheless, one-dimensional. It is troubling to find such close parallels between her stories and those told by French colonial writers from 1880-1960. Themes of witchcraft, mystery, failed assimilation, jealousy, betrayal, cultural clashes, exploitation and superstition pervaded that literature, which was true to the experience of Europeans who saw only one side of life in Africa. According to an internet page, "Biographical Information about Rosemary Nixon," the writer "accurately conveys a culture enmeshed in witchcraft." Can one summarize so easily the essence of another culture? According to the same document, Nixon claims to have found in writing a way to transcend "a rather simplistic view of what is right and wrong." Yet the very strength of her central image, the cock's egg, tends to leave out another side of life in Africa—the small victories of cross-cultural understanding, the missionaries who aren't naive fundamentalists, religious truth that cannot be reduced to illusion.

In her final story, "I seek. Emigration," Nixon draws upon a scene from childhood in Saskatchewan to paint a different picture of the Congo. A CBC school broadcast from Kinshasa evokes "joyous cacophony goat wails smoke-scented cries market bartering heel-calloused feet honey-citrus-textured music of Africa bone-light lizard-scuttle splash of hot pickpocket wind gourd clutter bright tomato pyramids pebble-scatter of desire coming apart. In me" (166). In that classroom the narrator is a young girl presiding at a Red Cross meeting, eager to escape from her Saskatchewan existence to transform the Congo.

Book Reviews

Although the description itself draws upon Nixon's recent experience, she places it within the context of a child's world. How else does one account for the positive cast of those images not found elsewhere in the book? It invites comparison with another collection of stories, *Swimming in the Congo* by Margaret Meyers (Minneapolis: Milkweed, 1995). The daughter of missionary parents in the Equator province of the Congo, Meyers uses a seven-year-old narrator to record her encounters with the Africans, missionaries, embassy personnel and other expatriates. The eyes of the child miss nothing; we condemn the gossip, hypocrisy, self-righteousness and vanity of the adult world, but we also forgive. Sketched by the child, these characters are too human to dismiss casually, unsympathetically. The world of little Grace Berggren includes witchcraft (in fact, it is the subject of the first story), but it does not function as a key to unlock the illusions of another culture. Life is too complicated and wonderful; Congolese cosmology cannot be summed up in a "cock's egg."

Reading *The Cock's Egg* evoked in me the disappointments, fears and frustrations that one finds in journals of cross-cultural students who struggle to make sense out of their initial experiences. The most intelligent and sensitive fight the hardest battles with despair and cynicism, sometimes winning, sometimes losing. Nixon is too honest in her portrayal of her years in the Congo to gloss over the contradictions of her existence with an easy optimism. Is there no escape from the longing for emigration, from the cycle of exploitation? Liberation, alluded to earlier in the book, does appear in the last paragraph, not as integration into the culture but as escape. The perfect falling of water at Vampa Falls dissolves the image of a blood-red cock; a gust of lemon-swallowed wind allows the writer to cast away her pen and to glide. That lightness of being, a new freedom, works aesthetically if not politically. It may also interpret more accurately than we would like to admit the experience of MCC volunteers (myself included) who have returned back home, who are free from the demands made upon them during their years abroad.

Eastern Mennonite University   CARROLL D. YODER

Man Under A Pear Tree. By Keith Ratzlaff. Tallahassee, FL: Anhinga Press. 1997. Pp. 70. $18.95.

Across the Known World. By Keith Ratzlaff. Arlington, TX: Loess Hills Books. 1997. Pp. 47. $12.

The narrator in Keith Ratzlaff's opening poem in *Across the Known World* warns the reader: "As a rule there's nothing here / to see" (3). But the poems in that volume, as well as in *Man Under A Pear Tree*, present a different view, for seeing is precisely what Ratzlaff helps us to do in his energetic and detailed look at the everyday aspects of life—whether it is a doorknob that breaks and "won't be ignored" (AKW 43) or a "woman in the purple trousers / on the bicycle" (MUPT 3). Although Ratzlaff writes in free verse, he incorporates an engaging array of stanza forms, from brief two-line stanzas to longer verse paragraphs. Using his wonderfully specific images of the land and people around him,

Ratzlaff reflects on sexuality and mortality but also offers suggestions of grace and hope. Although most of these poems do not overtly deal with Mennonites, these volumes contain a deep love of the land and a concern with living reflectively that will likely resonate with many Mennonites.

The two volumes, both published in 1997, reflect similar themes, while differing somewhat in subject matter and style. The title for each volume is aptly chosen, for in a general way each suggests the focus of the collection. Often using the work of Swiss surrealist artist Paul Klee as a starting point, the poems in *Man Under A Pear Tree* show considerable interest in people and particularly in the human body — its attractiveness as well as its tendency to break down. On the other hand, *Across the Known World*, growing out of Ratzlaff's long association with the Midwest, directs our attention to the land and the world around us.

The three sections of poems that make up *Man Under A Pear Tree* show a clear progression. In the first grouping, the poems focus primarily on the body, its sensuousness but also its vulnerability. "Mural from the Temple of Longing," for instance, suggests the power of our sexual nature. The speaker begins by extolling the glories of nature, but after watching the man and the woman across the street pull "A blind down / together," he no longer feels satisfied: "Now the jay / in the wind in the tree / is not what I want" (MUPT 14). In another poem in this section, Ratzlaff shows the body breaking down, pointing to "the sties and caries, / the eruptions and boils, / the limp that now my friend / takes up as she walks her body" (MUPT 12). This theme continues in the second section; indeed, I find the opening poem of this grouping, "Blue Jays," to be one of the most provocative in the volume. Ratzlaff points up the seeming randomness of death by linking a description of his cat's destruction of a blue jay with numerous references to people who have died, leading the speaker to wonder, "Who knows how long" we will live (MUPT 25). However, Ratzlaff moves to an image of resurrection in the final poem of this section — even if it is a resurrection that we may miss because of our preoccupations. The third section of the book shows less concentration on destruction and instead suggests a sense of the eternal, with several poems focusing on angels and the volume ending with a hint of grace in the image of a "woman flying / blessed for no reason with a great invisible gift" (MUPT 70).

"Map Flaws," the second poem in *Across the Known World*, ironically plays off its title to serve as a guide for the volume: the narrator points out that maps look only for the big picture, but "life is a long rite of smallness" (AKW 4) — a smallness that Ratzlaff examines closely. As a generalization (flawed, as all maps are), the two sections of the volume function as mirror images of each other: in the first part, Ratzlaff focuses primarily on the space where he lives, with characters occasionally entering that field of view; in the second section, Ratzlaff emphasizes more his interaction with others, with the land playing a secondary role. Ratzlaff's poems that look at place range from the rambunctious "Disciplining Grapes" —"I'm not polite. Instead of pruning shears / I use the axe. . . . Fear is what I want." (AKW 5) — to the more reflective: "After the Blizzard" —"Last night in the bed covered with blue light / I memorized the farm, measured the boundaries / hoping they wouldn't get away. They didn't"

(AKW 13). His people poems range from a focus on the piano-playing of an autistic child to his loving but violent struggle with a foster daughter to a love poem for his wife. Throughout, the volume yields a clear sense that even while Ratzlaff does not flinch from life's hardships, the goodness of life can be found even in planting "a long unbroken line of carrots" (AKW 18).

Preferences for one creative work over another are always deeply informed by personal matters, so it becomes difficult for me to sort out any "objective" criteria from my own interests. Certainly our family's fairly recent move from the East to the edge of the Midwest, as well as my extended family's solid presence outside of Hutchinson, Kansas (a town mentioned in the title of a poem), contribute to my being drawn to the poems in *Across the Known World*. But there is a difference in style between the two volumes, too, which suggests that the calm of the land has infused Ratzlaff's poems in *Across the Known World*. The energy in this volume is more disciplined, as if the "grapes" have indeed been forced into submission. There are fewer instances of the piling up of ideas and images that abound in *Man Under A Pear Tree*, as in this stanza from "Winterreise":

This is the white fog changing to yellow.
This is Klee's mother after tea in his studio.
This is Schubert dying of syphilis.
This is Schubert singing to the crows (MUPT 5).

Such a technique is engaging, but in the course of the volume finally becomes a bit repetitious.

My overarching response to these volumes is a renewed sense of wonder, a feeling of somehow having seen more clearly what has always been around us. In his weaving of these fine poems from the texture of our everyday lives, Ratzlaff, like the bird in the poem "In March," seems "As if / every time he sings four notes they make a song" (AKW 33).

Bluffton College   L. LAMAR NISLY

Our Asian Journey. By Dallas Wiebe. Waterloo, ON: MLR Editions. 1997. Pp. 449. $30.

Dallas Wiebe's novel is a quest for signs in the apocalyptic trek to central Asia by a band of Russian Mennonites from 1880-1884. It should send descendants of that band into their own attics of family story and memory, but this tragicomic and heroic story will have a much broader appeal as well.

The second chapter is a type of the whole. Two co-pilgrims-to-be on this mad journey have emerged from the Russian winter cold to join the narrator's light and warm fire. As they talk all night long, Wiebe's pilgrim narrator Joseph Toevs offers running commentary on the interaction of life and narrative, of dream and illusion. He is alternatively formal and colloquial, graphic and plain, and ridiculously precise (Abraham is five feet six and one- eighth inches tall). He becomes self-consciously postmodern as he plays upon debates over orality, semiology and consciousness. The symbolic landscape of the novel extends from Revelation to the Russian revolution and by implication to the silent pilgrims of

Heaven's Gate "waiting at the end of the world." The novel places our history as a people squarely in the middle of our own transition into the next millennium. It recreates a moment in Mennonite history in a way that is both hilarious and moving, ironic and heroic. Ambiguity reins.

For all its narrative complexity, the novel tells a pretty basic story in seven chapters named after John the Revelator's seven churches. The middle chapter, "Thyatira," which with 260 pages comprises over half the novel, presents "the great trek" in the form of the diaries of the narrator Joseph Toevs. It records the day to day visions and failures and deaths of the pilgrims who follow their increasingly mad "leader" — the Claas Epp of history who is never named. This section takes us from the Am Trakt colony in Russia to Tashkent and on to Khiva from where Joseph and others eventually defect and where the great leader later dies.

This central diary, which the author parenthetically claims to have translated before it was stolen from his car, is preceded by two chapters that lead up to the great trek, and is followed by two chapters that relate the events in Asia following the narrator's emigration to Newton, Kansas. Finally this "envelope" structure continues outward as chapters 1 and 7 combine to record the shadowy meditations of the aging narrator on the events and significance of his life now approaching its close in Aberdeen, Idaho.

As a journey into the memories of Russian Mennonites with biographical and religious roots in the great trek (see Fred Belk's *The Great Trek*, 1976), the novel will renew and give deepened meaning to family stories and legends, perhaps family pride and shame, and both ethnic and religious identities. But for all of us it illuminates a time and a people, and places them in a symbolic and historical context.

The novel also presents interesting characters. Joseph Toevs is the largely believable consciousness of a Mennonite minister who has lived through tumultuous times. His faith is real, yet he possesses a disturbing capacity for self-deception in his "construction" of meaning out of chaos. He sometimes seems to serve as the voice of his author. His wife Sarah is interesting and enigmatic. She was with Joseph on the trek, and she is still present cooking as he concludes his meditations. She is, in spotty but persistent ways, the voice of instinctive wisdom. She cuts ironically through Joseph's religiosity. She is both defiant and devout. Her wisdom finds voice in her proverb-making, in her laughter, in her tears and in her creative "making." She is the novel's minimalist.

Gerhardt Wiebe plays a very different role. He is a foil to Joseph, the quiet doubter to Joseph's pious faith, the enlightened reader of Dostoyevsky and Marx. He eventually joins the revolution, and thus represents some of the family left behind by immigrants to the West. But he is no simple apostate; he ministers to "the leader" in the hour of his death after his more pious followers have abandoned him. His is a solid integrity whose shoemaking and instinctive compassion carry the force of active love without pretense. "The leader" himself appropriately remains a more symbolic and distant figure who is never well developed as a character.

The novel also succeeds (perhaps revels) in its postmodern attempts to plunder the visions and signs of ancient and recent literature. Other readers will see their own echoes. Among those that stand out for me are the following. The book of Revelation, with the culmination of its apocalyptic visions still delayed at the end of the second millennium, provides the classic archetype for the novel—a technique similar to James Joyce's use of received archetypes to structure the chaos of modernity in *Ulysses*. Dostoyevsky, near the time of the great trek, figures importantly in Gerhardt Wiebe's reading and embodies the novel's struggle with symbolic dreams, religious apostasy, political revolution and restored faith. Gerhardt Wiebe echoes the heroic Solzhenitsyn in his denunciation of a western capitalism turned nearly as godless as its philosophical mirror in eastern communism. One sees in Joseph Toevs's (and author Wiebe's) endless quest for signs something of Humberto Eco's medieval yet postmodern quest in *The Name of the Rose*. Even Wiebe's ironic epigraph at the front of the novel ("We shall be changed. But into what?") bears a striking resemblance to the postmodern and also ethnic (Jewish) Brazilian novelist Moacyr Scliar's *Centaur in the Garden*, whose centaur-inspired epigraph reads irreverently and irrelevantly, "Since when do Jews ride horses?" Indeed: since when, or into what shall we be changed? Such "flip" questions are echoed within the novel as well, most notably when Joseph and Gerhardt decide to join the great trek after a bizarre evening with the great leader, not with somber deliberation but with casual abandon: "'Well, Gerhardt, shall we go to Central Asia?' And Gerhardt says, 'Why not?'" Extending such "why not" questions to the novel's artistry, one notes that key events or symbols seem to occur at the exact physical center of each chapter—such as the "sign of the beast" in chapter 3 and the gruesome death of Gerhardt in chapter 6. Are these signs? Ironic plundering of archaic commitments to "form"? Wiebe's intention? Does it matter? Why look for key signs in the precise middle of chapters? Well, why not?

Are there failings in this major novel? There is at least another side. Some may find the length of the central diary section to be excessive or tedious. I didn't. There are parts that are overdone. For example, Wiebe's persistent joke of having the six foot four and one-eighth Gerhardt bump his head on every low lintel in every house gets a little out of hand when Wiebe cannot resist having Gerhardt's nearly severed head strike the door post one more time as his body is carried in from the bloody streets of Khiva. And some may wonder whether the ironic and deconstructive Wiebe is compatible with the heroic and elegiac Wiebe.

But on the whole this novel will both entertain and instruct, and the blend of irony and aspiration is more than a literary game. This profound story is rooted in a significant chapter of Mennonite history. It narrates human failings of enormous proportions but is balanced by its roots in faith, in courageous struggle, in a vision of peace in a world torn by global forces. Its apocalyptic madness is both historical and current, its balancing range of human personality is believable, and its endless array of shifting signs and wonders will both amuse and intrigue. This epic novel is at once poetic and ironic—even to the oft repeated phrase with which its narrator and author concludes: "Even so, come, Lord Jesus." Why not?

Goshen College   WILBUR BIRKY